THE
SOMME

Published in 2016 by Times Books

An imprint of HarperCollins Publishers
Westerhill Road
Bishopbriggs
Glasgow G64 2QT
www.harpercollins.co.uk

© Times Newspapers Ltd 2016
www.thetimes.co.uk

A catalogue record for this book is available from the
British Library

ISBN 978-0-00-820975-9

10 9 8 7 6 5 4 3 2 1

Printed in UK

PUBLISHER'S NOTE

The Times Battle of the Somme has been created with extracts
from *The Times History of the War*, volumes 9, 10 and 11.

CHAPTER CLI.

THE BATTLE OF THE SOMME (I).

PREPARATION FOR THE OFFENSIVE—ARTILLERY BOMBARDMENT—WORK OF THE ENGINEERS—AIR
RECONNAISSANCE AND PHOTOGRAPHS—DESTRUCTION OF GERMAN CAPTIVE BALLOONS—THE
GERMAN DEFENCES DESCRIBED—GERMAN CONFIDENCE—AREA OF THE OPERATIONS—MAIN
FORCES UNDER SIR H. RAWLINSON—THE ARMY CORPS COMMANDS—THE ATTACK ON JULY 1—
FRICOURT—MONTAUBAN—THE ULSTER DIVISION—LONDON TERRITORIALS—THE FRENCH OFFEN-
SIVE UNDER GENERAL FOCH—RESULTS OF THE FIRST DAY—THE OPERATIONS FROM JULY 2 TO
JULY 6—THE "HORSESHOE"—RESULTS OF JULY 7 AND 8—CONTALMAISON AND MAMETZ WOOD.

THE time had now come when the
Allies were prepared to assume the
offensive and to continue it.* They
had troops enough available, and
these were amply provided with weapons,
ammunition and equipment of every kind.
The progress in armament which had been made
since the beginning of the year was enormous.
In former campaigns it was thought sufficient
to equip the first line of artillery with 500 rounds
per gun. At the present time 5,000 would be
insufficient. Moreover, the calibres of the
weapons employed had been much added to,
thereby augmenting enormously the power of
the shells. This had involved a corresponding
addition to the weight of ammunition which had
to be moved up to the front and deposited in
the advance depôts. In its turn, this taxed
severely the resources of the lines of communication ; but these difficulties had all been overcome.

A good idea of the effect of the greatly
increased power of the Allied artillery, as shown
in the preliminary bombardment, may be
gathered from the description given by a
German officer who was in the trenches near
the Somme. It was published in New York on

July 9 in an Associated Press cable. It said
that the Germans here had " rows of massively
built positions " which they had regarded as
" practically indestructible and impregnable,
but the event proved that the progress made in
offensive tactics since the September offensive
had not been realized." The German officer
went on to say :

At the beginning of the artillery preparation the
enemy showed us a new thing in the destruction of
observation balloons. Airmen swooped down on them
and shot fire-balls on them from above, a burst of
flame marking the end of each balloon hit.

The second day's bombardment, on June 26, brought
another surprise in the shape of aerial mines of unheard-
of calibre and thrown in incredible numbers. The
explosion of the first of these air torpedoes caused
such a tremendous detonation that the windows of
our bombproofs were shattered and a massive pillar
of black earth was thrown up, perhaps a hundred
yards, into the air. This showered the whole neighbourhood with turf, bricks, and earth. It was a
regular eruption of Vesuvius.

The destructive effects of this uninterrupted throwing of the heaviest mines were almost immediately
visible. The entrances of two bombproof shelters
were buried within a few minutes, and the inmates
had to be dug out. A few minutes later an orderly
who had been sent with a message to the left of the
company returned with the report that the trench
had been completely levelled. Going to verify this,
I saw as far as the eye could reach crater after crater,
each about 6 ft. deep. The earth in between was
thrown up in a wild, high-heaped chaos of trench
timbers and wire entanglements. Nine months' work,
day and night, had been destroyed in a few minutes.

Report after report arrived of " bombproof " shelters
demolished by these aerial torpedoes, the inmates

---

* For the events immediately preceding the Battle
of the Somme, see Chapter CXLI.

TWO OF THE BRITISH HOWITZERS ON THE SOMME.　　[Official Photograph.

being buried in the ruins. As the trenches became rapidly levelled, communication between the different sections grew difficult, and the communication trenches leading to the second and third lines were so heavily shelled that it was inpossible to traverse them. An orderly sent with a message to the captain was away for hours, and, finally, returned with his mission unaccomplished.

The left flank of my company's trench was by this time so obliterated that it was difficult to follow its trace, and the only means of progress was to dash from crater to crater, fully exposed to the enemy's fire while crossing the intervening ridges. I arrived finally, after a period of intense danger, and found the left platoon of the company in the same condition as the right platoon.

A number of the men were still buried in demolished bomb-proofs, and their comrades worked for hours excavating them. During this work our intrepid battalion surgeon arrived with an oxygen apparatus and stood for hours under heavy artillery fire administering the gas to the half-suffocated men, and attempting to revive those who had been asphyxiated.

The bombardment continued without a break, aerial torpedoes being hurled at ranges such as have never before been heard of for mine-throwers, while the French artillery was pounding every yard of the ground with an intense fire of big shells.

The Engineers and Pioneer battalions had been hard at work repairing roads or constructing new ones, improving existing railways or laying fresh lines and constructing sidings and platforms to facilitate the loading and unloading of stores, guns and troops so that a perfect system of approaches from the bases to the front was available.* The Army Ordnance Corps and the Army Service Corps had utilized these to the fullest extent. Besides

* Altogether some 3,000 miles of railway were constructed.

all this labour there was a constant succession of mines to be driven against the enemy's works and counter mines against those he was pushing forward against ours. The lighter forms of artillery, trench mortars and other engines for throwing heavy bombs over a short distance had been made in large numbers, grenades and rifle ammunition stocked by the million. Our air-planes had attained a distinct superiority over those of the enemy, their reconnaissance had furnished the directing powers of the Army with accurate photographs of the hostile defences, and the Royal Engineers had constructed from these excellent maps of the German trenches which would serve to guide our troops when engaged in turning their opponents out of them, and further by means of telephoto lenses had constructed panoramic views of the enemy's position.

The following description of the various uses to which aeroplanes were put is due to Lieutenant Réné Puaux, formerly on the staff of the Temps, who was attached to the staff of General Foch, commanding on the Somme. He wrote :

" The rôle played by the Franco-British aviation during the battle of the Somme will never be sufficiently appreciated. Pursuing aeroplanes, bombarding aeroplanes, aeroplanes for regulating fire, anti-captive balloon aeroplanes, aeroplanes for attacking infantry, photographer aviators—all these different

branches of the new arm have one and all contributed to victory.

"At the beginning of the war only a very
vague idea existed of the extent to which
aviation could be useful. The mind dwelt
especially on reconnaissances permitting of
information as to the movements of big enemy
units reaching the high command. Bombardment was at the beginning of the war merely a
sport.

"As for the service devoted to regulating
artillery fire, I recall at the Châlons front in
July, 1914, we were still at the point of manu-
facturing and testing an arrangement furnished
with brilliant plaques of metal at the end of
each of the wings—plaques which the pilot-
observer had to manipulate with a steel thread
in order to indicate to the artillerists who were
following his movements through binoculars—
'fire to the right'—'fire to the left.'

"We have gone a long way since then.
Wireless installations have been provided for
the aeroplanes, and now the regulation of
artillery fire is a duty carried out with quite
disconcerting ease. The aviators have become
the indispensable eyes of the artillery.

"One can understand the terrible incon-
venience caused by the Franco-British chasing

aeroplanes to the German artillery by reason
of their pitiless vigilance in preventing the
German spotters from performing their work.
Deprived of its aviators the German artillery
had to take to captive balloons—'sausages'—
which, from the fact of their height of 600 to
800 yards can dominate the horizon, observe
the flash of cannon, and report troops on the
march, and the arrival of masses of reinforcements.

"The Franco-British aviators have attacked
the 'sausages' successfully, thanks to certain
measures which they have taken, and the

AIRCRAFT ON THE WESTERN FRONT.
[*Official Photographs.*
Anti-aircraft gunners spotting an enemy aeroplane.   Smaller picture : an aeroplane on reconnaissance.

'sausages' fall in flames or descend precipitately as soon as our aviators are reported. One can imagine the disorganization of the fire-regulating service occasioned by these spasmodic descents.

"In default of aeroplanes or 'sausages,' the artillery can still fire according to the directing plan,* but this needs checking by observation or it is liable to be a mere squandering of ammunition. These plans have been furnished for the most part by the aerial photographic service. There is no more interesting service to be seen at work. Their apparatus, perfected to an immense focus, will take photographs with absolute detail at a height of 3,000 to 4,500 feet. Its mission accomplished, the aeroplane returns to the shed. The special photographic car is provided with developing rooms all ready prepared for the stereotype plates. Half an hour afterwards the print is on the geographical officers' table, while other prints are being despatched to the staffs, from which their charts are corrected to the slightest detail. The more numerous the photographs taken the more complete are the comparative indications.

"During the long period of two years during which the enemy armies faced each other without appreciable change of front, the German photographic aeroplane service was able to prepare excellent directing plans of the Franco-British positions. The Somme offensive has demolished all that work, however, and it is now impossible for the enemy to do it over again, since his aviators cross our lines only at very rare intervals.

* This is a map divided up into squares which enables the artillery to keep up its fire on any particular point because its position is known relatively to some particular square.

"At the present day, when the Franco-British artillery gives no respite to the enemy, the latter has no longer the opportunity of carrying on all this complicated work, and the photographs taken by our aviators tell us the naked truth. Very numerous, alas! are the aviators who have succumbed in this noble task of driving back the enemy aviators far from our lines and of flying ceaselessly over the German positions, but the value of the services they have rendered cannot be over-estimated, for they have saved the lives of thousands of their comrades by blinding the German artillery and by furnishing to the Anglo-French command the decisive elements of victory. It is owing to them that we can go on with firm step towards our common goal."

The line occupied by the British had been considerably extended. In April of 1915 it measured only 30 miles: in July, 1916, from Ypres to Frise, it was 90 miles in length.

The German view of the situation at the end of June was well shown in a typical article by the military correspondent of the *Berliner Tageblatt*, Major Moraht, actually published on July 1.

The writer began by declaring that "all the belligerent armies were now at a critical stage." The Allies had undoubtedly increased the energy and the uniformity of their conduct of war, and their great resources in money and men and their command of the sea would enable them to do everything possible "to hamper Germany's final victory." Major Moraht then went on to declare that the Russian offensive had brought no relief to the French at Verdun, and he was foolish enough to predict that "the decisive fights" before

THE NIGHT BEFORE THE ATTACK.   [*Official Photograph.*
Men of the East Yorkshire Regiment marching up to the trenches.

THE LANCASHIRE FUSILIERS

Fixing bayonets before the battle, July 1, 1916.

[*Official Photograph.*

Verdun were now imminent. Meanwhile, the defenders of Verdun were only "trying to gain time." The British offensive was about to begin, and "without a serious settlement of accounts with England on the battlefields in the west the Germans would not come a step nearer to peace." Major Moraht and the other German writers betrayed no sense of the immensity of the coming events, and it was clear that the Germans had not begun to dream of the defeats that were about to be inflicted upon them.

It was, indeed, almost as if the Germans had learned nothing from the previous fighting. Yet they must have been aware that in a series of rear-guard actions in the dark days of August, 1914, the British had held at bay four times their numbers. When on September 5 the Allies had turned against the Germans and pushed them back without a stop over the Marne to the Aisne, they must surely have felt that their opponents were their superiors in the open field. We held them beaten. But unfortunately the resources neither of the British nor French in men and equipment were sufficient to enable them to continue the pressure on their opponents. The Germans proceeded to dig themselves in and constructed the modern " *ne plus ultra* " lines by which they held us at bay for nearly 20 months while both nations were creating armies, organizing and equipping them, and, as Major Moraht said in schoolboys' slang, " cribbing " from the Germans. But the Germans were destined to find that the pupils had gone one better than their teachers, and that with the modern appliances of artillery they were capable of dealing effectively with the most perfect works of defence, while their infantries were able and willing to come to close quarters with their opponents. The German argument appears to have been that the French fought bravely at Verdun, but were exhausted and incapable of any offensive movement, and that, although the British fought well in their retreat from Mons to Le Mesnil, their old army was dead and their new a mere raw, half-trained militia.

It is desirable to understand the real nature of the task which our troops had before them.

It must be remembered that the Germans had had over a year and a half to prepare their works ; they were by no means the hastily thrown up defences characteristic of ordinary field operations, but were, in fact, permanent fortifications of the most perfect description. It is true there were no deep ditches to be crossed, but this obstacle was replaced by wide and strongly constructed continuous wire entanglements. These had literally to be swept away before the assaulting troops could reach the garrisons of the trenches. Moreover, the shelters constructed to protect the latter were of such a solid character as had never been found before in any fortress. Deep down with such an amount of solid earth above them that they were safe from any but the heaviest projectiles, and in some cases so deep that even these could not reach them, there had been constructed rooms in which the bulk of the troops could be kept until actually wanted to resist assault on the parapets, to which access was gained by numerous staircases. Many of the dug-outs were closed by a steel door, from which there descended a deep staircase, with the risers and treads made of wood. At the foot there were several rooms, of which the floors, walls, and roofs were boarded. The connecting passages were similarly constructed. Sometimes a second stairway led down to a second group of rooms. Some of these were arranged as hospitals, with two tiers of

[Official Photograph

LOADING WAGONS WITH FIELD ARTILLERY AMMUNITION

Standardized Steel Door and Scraper.

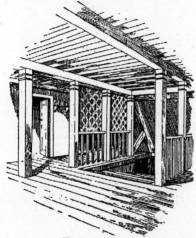

Timber Staircase.

Officer's Dug-out.
GERMAN TRENCH ARCHITECTURE.
By permission of the "Architectural Review."

bunks to hold the patients. The larger dug-outs could take a whole platoon. They were often 30 feet below the surface, and when there was a second tier this was still farther down.*

At intervals in the lines of trenches specially strong works had been constructed from which a flanking fire could be brought to bear on our men when they reached a line of German trench, and these also acted as reduits from which counter-attacks could be made on our troops. Cunningly concealed machine-guns protected by concrete were placed so that they could bring an oblique and sometimes even a flanking fire on the assault. These did not prematurely betray their presence by any general engagement against the advancing infantry, but waited until the near approach of the latter rendered their fire more deadly and decisive. On many occasions they had to be silenced before the advance could be continued.

One of these arrangements, which may be taken as the type of many others, may be here briefly described. A tunnel 20 feet below the ground ran in one direction to a large dug-out and in the other beyond and in front of the trench. At the most advanced point there was a small inconspicuous emplacement strongly roofed over, led up to by stairs from the tunnel. It was just sufficient for one machine-gun and its crew of two men, and had a wide loophole just about ground level which permitted a considerable lateral range. While the bombardment of the trench was in progress the machine-gun was safe down below in the dug-out, but when the infantry attack was imminent it was rapidly brought into position and was ready for action. It will easily be understood how difficult it was to detect and destroy so small an object.

Equal care was taken with the posts constructed for snipers. These were most carefully concealed, and often connected with the subterranean organizations by tunnels from the shaft, at the top of which the sniper was securely ensconced behind a steel loop-holed shield, the front of which was concealed by some means to make it look as like the surrounding ground as possible. Generally it may be said that the snipers' stations, whether in the special places just described or in artfully-

* There is no doubt that in some cases this great security was harmful to the defence as the defenders refused to come out to take an active part in the defence.

THE BEGINNING OF THE ADVANCE.

British Infantry attacking the German second line. To the right is the German zig-zag communication trench leading from the first to the second line of trenches. At its nearer end men are at work with entrenching tools.

selected positions, in houses, trees, etc., were most carefully placed.

The use of sniping was another of the introductions made by the Germans, who had raised this form of man-killing to a fine art. They had special telescopic rifles, range-finders, telescopes, etc., and apparently looked on the shooting of individuals from the point of view of the Red Indian collecting scalps.

The point, therefore, to be borne in mind by the reader is that the fighting on the Somme was like no other fighting which had ever taken place. In no former war had such formidable defences ever been met with. Never had the fire of infantry and artillery been so formidable, never had so many grenades been flung by hand, nor others, larger and more powerful, from trench mortars, been employed.* All these destructive weapons had to be overcome and the trenches they defended pulverized before the infantry could put the final touch with the bayonet to turn the undestroyed elements of the garrison out of their position or compel them to surrender.

But the result of the fighting was to show that, great as were the resources which modern science had given to the military engineer, all these could not oppose the mighty strides which science had also made in the construction of artillery, and, as had happened before, the offensive proved itself superior to the defensive.

Neither the British nor the French favoured the mass attacks employed by the Germans— viz., columns of infantry in close order driven forward in spite of loss. It is true that in 1914 and on some few occasions later the remnants of such formations succeeded in reaching the lines of the Allies. But for one such case there were fifty in which the only result was the wholesale slaughter of the troops using this clumsy plan. In others the exhausted remnants penetrated our front trenches only to be promptly turned out by counter-attack. In the period now under description we employed the method of successive waves of infantry following at a short distance one after the other. The way for these was always prepared by the preliminary bombardment, and then when the infantry went forward they were always supported by the artillery keeping their fire a little ahead of them, and also making a barrier or screen of shell and shrapnel behind

[*Frederic Robinson.*

LIEUT.-GEN. SIR L. E. KIGGELL, K.C.B.
Chief of the General Staff in France.

the enemy's line to stop him sending up reinforcements. This action was rendered possible by the large provision of guns and of shells with which our armies were now supplied, with the result that our attacks were nothing like as costly in life as they formerly were and far more lasting in results.

Confiding in the strength of their position, but, above all, believing that they were superior in every respect to the troops opposed to them, the Germans awaited calmly the Allies' onslaught. To them it was inconceivable that they could under any circumstances be beaten.

For the past fifty years the Prussian Army had been nurtured on a continuous diet of lies. It had been taught by mendacious history that the Germans were invincible. Frederick the Great's victories were belauded— his defeats slurred over. Rosbach was praised as the kind of result which would always be obtained whenever the Prussians met the French. The miserable results of their arrogant conceit when they went down before the French in 1806 like corn before the sickle; when the two victories of Jena and Auerstedt gained by the Imperial Troops on one day served to crumple up the whole Prussian Army so that for the remainder of the war they owed

---

* The various kinds of mortars made use of for these purposes have been already described. See Vol. IV., p. 376.

their defence entirely to their Russian Allies, counted as nothing. Prussia had never played a losing game well. The reason is that the Prussian system had always aimed at crushing the individual soldiers into one unthinking man, who may, indeed, be forced on to victory, but who is extremely likely to lose all heart when the balance of battle tends to turn against him. The French from the days of the Republic, for reasons which are too long to give here, had developed the fighting capacity of the individual. Even in the days of the Peninsula this was not lost sight of in our army, and of late years it had been followed to a higher pitch

[*Lafayette.*

LIEUT.-GEN. H. S. HORNE, C.B.
In command of the 15th Army Corps.

than in any other. Deprive the Prussians of their tyr anical leaders and they are unable to rise to the situation. In the British and French armies all the officers may be killed off, the non-commissioned officers are still there; even if they are absent the men know how to act. In both armies there are always leaders to be found. In the German army, without their directing officers the machinery comes to a standstill.

But they pointed to 1813 as sponging out 1806. Those who know military history are aware that the Prussians owed their resurrection largely to English gold, English equipment, English weapons. They claimed the great victory of Leipzig, but forgot the parts played

in it by the Austrians, the Russians and the Swedes. They ignored Lützen, Bautzen, and Dresden. It was numbers which beat Napoleon in 1814, and yet he was enabled to defeat many times his Prussian opponents. In 1815 they were again beaten at Ligny, and it was the British stand at Waterloo which finally held the Emperor and gave the Prussians time to come up to complete the victory. But for 50 years they had lived on the reputation of 1866 and 1870, and exalted themselves on the results then won without pausing to enquire how, or why, they were obtained. Hoenig had shown that in the latter war they made many mistakes. France was beaten because her forces were badly led and because after the old professional army had gone into captivity there was nothing available but raw recruits in the shape of the Mobiles. Even with these, if they had been used against the German communications instead of being uselessly expended in direct attacks on the armies blockading Paris, the result might have been very different. In 1866 the Austrians and minor States of Germany were crushed in the Seven Weeks' War because they were vilely led and because they opposed the quick-loading needle-gun with the slow-loading muzzle-loader.

In the Great War Britain had had to improvize her armies ; France had to organize ; each had to provide new armaments. Now they possessed both numbers and weapons. In the long struggle at Verdun since the third week of February the armies of the Republic had shown that they possessed the same military capacity as was displayed by their grandfathers in the wars of a hundred years ago. Our troops in the Retreat from Mons fought as troops had seldom fought, kept back the invading hordes, and gave Joffre time to rearrange his plans, till on September 5 he turned and pressed back the Germans without a check from the Marne to the Aisne.

Truly it might be said of our own men in this terrible fighting :—

> They fell undaunted and undying,
> The very winds their fate seemed sighing,
> The waters murmured of their name,
> The woods were peopled with their fame ;
> The meanest rill, the mightiest river,
> Rolls mingled with their name for ever.

During the last week of June * a most intense and destructive bombardment had been directed against the enemy's lines, and

---

* Chapter CXLI, p. 177.

BRITISH HEAVY GUNS IN ACTION.

[Official Photograph.
GEN. SIR HENRY RAWLINSON, BART.,
K.C.B.
In command of the Fourth Army.

had been combined with numerous raids sent out by the British, which brought in much valuable information of the composition and distribution of the German forces. Similar action had been taken by the French. The bombardment had been maintained against the whole 90 miles of front facing our trenches, so as to keep the enemy in ignorance of the particular region selected for attack, and to prevent him from concentrating his reserves against it. Added to this were local smoke and gas attacks. The Germans were conscious that attack was imminent; indeed, prisoners subsequently taken stated that so great had been the effect of our artillery that they had expected an assault three days before it took place, but they were uncertain as to where to expect it, so general had been the bombardment. The Belgians on the extreme left had contributed their share to this bewilderment of the enemy by keeping up a constant artillery fire. Meanwhile our infantry were waiting impatiently for the moment when they should be let loose to storm the German trenches.

The area of operations was of a very different character to that over which Lord French had had to manœuvre in the previous year. It was an agricultural, not a mining, district, and there were none of the large villages, mounds of spoil-bank and slag such as were found in the mining centres more to the north, and which were of great tactical utility to the Germans because they offered easily fortified supporting points. In Picardy, on the Somme, the ground was open though undulating. The villages were small, rarely containing more than a few hundred inhabitants, and the ground being not so much cut up afforded a better field of fire for our guns, and was also more favourable for the movements of troops. Assuming that, roughly, the objective of the British was Bapaume, and that of the French Péronne,

LIEUT.-GEN. SIR T. D'O. SNOW, K.C.B.
In command of the 7th Army Corps.

the first step was to capture the dominating ridge extending from Thiépval to Combles, the possession of which commanded the ground for a farther advance and was important as enabling the Allied heavy artillery to be brought forward from the places in which it had hitherto been posted. This is clearly shown on the accompanying map.

The ridge in question was the main watershed of the whole system of hills stretching from the Somme Valley in the south to the tract of low ground between Lens and Cambrai in the north-east, beyond which there was the flat ground round Douai. From the ridge the ground sloped down to a small tributary of the Ancre, and then up another slope past Bapaume to a ridge some hundred feet lower than the first, covered with woods. Beyond this the country gradually descended with a series of parallel folds of the ground of constantly decreasing height, which presented no great tactical difficulties. From the main ridge the Germans commanded the ground up which our men had to advance, and from it they were able without aeroplanes or captive balloons to watch our movements. This advantage they would lose completely when turned off the ridge. The ridge on the Allies' side was difficult to advance up because of its cut-up nature and slopes which were steep. On the other hand, the slope behind the ridge, being gentler, gave greater facility to the Germans in bringing up reserves.

The French battlefield south of the Somme may be divided into two parts, differing widely from one another in character. In the more

LIEUT.-GEN. SIR A. G. HUNTER-WESTON,
K.C.B.
In command of the 8th Army Corps.

northern sector the French advance moved up the Valley of the Somme. The river, which was sluggish, formed at intervals large reed-covered ponds and marshes, which interrupted the movements of troops. There were also clumps of trees and occasional woods. The southern portion was bare, and formed an undulating plateau.

The operations which we are about to describe were the first on a large scale which had fallen to the lot of Sir Douglas Haig and his Chief of the General Staff, Lieut.-General Sir L. E. Kiggell, to carry out. The career of the Commander-in-Chief is well known and has been previously described in these pages. General Kiggell was one of those who had combined with a thorough theoretical education consider-

able practical experience. He was a professor and subsequently Commandant of the Staff College. At the War Office he held the post of Director of Staff Duties, and subsequently Director of Home Defence and Assistant to the Chief of the Imperial General Staff. When Sir William Robertson was brought home to succeed General Murray as Chief of the Imperial General Staff, General Kiggell went to France to serve as Chief of the General Staff to General Haig.

The actual supervision of the British troops engaged in the great advance was entrusted to General Sir Henry Rawlinson, in command of the Fourth Army. General Rawlinson had served without a break in France since the retreat from Mons and had continuously rendered good service. Under him were, with others, Generals Congreve, Horne, Hunter-Weston, Morland, Pulteney and Snow.

While Lieut.-General Sir T. D'O. Snow (7th Army Corps) was in charge of the operations about Gommecourt, the main forces engaged from Serre to the point of junction with the French were at the beginning of the operations on July 1 as follows :

Eighth Army Corps (Lieut.-General Sir A. Hunter-Weston) ;

[Russell.

LIEUT.-GEN. SIR W. P. PULTENEY, K.C.B.
In command of the 3rd Army Corps.

[*Langfier.*

LIEUT.-GEN. SIR T. MORLAND, K.C.B.
In command of the Tenth Army Corps.

Tenth Army Corps (Lieut.-General Sir T. Morland);

Third Army Corps (Lieut.-General Sir W. P. Pulteney);

Fifteenth Army Corps (Lieut.-General H. S. Horne);

Thirteenth Army Corps (Lieut.-General W. N. Congreve, V.C.).

During the night of June 30-July 1 the bombardment had gradually increased in power, and for an hour and a half before the assault began it was raised to the highest pitch of intensity. Parapets crumbled beneath the impact of the shells, cover hitherto thought bombproof was crushed and destroyed, and the garrisons of the enemy's works, sorely shattered in *moral*, were driven down into the deepest dug-outs to seek shelter from the pitiless hail of projectiles. The artillery had played its part with unrivalled excellence; the infantry was eager to carry the bayonet into the devastated trenches and complete the work.

At half-past seven on the morning of July 1 the word was given and the British infantry leaped to the attack. It was launched over a front which extended from Gommecourt to Montauban, roughly a distance of about twenty

miles, while the French continued the line of advance for another five miles on both sides of the Somme, as far as Fay to the south of the river.

Passing rapidly over the ground which separated them from their opponents, our men carried the enemy's front line trenches with an irresistible rush which the dazed and demoralized occupants were quite incapable of withstanding.

Many important tactical points were rapidly won, Mametz, Montauban and the Bernafay Wood being taken, while Fricourt was vigorously assaulted, as also were Beaumont Hamel, where the Newfoundlanders distinguished themselves and lost heavily, and La Boisselle.

At first the resistance of the enemy was not great, he had been so knocked to pieces and intimidated by the preparatory artillery fire; but as the day wore on it grew stronger, and the fighting, especially north of the River Ancre, became particularly severe. Many of the villages were clung to by the Germans with extreme tenacity, and afforded a strenuous opposition to our attacks. But our men were not to be denied, and at many places flowed round the points of resistance, thus threatening the line of retreat of the garrison. This was especially the case at Fricourt. Farther north,

LIEUT.-GEN. W. N. CONGREVE, V.C., C.B.
In command of the 13th Army Corps.

[Officia. Photograph.

A ROLL CALL
In the trenches on the afternoon of July 1.

Gommecourt, which formed a salient, was attacked on both sides, and a German counter-attack against Montauban was successfully repulsed.

By the end of July 1 we had made considerable progress. The right of our attack had captured German trenches on a front of seven miles and to a depth of 1,000 yards, besides taking several strongly fortified villages. In the centre of our attack we gained ground over a front of four miles, capturing many strong points; but up to the evening the enemy still held out at many others, and the struggle continued to be very severe. North of the Ancre valley we were very much less successful, and German counter-attacks even compelled us to yield a portion of the ground we captured.

Round Fricourt on July 1 the fight raged with extreme vehemence, which was prolonged into the night and next day. The high ground to the south of the village and the greater part of the Fricourt Wood were in our possession by the evening, but it was not till 2 p.m. on Sunday, July 2, that the village was finally captured.

Fricourt was situated to the west of Mametz, and combined with this village formed a strongly-organized position which it was necessary to reduce before advancing farther up towards the main ridge on the road to which Contalmaison and Mametz Wood, and behind them the two Bazentins, the wood of that name, and Pozières would still block the way to the Bapaume road. The position formed an extended portion of the German first line, and had a frontal of about 2¼ miles.* Fricourt

* When the expression "first-line" is made use of it does not mean a single line of trench, but the series of trenches which together constitute the front portion

Official Photograph.

THE BRITISH ADVANCE AT LA BOISSELLE.

A photograph taken on July 3. In the foreground is the original British front-line. In the centre is seen a crater caused by the explosion of a mine just before the assault.

itself was in a hollow west of Mametz, but the Fricourt wood slopes upwards, and was considerably lower than Mametz, so that the latter could bring a flanking fire to bear on any attack on the top end of the village and on the wood above it, the Fricourt Wood. So far as the village is concerned, its sheltered position was very favourable, and prevented the British artillery bombarding it with the efficiency it might have attained had it been less well concealed. Thus it was that heavy as was the deluge of shells poured on it, while the outer edge of trenches and obstacles had been pulverized, the dug-outs had been but little injured. When, therefore, the British attacked on July 1 the assault came to a standstill owing to the machine-guns which had been brought out from their hiding places in the dug-outs and placed on the positions prepared to sweep the streets in the interior. Thus, although the village was entered, our troops made no substantial impression on it that day, and it was not till 2 p.m. on Sunday, after more and severe shelling, that we finally took it. Behind the valley was a wood which had been strongly prepared for defence, and indeed its bombardment had in some ways increased its power as an obstacle, for it had so cut down and entangled the trees that they formed an almost impassable entanglement. Nor was this the only obstacle to an advance from Fricourt up the slope. Beyond the wood was an open space of some two hundred yards, commanded by a trench known as " Railway Alley." Farther up the slope was a copse, " Bottom Wood," which served as a gathering place for snipers and machine-guns. To its left, lower down the slope, on the western edge of Fricourt Wood, was another clump of trees, " Lonely Copse " behind which was the trench called " Lozenge Alley." A cluster of trees, known as " The Poodles," divided Lozenge Alley from Railway Alley. North of the Poodles was a triangular patch of woodland, to which the name of " Shelter Wood " had been given. After all these plantations had been cleared of their German garrisons the next point was the Quadrangle, which formed a

detached work defending the approach to Mametz Wood on its south-western side. The Quadrangle, which was in open ground, was a fortified area of trapezoidal form wider at its southern than its northern end. The bottom trench, i.e., that nearest our troops, was known as Quadrangle Trench ; that which ran · back from its right extremity was " Quadrangle Alley " ; that from its left was designated " Pearl Alley." The top and shorter side had the name Quadrangle Support, and was protected at each end by a redoubt. Moreover, it was commanded by the fire of the enemy from Contalmaison and Mametz Wood.

THE GROUND ROUND FRICOURT.

Altogether it formed a strong position which could be easily reinforced from the German works behind. From this brief description it will be seen that the task set the British was a difficult and complicated one. To arrive from the region of Fricourt at the outskirts of Contalmaison and the Mametz Wood they had to work their way up through or round the Fricourt Wood, descend thence into dips and hollows, and ascend the heights beyond. Every yard of the ground was under the fire of machine-guns, trench mortars and rifles, and in addition there was the fire from batteries farther up or behind the ridge. The ranges of different points over which our troops had to pass had been carefully plotted on the German maps, so that it was always possible by the use of telephones and other signalling methods to let the gunners in rear know where the assaulting troops were, and

of the defences, and which is never less than two lines of trench, and very often, in accordance with the requirements of the ground, several more. No trench is safe in front line that has not a support close up to it to stop the enemy if he should break through the trench. This second trench is also necessary to hold supports and as a basis for counter-attack against any enemy who might force his way through the first.

A FRENCH OUTPOST
Working a wireless installation.

thus concentrate gunfire on them. The garrison of the work were stalwart troops, fully impressed with the necessity of holding the posts entrusted to them, for they protected the approaches to the main line of communication of the Germans in France, which were of such vital importance to them.

Early in the afternoon of July 2 a brigade which had been held in reserve, but which, however, owing to being under shell-fire, had had no rest or sleep the night before, replaced the troops who had carried the village of Fricourt, proceeded to advance from it, and marched up across the lead-swept narrow open space at the southern edge of the wood. Met by a storm of machine-gun and rifle fire at almost point-blank range, struck by gusts of bursting shrapnel, their ranks rapidly thinned, but still the survivors pressed on and entered the wood. A bitter fight ensued with bayonet and point, in which our men slowly gained ground, pushing their opponents back through the terrible entanglement of wood and wire. But so desperate and stubborn was the resistance that it was only in the early evening that the northern edge of the wood was reached. Here the wearied soldiers hastily dug themselves in under fire from the Railway Alley trench, into which the survivors of the garrison of Fricourt Wood had bolted. All night long the enemy hurled projectiles at them, but our troops did not reply.

The next morning (July 3) the attack on Railway Alley trench began. It had been heavily bombarded on the 2nd, and after daybreak the artillery fire began. The wire entanglements were destroyed, but, for some reason or other, the trench itself escaped severe damage. Taking advantage of a dip in the ground, a company entered the communication trench on the right, while a battalion slipped beyond it and made for Bottom Wood, where they dislodged the enemy. From Bottom Wood a part of the battalion, bombing as they went, descended on the rear of Railway Alley and joined the company in the communication trench. A small body of Germans in Railway Alley ran back up the slope. Believing, but wrongly, that this masked the beginning of a general retreat, our troops in Fricourt Wood were ordered to make a frontal attack. They left cover and dashed forward. Unfortunately for them the main body of the enemy still held the Railway Alley trench. A terrific fire was opened by the Germans, which completely knocked over the first wave of the British, and of the supporting wave few reached the trench unhurt. But behind came a third, fourth and fifth wave, and they would not be denied. Over the parapet and into the Germans they leapt. The result was never in doubt for one moment. For a brief time they were completely masters. Several hundred prisoners were taken, and those of the garrison who had not been killed, wounded or captured took refuge in Poodles and Shelter Wood, from which they were quickly driven, leaving behind them another 400 prisoners.

While these events were occurring, troops of the same brigade, in face of a vigorous defence, gained Lonely Copse and Lozenge Alley, and 150 prisoners fell into their hands. So far the operation had been successful, but the Quadrangle had yet to be stormed, and here we may, slightly anticipating events, deal with its final capture.

To reduce it, it was necessary to move up the western and eastern faces. Between July 4 and July 9 three separate frontal attacks on the Quadrangle Support (i.e., the rear side) were made. The first two failed, but on the 9th, at midnight, our men reached to within a few yards of the central portion of the trench. Then, with a yell of " Stafford," they crossed the parapet and bayoneted the defenders. At dawn, however, the machine guns from the untaken redoubts at either end forced our men to retire back over the parapet, and it was not till after the fall of Contalmaison and the Mametz Wood, to be described later, that the British succeeded in finally capturing the Quadrangle Support trench, and with it the whole work fell into their hands.

Fricourt was a point of importance, situated at the apex of the salient formed by the German lines at this part of the field and had been fortified with the greatest care, and its strength had enabled it to hold out for nearly a day after we had taken Mametz and Montauban, which were relatively much deeper in the German lines. Its neighbourhood had already been the scene of much severe and bloody fighting.

The following description, by the special correspondent of The Times, of the ground round Fricourt gives some idea of the terrible effects of the bombardment on the German defences and the village itself :

For some hours before the storm broke, I had been going over the ground newly won from the enemy, in and around the village of Fricourt. It is a dreadful sight. From what were our front line trenches you go through remnants of rusted and torn barbed wire over the narrow strip of ground between the lines, across the writhing, twisted rails of what was once a railway line, through the wreckage of the enemy's wire to the German front line.

You must not imagine yourself to be walking over level ground. It was level ; but it is now all ridge and pit and hummock. Nowhere—not for one single square yard, I think—can you see the true surface of the ground. You go down the sides of a huge shell hole, the bottom full of a litter of equipment, and up the other, jump across a smaller one, follow for three paces the obliterated line of an old trench, then into another shell hole. So it is over the whole of Fricourt, except that in the village itself the shapeless piles of brick and masonry, here heaped man high, there battered flat, cover all the earth.

There are no streets or houses ; merely so much of the earth's surface covered with ruin and wreckage. And everywhere are the more immediate, the more terrible, relics of the fighting.

The German trenches are, as always, more elaborate than ours. Here they are deeper and wider. They are, therefore, more open to a shell bursting directly above ; but, when under fire, the German soldiers keep as much as possible in their dug-outs, which are—here as always—more extensive, deeper, and better built than ours. The trenches immediately about Fricourt were not very seriously damaged by our bombardment, in contrast to other points near here, as about Montauban, where they were practically destroyed. The barbed wire in front had been cut and blown to bits, except in certain spots, and all the ground around was, as I have said, devastated beyond description. But the direct damage to the trenches themselves was comparatively slight.

The taking of Montauban was a particularly brilliant piece of work. It was achieved by our

FRENCH BOMB-THROWER.
Explosion of a bomb after being shot from a compressed-air bomb-thrower.

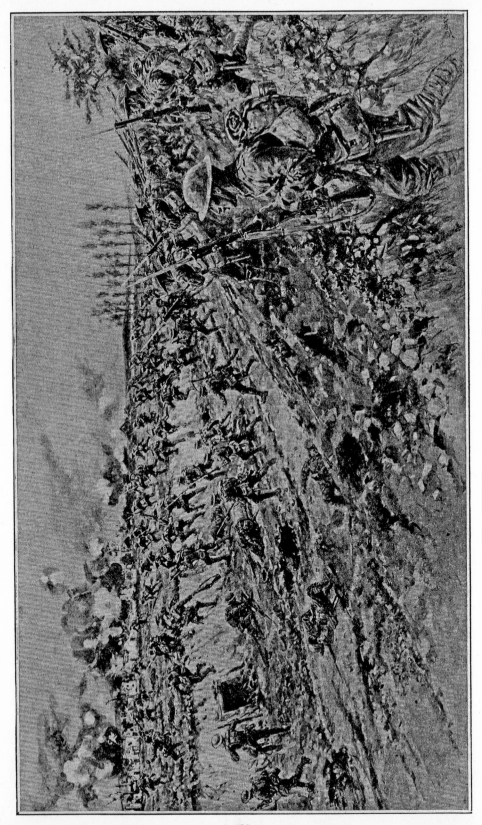

THE BRITISH CAPTURE MONTAUBAN, JULY 1.

Infantry, mainly Lancashire troops, supported by men from the Home Counties, including Surrey, Kent, Essex, Bedford, and Norfolk.

troops at the southern end of our lines nearest the French advance. The garrison was composed of Bavarian troops, men of tried experience in war. Against them went our newly composed armies, which had had but little previous fighting experience. There were present, among others, the Manchesters, composed largely of young clerks and warehousemen, and they went forward with a dash that veteran troops might have envied. On their way they cleared out some German advance posts and then arrived at their main objective, the village of Montauban. It was captured with very little resistance and with but slight losses. Artillery fire had rendered the village a mere rubbish heap and destroyed most of the German trenches. The left flank of the Manchesters, who appear to have been on the left of our assaulting forces, was protected by a powerful barrage fire. On the right of this regiment were other gallant troops who advanced with equal bravery, but having more difficult ground to pass over did not make such rapid progress. Notwithstanding, they still managed to move forward on the right of the force attacking Montauban in spite of the opposition they received, until they reached a difficult point called the Warren, which was full of shell craters occupied by the enemy. To turn him out took some time, but a severe bombing, followed closely by an advance with the bayonet, drove him out, and then our troops swept onwards towards the brickworks, on the right rear of Montauban facing the Bernafay Wood. This they captured almost by surprise, so unexpected was their quick advance.

The right of the British attack was well supported by the French, whose left wing never lost touch of the British right, and this correlation of forces had largely to do with the success we gained. All through this advance our men displayed individual superiority over the Germans. Where they were made to pause it was because, for each rifle they had, their opponents had a machine gun. When they came to real close quarters, in spite of opposition, they were soon able to settle the question. The German does not take kindly to the bayonet, as the Briton does, and once the machine guns were captured or silenced a decision was quickly reached.

The Ulster Division covered itself with glory in this day's fighting, and paid a heavy toll for their gallant deeds. Even in their position of rendezvous before going forward to the assault their losses were heavy, but, notwithstanding this, when they went over the parapet they formed up as if on parade, the Irish Fusiliers, the Irish Rifles and the other Northern Irish units advancing slowly at first and then, when nearer the enemy's trenches, with a huge shout of " No surrender, boys," they charged over the two front lines of enemy's trenches. They were met in front by heavy fire and struck on both flanks, but still battalion after battalion continued to advance with the greatest steadiness. On from the second line to the enemy's third line they went, and this was soon taken ; still onward until the fourth line fell to their arms, and now it was felt that a further advance was impracticable until it could be made on a wider front than the division was capable of, and unfortunately the troops on their right and left had not been able to progress with the same rapidity. Instructions were therefore sent to stop, but, notwithstanding, on they went. It may be that the order arrived too late, or perhaps the successes they had gained and the remembrance that it was the anniversary of the Battle of the Boyne urged them to greater exertions, and into the fifth line of German trenches what remained of the gallant Ulster Division reached. It was impossible to remain there, for the position was a salient, and was liable to concentric fire against which no human beings could live, and back they went again to the second German trench, bringing with them 500 prisoners. Here they stopped and firmly held it.

The General Officer Commanding the Ulster Division issued the following special order in recognition of the gallant conduct of his men :

The General Officer Commanding the Ulster Division desires that the Division should know that in his opinion nothing finer has been done in the war than the attack by the Ulster Division on July 1. The leading of the company officers, the discipline and courage shown by all ranks of the Division, will stand out in the future history of the war as an example of what good troops, well led, are capable of accomplishing. None but troops of the best quality could have faced the fire which was brought to bear on them and the losses suffered during the advance.

Nothing could have been finer than the steadiness and discipline shown by every battalion, not only in forming up outside its own trenches, but in advancing under severe enfilading fire. The advance across the open to the German line was carried out with the steadiness of a parade movement under a fire, both from front and flanks, which could only have been faced by troops of the highest quality. The fact that the objects of the attack on one side were not obtained is no reflection on the battalions which were entrusted with the task. They did all that men could do, and, in common with every battalion in the Division, showed the most conspicuous courage and devotion. On the other side the Division carried out every portion of its allotted task, in spite of the heaviest losses. It captured nearly 600 prisoners, and carried its advance triumphantly to the limits of the objective laid down. There is nothing in the operations carried out by the Ulster Division on July 1 that will not be a source of pride to all Ulstermen. The Division has been highly tried, and has emerged from the ordeal with unstained honour, having fulfilled in every particular the great expectations formed of it. Tales of individual and collective heroism on the part of officers and men come in from every side, too numerous to mention, but all showing that the standard of gallantry and devotion attained is one that may be equalled, but is never likely to be surpassed.

The General Officer Commanding deeply regrets the heavy losses of officers and men. He is proud beyond description, as every officer and man in the Division may well be, of the magnificent example of sublime courage and discipline which the Ulster Division has given to the Army. Ulster has every reason to be proud of the men she has given to the service of our country. Though many of our best men have gone, the spirit which animated them remains in the Division and will never die.

At a part of the field, between Hébuterne and Authuille, a distance of roughly five miles measured in a straight line, the Allies faced the Germans from opposite sides of a gentle slope with a narrow level bottom between them. On the German side the highest point

was Serre, but the top was fairly level as far as Beaumont-Hamel, where there was a steep slope down to the valley of the Ancre; then the ground rises again to another plateau which continues to Ovillers-La Boisselle. The highest elevation on this side is behind the village of Thiépval. The points mentioned were all strongly fortified with connecting trenches between. The whole position was indeed of a most formidable character, yet part of our troops managed to dash through and reached the point known as the "Crucifix," behind Thiépval; others actually reached Serre, which was taken, while some of our Southern regiments pushed their way over successive trenches of the German first-line system till they, too, were on the plateau. All this was done within an hour and a half of the attack commencing.

At another portion of our front battalions of the East Lancashire and York and Lancaster regiments advanced with great gallantry. The part at which these troops were assembled had been heavily bombarded during the night, and as the hour of attack approached the enemy

[*Official Photograph.*

THE LONDON SCOTTISH MARCHING TO THE TRENCHES.

A CAPTURED GERMAN TRENCH NEAR OVILLERS. *[Official Photograph.*

opened a tremendous barrage 50 yards before and 50 yards behind it with heavy explosive shell At the same time the whole of the space which divided our trenches from the enemy's was swept by him, with a storm of machine-gun and rifle fire. It was through this hail of shot that our men advanced and seized the German front line, and actually fought their way over successive lines behind them.

London Territorial battalions played a considerable part in the great attack of July 1, including the Central London Rangers, the London Scottish, and the Queen's Westminsters. They attacked with irresistible fury and penetrated to the third German line, but here they were brought to a standstill, for the enemy had massed many guns and much ammunition at this point. As, moreover, the

THE BLACK WATCH
Marching back from the trenches, headed by their pipers.

Germans had made a barrier fire behind our attacking troops it was impossible to send up reinforcements or supplies, and the victorious troops were compelled to fall back.

The operations of July 1 were aided by great activity on the part of our airmen. An important railway depôt was attacked by bombs, and others were dropped on railway junctions, batteries, trenches, and other points of military importance. Our machines also attacked a railway train between Douai and Cambrai with considerable success ; one airman, descending to a height of less than 900 feet above the train, dropped a bomb on one of the trucks, which exploded. The resulting fire spread to others, and it was observed that the whole train was alight, and many explosions were heard. Numerous enemy headquarters and railway centres, including the important station of Lille, were also attacked. Twenty Fokkers attacked our machines, but they were driven off, and two of them were destroyed, while all ours returned in safety. Many of the German stationary balloons also were brought down, thus depriving them of a great deal of their power of observation. Altogether we took 3,500 unwounded prisoners.

At 7.30 a.m., the same time as the British commenced their attack, the French north of the Somme advanced against the German line over a front of some three miles. The position to be captured was composed of three and four lines of trenches bound together by numerous communications and having as a central point the fortified village of Curlu, while several clumps of trees prepared for defence formed good supporting points. The first German trenches were carried without a check ; then going up the chalk slope to which the name of the "Gendarme's Hat" had been given, the troops arrived at the outskirts of Curlu. When, however, they penetrated more into the interior they were brought to a standstill by the fire of machine guns posted near the church, which had hitherto been silent. In accordance with the orders received the advance was then stopped, while a heavy fire of artillery was poured for half an hour on the village. The advance was then continued and by nightfall the whole village was captured. Three desperate counter-attacks were made from the north (from the direction of Hardecourt) but were raked by the barrier fire of the French artillery and finally driven off by the infantry fire from the captured village of Curlu.

On the south side of the Somme the assaulting troops did not move forward till 9.30. Here, too, in a few hours the French gained the object of their advance. The effect of the preparatory bombardment had been so great that the trenches had been practically destroyed, while the villages were a mass of ruins. By the evening the first lines of trench from the border of Frise to the outer edge of Estrées had been captured, the villages of Dompierre, Becquincourt and Fay taken, and beyond these the advance continued in the same methodical fashion—destruction by the artillery, advance of the infantry, and occupation of the line of ground previously determined on, which was then put in a state of defence. The advance penetrated to a depth of one and a quarter miles and 3,500 prisoners were taken, besides guns and machine guns.

The whole attack had been under the command of General Foch with General Fayolle ; the troops were chiefly the Colonial Army Corps on the left and the 20th Corps on the right.

The result of the first day's fighting was, upon the whole, very satisfactory for both the British and the French. It was not a lightning-like stroke intended to pierce the German lines right through, but rather a continuous and methodical push to make sure of the ground which had been devastated by artillery fire. This involved less loss of life and more certain results. Rapid advances are like rapid rises of the barometer, liable to quick reversals.

The German report on the first day's fighting was curious and somewhat amusing. It stated that the great Anglo-French attack which had been prepared during several months with unlimited resources was made over a front of twenty-five miles, with the result that the British gained no appreciable advantages between Gommecourt and La Boisselle. On the other hand, it admitted that the Allied troops did penetrate the German first line and consequently " we withdrew our divisions from the completely destroyed first line trenches to positions between the first and second positions." It also admitted that " as is usual in such cases material which had been solidly built in was lost." Further it added that many minor attacks west and south-west of Tahure and at points adjacent to the main attack were made, but these failed everywhere. A few days later Berlin thought the attack had not reached its highest intensity, but, on the 8th, Major Moraht returned to the charge in the *Berliner Tageblatt.* " It was doubtful," said he, " whether, from the point of view of preparation, the British offensive had not started too early." Further, he remarked " The British attack is far behind the French attack, and because *it has not succeeded* " the enemy mysteriously hints that the main blow will fall at a different place. " This makes no impression upon us, because there, as here, what we expected will be confirmed—viz., that the British are not sufficiently seasoned to drive us on to the Rhine."

During Saturday night and the next day July 2, the fighting north of the Somme

[*Official Photograph.*]

IN RESERVE : ROYAL WARWICKS RESTING.

continued with great fierceness, and several violent counter-attacks were made by the Germans against the French new positions in the neighbourhood of Hardecourt, but they were all driven off with heavy losses in killed and wounded, besides 200 prisoners. Following up the advantage gained on the right bank of the river, our Allies completely occupied Curlu.

On Sunday more progress was made, as has been seen. Fricourt was captured and 800 additional prisoners were taken. A further advance was also made to the east of Fricourt, and fighting went on in the neighbourhood of Boisselle, but here the enemy resisted stubbornly and we were compelled to give up Serre. A large amount of material was taken by our troops during the fighting and many counter-attacks were driven back.

South of the Somme the positions gained the previous day were held against all counter-attacks, and round Hardecourt and Assevillers some further progress was made. The severe fighting continued during the whole day, and some further advantage was gained in the region of Hardecourt and Curlu. A strongly fortified quarry east of the latter was captured, and a footing was gained at numerous points in the second German position between the river and Assevillers. Frise was captured as well as Méreaucourt Wood somewhat to the east of the village. A considerable number of guns and a great quantity of material on all fronts fell to the Allies, and the prisoners captured by the French alone on July 1 and July 2 exceeded six thousand, besides guns, machine guns, and a large quantity of war equipment.

North of the Somme the next three days were spent by the French chiefly in con-solidating the positions won, and taking points necessary for this purpose. They advanced up the Valley of the Somme, pushing their attack from Méréaucourt Wood towards the village of Feuillères, where there was a bridge leading northward across the Somme Canal and river to Hem. Feuillères was captured with a rush, the fighting being chiefly done with bomb and bayonet, and the Hill 105 to the south of it was also taken. Then, striking north-east, the Division employed here pushed through the Chapitre Wood, and captured the little village of Buscourt. The advance of the French in the top corner of the battlefield carried them right through the German second line, which was of great strength at this point. The first German line here consisted of three separate rows of trenches. The second line from Herbecourt, four miles west of Péronne, to Assevillers, five miles south-west of Péronne, had only two lines of trenches. North of the first-named village these stretched out to Feuillères, but had in front of them an advanced line of defence which stretched from Herbecourt to Méréaucourt Wood. By capturing Chapitre Wood a position had been gained through the three main defensive German positions, and the fact that this was done so rapidly was of great importance. The position at Feuillères and Hill 150 enabled the French guns to support the attack north of the river against Curlu, in which direction the advance had been much slower. Assevillers also was captured with great rapidity. Another important advance was made by the French troops, which, having taken Herbecourt on the 2nd, advanced and captured the whole of Flaucourt and its surrounding defences, and established themselves to the east of the

FRENCH TROOPS ADVANCING THROUGH BARBED-WIRE.

THE FRENCH OFFENSIVE.
Hoisting a 16-inch shell.

village. This was an exceedingly important gain. With Buscourt and Flaucourt in their hands they were within three miles of Péronne. From Flaucourt the German troops were driven back towards Péronne, and thus their communications with the south portion of their lines were much interrupted. The ever-winding Somme, which flows in varying directions now north and south, now east and west, rendered communications difficult.

Across the Somme the bridges were of the usual fragile character met with all over France on unimportant roads, and could easily be destroyed by artillery fire, and the road in question for nearly one thousand yards was borne on these bridges across the marshes, the Somme Canal and river. From the plateau at Flaucourt the French commanded all this country with their artillery fire, although to the south the villages of Belloy-en-Santerre and Barleux, both strongly fortified, were at this time untaken. Once they were captured there would be nothing but open country between the French and Péronne.

Monday, July 4, was a day of comparative quiet chiefly devoted to consolidating the ground already won. Bernafay Wood, into which our troops had penetrated on the 3rd, was this day completely captured before noon. By Authuille a slight gain was made in the German front line, and saps were run out from our line to connect it, thus making it part of our position. In many places slight gains were made, prisoners and material taken.

The line now held ran from Fricourt, Mametz to a line running from La Boisselle and Contalmaison through the Bois de Mametz past Bois Montauban to the Bernafay Wood. The village of this name was completely occupied by noon. Fighting went on all day and into the night on the outskirts of La Boisselle, where the village, although practically taken, was held by the enemy to a small extent. There was also fighting around Contalmaison. No further attacks were made by the Germans on Montauban; the only thing they did was to direct a barrage fire on the near side of the village to hinder the bringing up of reinforcements. The German artillery did not distinguish itself by any special efforts, although Mametz was somewhat severely shelled. On the other hand, our artillery brought a heavy fire to bear on the part of La Boisselle which the Germans still held. About three o'clock a tremendous thunderstorm broke over the whole of this portion of the field. The rain was torrential, made it impossible to observe, and turned every trench into a running brook, and this for a time much impeded the operations.

Near Thiépval, a German, above a battered parapet, waved a Red Cross flag. He was allowed to come down and lift back something into the trench, and just as he got it over and into it, it was seen that what he landed was not a dead or wounded man, but a machine gun.

Heavy fighting went on throughout the night of July 4–5 in the neighbourhood of the Ancre and the Somme, and further progress was made at certain points. On Wednesday, the 5th, there was considerable artillery fire from the German side, and two determined attacks were made on our new trenches near Thiépval, but these were easily beaten off with loss to the enemy. The fighting was indeed almost continuous along the battle front, but was chiefly confined to local struggles for certain points of importance to us, the result being that we made some advance in certain places, and also defeated all offensive attempts of the Germans. More prisoners fell into our hands, and the total number taken from the first of the month was well over 6,000.

On the same day the French, to the north of the Somme, advanced again, and during the night of the 4–5th captured a line of German trenches to the east of Curlu. To the south of the Somme the Sormont farm was captured on the left bank of the river opposite Cléry. The final result from the 5th was that the whole of the ground south of Sormont Farm and Hill 63 on the road from Flaucourt and Barleux were gained by the French. On the same night (4–5th) the Germans made an attack on Belloy-en-Santerre after a very severe artillery preparation. This had been taken by the French on the 4th. For a short period they gained a footing in the village, but the French counter-attacked and drove them out. The village of Estrées was still partly held by the Germans, and here the fighting was very severe, but by night the last of the Germans were driven out, and a detachment which was holding a mill to the north of this village was forced to surrender. None of the attacks on the French position came to any result, all being stopped by the French fire. Further prisoners were taken, and the total number was raised to 9,000.

North of the Somme the French continued their advance, and captured in the course of July 5 the southern slopes of the knoll north of Curlu, and also several small woods which had been prepared for defence. To the east of this village the French infantry shelled the second German position, which was completely captured on a front of about 1¼ mile from the Cléry-Maricourt road as far as the Somme. Pushing on, the French attacked the village of Hem, which they captured after a smart fight which lasted till seven in the evening. They also took the farm of Monacu. This gave them an addition of over 300 prisoners to those already taken.

The capture by the French of the trenches connecting Estrées and Belloy involved the whole of the German second position to the south of the Somme on a front of about 6¼ miles.

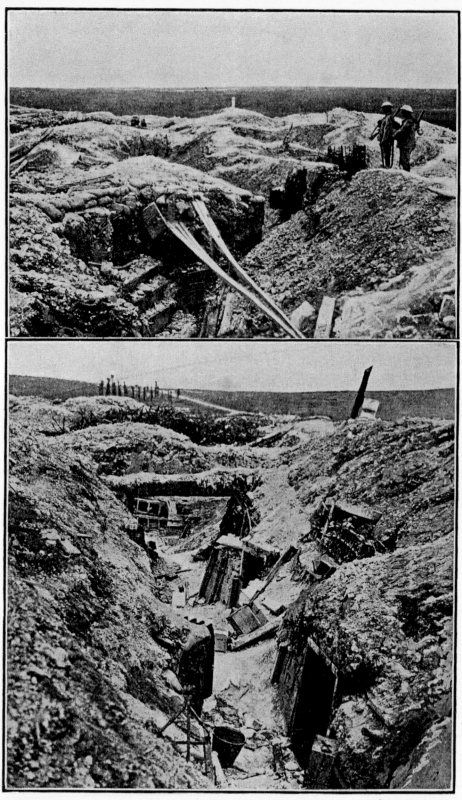

THE EFFECTS OF A BOMBARDMENT
On the German Trenches near Ovillers.

On the 6th low clouds interfered with aeroplane work, but a British machine, by descending through them to within 300 feet from the ground, succeeded in surprising and bombing a train in the Bapaume area, just as German reinforcements were alighting. One of our heavy batteries inflicted severe losses on a German battalion in column of route. On the left, near Thiépval, a slight advance was made and some prisoners secured. North of La Boisselle, and eastward of that village, a determined attack was completely crushed.

At nightfall the Germans were driven from a trench on a front of a thousand yards. There was, besides, violent bomb fighting at other points between Thiépval and the northern end of Foch's left wing, where the enemy were attacking in force. North-east of Hem he recovered two little woods a thousand yards from the village; but to counterbalance this the French drove the Germans from another wood in the vicinity and easily repulsed an attack south of the Somme directed against Belloy.

The last-mentioned attack came not from Péronne, which was being shelled by the French artillery, but from the direction of Chaulnes, 10 miles south-west of it. Péronne was no longer a railhead, German reinforcements being now detrained at Roisel, nine miles away, or at Cartigny, four miles to the east of the town.

From Chaulnes, through Berny, the Bavarians were six times led to the shambles, the heaviest attack being launched at 3 p.m., when two regiments in massed formation staggered forward through the curtain of shells only to be dispersed by the bayonet. A company of Bavarians which had occupied some farm buildings on the cross-road from Belloy to Berny was obliged to surrender. By this date our Allies had captured 76 guns and hundreds of mitrailleuses.

In the night the offensive was resumed by the Germans at both ends of the French section of advance. The counter-attacks north of Hem were shattered by gun and rifle fire and several prisoners taken; the charges delivered from Berny-en-Santerre against the French lines from Estrées to Belloy were stopped by curtain fire, the enemy losing heavily. Two companies enfiladed by French machine-guns were annihilated.

To interfere with the reinforcements of men and munitions which were being hurried up by the German Staff to the Somme, French aeroplanes bombed the railway from Nesle to Ham. Fires were observed to break out in the stations at Ham and Voyerres, both south-east of Péronne.

On the 7th the British forward movement was resumed. In anticipation of it, the enemy, during the night of the 6–7th, had been bombarding with ordinary and lachrymatory shells the British position at La Boisselle, in Montauban, and in the Bernafay Wood. Our guns took up the challenge. "Such a night!" observed an eye-witness. "I never saw anything like it. Exactly like hell, only worse; a sky full of shells and lights bursting like blazes. A regular Brock's benefit." But our troops did more than merely reply to the German fire. Early in the night of the 6–7th we made fair progress, advancing in the neighbourhood of La Boisselle and capturing 50 prisoners, moving also nearer Contalmaison, which was to be the main object for the next day. There were little woods which served as advanced posts for the Germans, called Bailiff's Wood, Peake's Wood, and Birch Tree Wood. The last named we had gained some days before. Above and a little west of Peake's Wood was an intricate nest of German trenches to which we had given the name of the Horseshoe. This we attacked at its northern and southern ends. At the former there was a strong redoubt with many machine-guns, and altogether the position was a formidable one. Our troops made good their entry. But the two assaulting bodies made no connexion with one another in the Horseshoe, and neither was aware that a considerable body of Germans lay in between them until the fire from the latter revealed the true state of affairs. To relieve the situation it was necessary to take Peake's Wood, which lay somewhat behind the Horseshoe, and which, when captured, would render the latter untenable. This was done by a separate force of troops, and then the Germans were entirely cleared out of their position.

The day broke hazy, dull, and humid; everything for miles round was shaken by the explosions of the artillery and by the bursting shells. From the north-west of Thiépval, away towards the banks of the Somme, the battle once more was joined.

On the extreme left our men met with a reverse, and the enemy temporarily regained two or three hundred yards of lost ground.

FRENCH COMMANDER ON THE SOMME.
General Fayolle (third from left) with General Balfourier (in dark uniform).

South of Thiépval the struggle centred round the Leipzig Redoubt, at a salient in the German line. For 20 months the most up-to-date engineers had been busily strengthening this formidable work, which, it was believed, would, like the Hohenzollern Redoubt on the Loos battlefield, be sufficient to hold in check for months the advance of the Allies. Our men, who had already worked their way into the redoubt, made during the 8th further progress. On their right a British brigade broke through 500 yards of trench in front of Ovillers, and entered the village, where a desperate struggle went on till nightfall. Farther to the south and east of La Bois elle our line was advanced 200 yards or so over a maze of German trenches 2,000 yards in length.

It was round Contalmaison, however, that

ON THE SOMME.
General Foch (on left) and General Fayolle.

the chief incidents of the day occurred. Contalmaison is about a mile and a half to the east of La Boisselle. It is flanked by woods on both sides, the Bailiff Wood on the left, the larger Mametz Wood on the right. Eastwards are Bernafay Wood, and beyond it Trônes Wood. The main trench leading up to Contalmaison was the sunken road between Round Wood and Birch Wood, woods only by courtesy, for the shell fire had felled the trees in them. The sunken road was enfiladed from Bailiff and Mametz Woods, both in the German possession. Behind Contalmaison lay the hamlet of Bazentin-le-Petit and an adjacent wood. In these some of the German reserves were hidden.

During the previous night's fighting the British, after securing the Horseshoe Trench, had moved up to the outskirts of both Contalmaison and Mametz Wood. On village and wood our batteries discharged salvo after salvo of shells. Behind the barrage of fire the British infantry advanced to storm the village. Advancing both to right and left of Mametz Wood our troops swept steadily onwards, and by 10 a.m. some were getting through the wood to take Contalmaison in flank while others

went straight for the village. Between the wood and the village five battalions of the 3rd Division of the Prussian Guard, probably at the orders of the Kaiser himself, advanced in close formation. They had left Valenciennes a few days before and, via Cambrai, had been hastily brought to the scene of action. No time had been given them for studying the ground and it is not, therefore, surprising that they marched straight into the barrage which was covering our advance. One of the battalions was wiped out, the others, who closed with the British, were killed, wounded, dispersed or taken prisoners. At first the Germans thought they had been defeated by British Guards. They were extremely surprised and disgusted to find they had been beaten by men of the newly raised army.

Flushed with their success our troops, mostly Yorkshiremen and other Northerners, carried Contalmaison and released several captive comrades. But at this moment rain descended in torrents and, under cover of the deluge, the Germans counter-attacked from the Mametz Wood. At the same time Contalmaison was heavily shelled. It was decided that for the time being we should evacuate the village, which was accordingly done. In the afternoon the cemetery to the south-east and the Acid Drop Copse near it were taken and our men ensconced themselves on the edge of the Mametz Wood.

Although the rain which had filled the trenches and rendered the ground slippery and sodden had impeded the advance, we had done well. The German reserves in the hamlet of Bazentin-le-Petit had suffered from our shell fire, as had large numbers of troops retiring across the open. An enemy battalion marching to the front had been peppered by the machine guns of an aeroplane flying low and had subsequently been thinned by the shells of our heavy artillery. An extract from the diary of a captured Bavarian officer, Colonel Bedall, may interest the reader :

July 7.—The English once again let off gas. Bazentin-le-Grand and the positions of the 16th Regiment were subjected to a lively bombardment on the evening of the 6th inst., which has completely wrecked them. The attack which started in the afternoon of July 6 near Contalmaison was continued without a pause and with varying success ; on July 7 the line was pierced as far as Contalmaison ; 14 companies of the 3rd Guard Division were ordered to counter-attack, coming from the direction of Martinpuich and Flers and advancing south-west on Contalmaison.

At 10 p.m. Bazentin-le-Grand was subjected to half an hour's surprise fire by the enemy's artillery. This was of unprecedented violence and destroyed the village to such an extent that there is nothing but a heap of bricks to be seen there now.

Waiting at the station.

On the way to the Internment Camp.

GERMAN PRISONERS ARRIVE IN ENGLAND.

On the 8th, in cloudy weather, our aeroplanes and kite balloons took photographs, directed the fire of batteries, and bombed the rain-soaked billets of the Germans, and also a depôt of ammunition, which exploded with a loud report. Few enemy machines went up, but three of them attacked one of our own, which, however, though disabled, landed safely at its own aerodrome. The heavy rain of the day before impeded operations on the ground, but hand-to-hand fighting went on in the ruins of Ovillers, the Germans getting the worst of the encounter. East of Montauban and of the Wood of Berna-fay, after a violent bombardment, our men effected a lodgment in the Trônes Wood, capturing 130 prisoners and several machine guns. Up to then we had secured in the Battle of the Ancre-Somme 20 guns, 51 machine guns, numbers of trench mortars, *minenwerfer*, bomb-throwers, searchlights, and other war material. The French to our right by the fire of their artillery greatly assisted us, and masses of Germans counter-attacking across the open melted away under the fire of the " 75 " guns and of our 18-pounders. The British had attacked the Trônes Wood and a farm south-east of it, while through rain and fog the French

in the morning had successfully assaulted from trenches filled with water the knoll north of the village of Hardecourt, situated between Longue-val and the right bank of the Somme. The Germans in the Hardecourt action lost in prisoners alone 623 men and 10 officers.

During the 9th the hostile artillery was more active. Nevertheless in Ovillers, now a mass of levelled trenches, ruins, and craters filled with mud and corpses, the British continued to push forward.

At night, after a gruesome fight with bomb, knife and club among the broken trees, under-growth and tangled wire, the British secured Bailiff Wood on the edge of Contalmaison. Two vigorous German counter-attacks on our position in and near the Trônes Wood met with the fate of those delivered the day before.

This wood, triangular in shape and 1,400 yards from north to south, with a southern base of 400 yards, had been strongly defended by the Germans with trenches and wire entanglements. We had captured the southern end of the wood. In the evening the enemy bombarded it and delivered four separate and unsuccessful charges in the hope of recovering the lost ground.

IN A TRENCH AT OVILLERS.   [*Official Photograph.*

[*Official Photographs.*

LOOKING AFTER THE WOUNDED.
Attending to the slightly wounded.
Circle Picture : In a trench.
Bottom Picture : The helping hand across a trench.

Meanwhile, Foch, after two days' preliminary bombardment, had launched another offensive south of the Somme, and the position attacked was a front of 2½ miles from Flaucourt to Belloy. The French crossed two entrenched ridges and reached the plateau capped by the Maisonnette Farm.

The village of Biaches, in the western environs of Péronne, was assaulted from three sides. At 2 p.m. the French were holding the northern end, but the Germans, with machine-guns in a group of ruined houses between the market-place and the road leading to Barleux, offered stubborn resistance. Suddenly bugles sounded the charge, and a French force moved on the enemy's burrows. The Germans were dislodged, although, in a farm-house, near the church, 60 of the enemy held out for some time. By 2.45 p.m. Biaches was in the hands of our Allies, and what remained of the garrison was scampering off into the Ste. Radégonde suburb of Péronne, south of Biaches. Round Barleux there were desperate combats. By nightfall a line of trenches stretching north-eastward from Barleux to Maisonnette Farm had passed into the possession of the French. These lines now ran from Hardecourt, where they joined the British, to a point on the Somme between Hem and Cléry. Thence they follow the south bank of the river from Buscourt, by Sormont Farm, past the junction of the Nord and Somme Canals to Biaches, and over the plateau of La Maisonnette to Barleux. The French looked down on the city where Charles the Bold had outwitted the treacherous Louis XI.

The time had arrived for the completion of the British operations against the enemy's 14,000 yards long front system of defence. Our main efforts were concentrated on Contalmaison and the Mametz and Trônes Woods. The next day (July 10) there descended on the doomed village hurricanes of shells. Part of the garrison, panic-stricken, bolted back into the open, where they were caught by our guns and the mitrailleuse of the brigade in the "holding" positions to the right and left. This retrograde movement was but natural. As a German prisoner who had taken part in the Verdun fighting subsequently remarked, "the shell-fire on the Somme was much worse than that in the region of the Lorraine fortress."

At 4.30 p.m. two companies of British infantry left Bailiff Wood, moving on the north-west corner of Contalmaison. Simultaneously on their right two battalions in four successive waves made for the village. The Germans had expected an attack from the south. To reach the shallow trench protecting the western face of Contalmaison 1,500 yards had to be crossed. The men were in open order, but, held up in places by wire and subjected to machine-gun fire and shells, their numbers were terribly depleted by the time they reached the trench. The sight of cold steel, however, was too much for the more numerous Germans, who retired from it, decimated by their own machine-guns.

Lying in the trench the survivors of the British battalions recovered breath. Then,

with a shout, they rushed for the village. Hedges interlaced with wire had to be negotiated, but the gallant band pressed on. The Germans in Contalmaison were numerically superior, but British individuality gained the day over German automatism. Some of the garrison flew for their lives, most surrendered, a few died at their posts.

Scarcely had the British taken cover in Contalmaison when, towards 6 p.m., the German reserves advanced to retake the village. Reinforcements were hurrying up to the support of the heroic groups of British; one of which groups, led by a second-lieutenant, emerged from the village flinging bombs at the oncoming enemy, who was driven back.

During the night the Germans counterattacked, but were beaten off with heavy loss, and by the morning of the 11th the village was definitely in our hands. The Germans in Ovillers, as a result of the fighting, were now in a dangerous salient.

To the south of Contalmaison an equally fierce struggle was proceeding for the Mametz Wood, some 220 acres in extent. At the south-westerly end the wood was fairly open; elsewhere the saplings were so close together that it was difficult to squeeze one's way between them. Lanes had been cut through them, and a German railway ran from southwest to north-east in the northern portion of the wood. At points on the edge and in the interior machine-gun emplacements had been made. A heavy howitzer and three field guns were hidden in the undergrowth.

On July 5 some of our men had entered the tiny Marlborough Wood to the east of the Mametz Wood, whose exits on that side became commanded by reverse machine-gun fire. The next day our patrols entered Mametz Wood on its southern side. By the 10th our troops had broken through the mazes of fortified area known as the Quadrangle on the south-west. On that day the real struggle for the Mametz Wood began.

END OF VOLUME NINE.

CHAPTER CLIV.

THE BATTLE OF THE SOMME (II.).

JULY 10, 1916—THE ATTACK ON MAMETZ WOOD—ITS CAPTURE BY WELSH TROOPS—TRÔNES
WOOD—THE FRENCH SOUTH OF THE SOMME—GERMAN PRISONERS—BRITISH MASTERY OF THE
AIR—STRATEGIC POSITION ON JULY 13—GENERAL JACOB AND GENERAL BIRDWOOD—THE GREAT
BATTLE OF JULY 14—FRANCE'S DAY—THE TWO BAZENTINS—SOUTH AFRICANS AT DELVILLE
WOOD—CAPTURE OF OVILLERS - LA BOISSELLE—FRANCO-BRITISH COOPERATION—BATTLE OF
JULY 20—THE ATTACK ON POZIÈRES—WORK OF THE FIRST ANZAC CORPS—"THE WINDMILL"—
CAPTURE OF POZIÈRES—RESULTS FROM JULY 1 TO JULY 26.

CHAPTER CLI. took the narrative of the Battle of the Somme up to the preparatory measures for the attack on Mametz Wood. It was on July 10 that the expulsion of the Germans from this stronghold began. The garrison obtained some help from their artillery farther back from the Quadrangle and from a machine-gun emplacement near Acid Drop Copse, but otherwise had to depend on their own exertions.

The German gunners in the background were deceived into believing that the eastern edge was most in danger, and consequently the barrage of German shells was sent down between it and Marlboro' Wood. But our real attack was delivered from the south and also against the Quadrangle position. So long as the redoubt at the east end of the Quadrangle Support Trench was not won, an advance up the northern part of Mametz Wood would be very difficult, if not impossible.* It was, therefore, necessary to take it, and all day long desperate fighting for its possession went on. By nightfall it was in the possession of Welsh troops.

Our artillery prepared the way by a devastating fire directed on the wood, and kept carefully ahead of the advancing infantry, which could be seen moving forward in scattered

parties towards the southern edge. The German machine-guns at that point were destroyed or buried, and our artillery lifted their range on to the northern edge of the enemy's second line and positions beyond it. Gradually the garrison, or rather what remained of it, withdrew to the upper part of the wood, followed by our ardent and cheering infantry and by the Pioneers, who wired and entrenched the positions immediately after they were taken. At sunset the British line ran along an open drive and the railway which ran through the wood. During the night the enemy vainly counter-attacked. How the contest was regarded by the Germans may be fairly imagined from the entry under July 10 in Colonel Bedall's diary already referred to :

July 10.—There was very heavy fighting in the Mametz Wood in which No. 1 section of the machine-gun company of the 16th Regiment suffered the exceptionally great loss, by a direct hit, of 15 men and one platoon commander killed and 12 men wounded.

Towards evening a furious struggle began in Mametz Wood. This lasted the entire night until the morning. The 3rd Battalion of the 16th Regiment and the 2nd Battalion of the Lehr Regiment were heavily engaged.

To-day a draft of 300 men arrived from the recruit battalion. Each battalion received 100 men to make up for losses.

Bazentin-le-Grand was repeatedly shelled to-day, but during the night less so than usual.

At break of day (July 11) the four Welsh battalions in Mametz Wood pushed onwards to east, north-east, north and south-west. Under

---

* See small map, Vol. IX., p. 493.

AUSTRALIAN TROOPS BRINGING UP A HEAVY GUN.

the hottest fire from *minenwerfer*, machine-guns and rifles our men got within 50 yards of the edge. Yet the narrow strip could not be passed except at the price of too great losses. Orders were given for a retreat to the drive and railway trenches, and our artillerymen were requested to concentrate their fire on the position, which had stopped our advance into the open. For half an hour the northern and north-eastern edge and eastern edge of the wood seemed to be convulsed with struggling men. That anything could live in this inferno seemed impossible. Nevertheless, at the north-east and north-west angles, machine-gunners remained entrenched, and when the British once more went forward through the fallen timber they were met with a hail of bullets. Not until 4 p.m. was the north-east corner, with its *minenwerfer* and machine-guns captured. Later in the day the north-west corner was secured, and by nightfall nearly every German in Mametz Wood was killed or a prisoner. We were within less than 300 yards of the German second line position. The bulk of the prisoners taken came from the 3rd Reserve Division of the Prussian Guard and the 16th Bavarian and 122nd Wurtemburg Regiments. The Wurtemburgers had been brought from the Russian front. They had arrived four days before and

complained of the bad weather and of the poor food now supplied to them.

"What sort of a time have you had in Contalmaison?" inquired a war correspondent of a German soldier who, in (for him) happier times, had been a cabinet-maker in the Tottenham Court Road. "Hell, perfect hell," was his answer. "The artillery fire was terrific. I never thought you English could do it."

The last sentence revealed the dominant feeling of the nation-in-arms which had been taught for two generations to regard peaceful projects with contempt and peace as merely an interlude in a perpetual warfare for existence. That British men, mere cricketers and football players, should, in under two years, have been made into warriors more than a match for the pick of the German Army; that the manufacturers and chemists of Great Britain should in the same period have mastered the gunner's craft and surpassed the skill of Krupp was quite incredible. The Germans had fought bravely and even stubbornly, but they felt themselves beaten at their own game.

The centre of the German first line had been broken. To the north and south of Contalmaison and the Mametz Wood the battle continued to rage. In the neighbourhood of

Ovillers, a shapeless mass of ruins, its chalk foundations tunnelled and honeycombed with deep dug-outs, the Prussian Guards still held out.

The road from Ovillers to Contalmaison had been secured by, among others a battalion of a South Country Regiment, which had been relieved on the 9th. During the two preceding days it had been fighting in a quagmire of yellowish-white mud, so tenacious that the very boots of the men stuck in it and had often to be wrenched off. The German soldiers, if not the officers, who appear to have remained in the background of the battle, had proved tough opponents. "These fellows," observed an officer, "fight like blue glory. I can't think how some of our people at home have got it into their heads that we are up against old men and immature lads. All the men we have fought have been fellows of fine physique. There have been exceptions, of course, but the old Boche is still a sticker and stands a lot of beating before he will hand in his checks." As *The Times* Military Correspondent had remarked, it was a tribute to the quality of our troops that some of the finest fighting material in the enemy's armies had been detailed to stem the British advance. Against a less tenacious foe they

would probably have succeeded. But our men were made of sterner stuff. One of them, for example, carrying bombs, had crawled up to a machine-gun emplacement and blown up gun and crew. The captain of another regiment had continued to lead his company after being hit in the heel, thigh and arm. Finally he fell pierced through the chest. Of deeds like these there were many.

Two and a half miles to the east of the Mametz Wood, away to the right of Montauban,

[Official photographs.

BEHIND THE LINES.
Trench-mortar ammunition. Smaller picture : Taking the ammunition up to the trenches.

[Official photograph.

GUNS IN ACTION AGAINST CONTALMAISON.

more stiff fighting had taken place. The Trônes Wood, through which lay the direct route to the important fortified area of Longueval, in the German second line, had been elaborately prepared for defence. At an enormous expense of labour, a labyrinth of interlacing trenches and redoubts had been constructed. Our troops had entered this nest of machine-guns, and fierce had been the struggles there. Time after time they had had to meet and repel determined charges. On the evening of the 10th it almost seemed as if they would be expelled from their dearly-won trenches and driven down the slopes towards Hardecourt. But fortunately the bulldog courage of the British, never better displayed than in such a crisis, did not desert them. They hung on through the night to the skirts of the wood, and on the 11th once more took the offensive. At 8.30 p.m. the British General Headquarter Staff reported that we had gained the whole of the wood with the exception of the northern end.

Up to this date we had captured 26 field guns, one naval gun, one heavy howitzer, an anti-aircraft gun, and over 7,500 prisoners. That the " Archibald " was not an insignificant item in the booty was apparent from the fact that, worsted, as a rule, in aerial duels, the Germans were more and more inclined to pin their faith on such artillery.

While General Haig was driving his wedge through the German first line between the Ancre and Hardecourt, General Foch had not been idle south of the Somme.

Péronne lies in a slight depression. To its west is the plateau of La Maisonnette, facing, on the opposite side of the Somme, the dominating hill of Mt. St. Quentin north of the town. During the night of the 9–10th our Allies, in the Barleux region, captured the trenches between that village and La Maisonnette, together with 950 prisoners, some of whom had been taken on the previous day. On the 10th, in the outskirts of Biaches, a redoubt with 103 men and 10 officers in it fell into the hands of the French. More important than this, after a desperate struggle Hill 97 and the Maisonnette Farm on its summit were at last carried, together with most of a copse to the north of the farm. The disingenuous German account of this action is worth quoting. "South of the Somme," it ran, " a strong attack made by French black troops against the La Maisonnette Height was

[*Official photograph.*

BRITISH BIG GUNS GOING UP TO THE FRONT.

met by overpowering fire. A few coloured troops who penetrated into our lines fell at the point of the German bayonets or were taken prisoners." The German General Staff forgot to add that the "overpowering fire" and "German bayonets" had not saved the hill and farm from capture. The next day the Germans were entirely dislodged from the copse, and some communication trenches between Estrées and Belloy, in which parties of the enemy still lurked, were occupied. Foch had secured nearly the whole of the loop of the Somme, and was within a few yards of the suburbs of Péronne.

On the 12th Sir Douglas Haig was able to announce that, despite the desperate efforts of the enemy, the whole of the Mametz Wood was in possession of the British, and that two German attacks against Contal-maison had broken down under our fire. The moment approached when the German second line would be breached. We had smashed our way to various depths of from 2,000 to 4,000 yards, reduced five strongly fortified villages, a large number of extraordinarily strong redoubts, and numerous heavily wired and entrenched woods. Altogether the Allies had

taken over 20,000 prisoners, a hundred guns, besides many machine-guns and bomb-throwers.

The special correspondent of *The Times* wrote of these events as follows :

"The prisoners are constantly passing through both the French lines and ours in batches, being kept for a while in paddocks enclosed with barbed wire, for the necessary examination, and then, as rapidly as possible, to the rear. Every time that one visits one of these depôts one finds it full of a new lot. And they vary extraordinarily. Many are fine, robust-looking men in the prime of life. As many others are weedy and poor, some old, some very young. And it is by no means the 'best' regiments which are now composed of the best material. I have seen none who looked under-nourished, though many had plainly endured great privations immediately before their capture.

"As for the guns, one meets them on the high roads and being dragged back from the battlefields, and they are being parked for exhibition purposes about Corps and Division and Brigade Headquarters. At a certain Headquarters there is quite a museum being accumulated on the lawn, which includes already a variety of designs of German trench mortars and the like and a row of *minenwerfer* made almost entirely of wood bound with wire, with the hollowed wooden blocks to take the recoil and the ingenious sundial-like stand of light iron bars to which they are braced forward to prevent them kicking over on discharge. The whole thing is so light that two men can easily carry it about : and they make, at practically no cost, very useful weapons.

" A gentleman who has just returned from a visit to the French Army tells me that German prisoners there said (what we had in effect heard here before) that they all thought that what they had to do was merely to overrun the new British Army— which they would do as soon as they tried conclusions with it—to have the war won. I was with the French Army myself 10 days ago and I know how utterly unlike a beaten army it looks. I never saw an army gayer or more evidently fit and confident. The German prisoners seem to be utterly astounded and disgusted by what they see there ; and their spirits are not raised by what they hear of what has been going on with the new British Army. The whole thing, including the fact that the French could hit as hard as they have hit and that our new armies were made of the stuff that

GETTING READY FOR ACTION.
A howitzer and its shell.

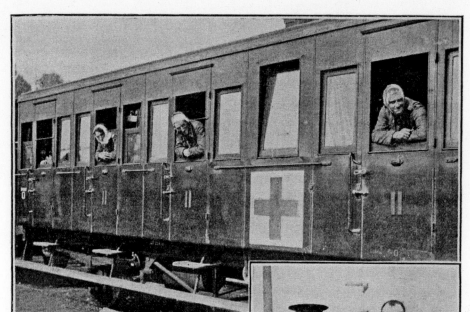

FROM THE BATTLEFIELD.
Wounded coming back from the Somme.

Of the six unhappy men three died on the fifth day. Of the others who survived and were rescued by their comrades one has since succumbed.

they have shown themselves to be made of, has evidently been a complete surprise to them.

"By this time I have had the opportunity of familiarizing myself with the events of the earlier days' fighting on the front of practically every brigade in the whole of our line. A few days ago I was very careful to report that at one point the Germans had shown humanity in allowing us to recover our wounded and in taking those of our wounded within their reach back into their trenches. I am sorry to say that this was most exceptional. The contrary (which I have also reported) was the rule. In general, they have bayoneted our wounded and have played machine-guns over the fields where the dead and wounded lay together to make sure that none would fight again. The evidence comes authoritatively from too many quarters to admit of doubt."

Another instance of German brutality was reported by a French paper, the *Journal:*

Six of the soldiers left behind were taken prisoners. The Germans kept them in an advanced trench without giving them bite or sup. Several times a day they were hoisted on to the parapet and thus made the living target for ball and shell, and as their blood flowed their captors would approach them and taunt them with gibes about the meals they had not had.

Prisoners and wounded were brought over to England shortly after the great advance. A writer in *The Times* gave a dramatic account of a meeting of two trains near Southampton Docks, the one filled with wounded returning from France, the other with reinforcements going out to make good the losses :

A long Red Cross train, just filled from end to end from one of the hospital ships—casualties from the present offensive in France—was pulling slowly out

SCENE NEAR LA BOISSELLE: SHELLS BURSTING IN THE BACKGROUND.

for its run to London. Almost every window served to frame an outward-gazing soldier, officer or man, in ragged, bloodstained, muddy khaki. These were the sitting-up cases, nearly all with heads bandaged or arms in slings.

Just near the dock gates the hospital train met another equally long train coming in, and packed from end to end with fresh troops bound out for France from some English depôt camp. Each of its windows framed not one, but two or three men in khaki, red, lusty faces, well sun-browned, looking out over the close-cropped heads of their mates ; full of eager curiosity and expectation and fresh clean robustness.

For 50 yards or so, and at a foot pace, the two contrasting trains of King George's soldiers glided side by side in an uncanny silence.

The writer watched them from an office window overhead, and could plainly see in the faces of the untried troops their eager interest, their profound respect for their comrades who had been tried. A strange, dumb kind of promise shone out from many of the eyes in those fresh faces. The assured pride, the easy fearlessness of the man who has proved himself in the very teeth of death ; this was marked in the faces of the wounded. But no man spoke a word. Silent and inarticulate, the man to be tried gazed into the faces of the men tried as they were carried past.

Suddenly then, in a rather quavering voice, most singularly vibrant with emotion, a very young lance-corporal, whose right arm was in a white sling, and whose head was swathed in bandages, cried out, in all the sunny silence :

" Are we downhearted ? "

And then the tension snapped. It seemed that hundreds of these brave fellows—coming home and going out—heaved long sighs. All had wanted to give expression to the powerful emotions inspired by the chance juxtaposition of those two trains ; and none had known how. Here was a way. The music of the roar which rose now from the cabined hundreds of both trains was something to penetrate the vitals of a Briton ; to touch with magic of some kind the least impressionable mind in all this realm. Those wonderful rising and falling waves of sound I shall never forget. It was only when the two trains were divided by a gap of fully 200 yards that the music of it died away, slowly in the soft summer air.

Incidents like this showed the spirit of the New Army.

The progress of the Allies to July 12 had been considerable and continuous. It had also, in contrast with earlier operations, been carried out with losses which, upon the whole, may be described as comparatively small. For this there were three reasons. In the first place the cooperation between the artillery and infantry already described had become more and more perfect as the fighting went on. Secondly, the aircraft had become the close allies of both the foot soldiers and the guns. Thirdly, the operations of the Allies were carefully and skilfully planned, and fully adapted to meet the situation. The intimate relationship between the artillery and infantry was not only shown in the way the artillery prepared for the advance of the infantry, but even more in the absolute unison of effort between the

gunners and the infantry during the attack. The positions of the German guns were known by means of the aircraft observations and they were carefully battered, reducing many of them to silence and always diminishing the value of their fire. While this was the task of part of the Allied artillery, the rest overwhelmed the trenches with a fire of great severity so that they could hardly be manned. The guns also put a barrier of fire behind the position attacked, to prevent reinforcements coming up to the threatened points, to keep down counter attacks and protect the flanks of the attacking units. Step by step, as the infantry advanced, the artillery changed its target to suit the situation.

The Flying Corps had, as the war progressed, taken a constantly increasing share in the operations. In the first place the boldness of their flights had enormously impressed the German airmen. The latter could no longer roam over the British lines, while ours constantly went over the German, bombing important points, destroying stores and supplies, railway stations and railway trains, even coming down to low altitudes and using their machine-guns in support of our infantry attacks. The proof of the audacity of our flyers was clearly shown by the increasing numbers of casualties among them. Yet these losses had been justified and more than justified by the gains. They had blinded the enemy's observers and increased the range of their own observations. How their activities were regarded by the enemy may be surmised from the statement of a German prisoner describing the bombardment of St. Quentin on July 10:

At the end of June the 22nd Reserve Division, to which my regiment was attached, was sent to rest in the neighbourhood of St. Quentin. An order came to us on July 10 to proceed to the Somme front. About three o'clock in the afternoon the first battalion of the 71st Reserve Regiment and the 11th Reserve Battalion of Jaegers were in St. Quentin Station ready to entrain. We had placed our arms and equipment in the carriages.

At this moment some British aeroplanes appeared and dropped bombs. One fell on a building full of ammunition and caused a violent explosion. There were 200 ammunition wagons in the station and 60 exploded. The remainder were only saved with difficulty.

The train which was to have carried the troops, together with all the equipment and baggage, was destroyed, in addition to a large quantity of war material stored on the platforms. The men, seized with panic, fled in all directions. A hundred men of the 71st Regiment and 80 men of the 11th Jaegers were killed or wounded. It was not before several hours that it was possible to reassemble the battalion of the 71st Regiment, which was sent to rest, and the next day it entrained at another station in order to be entirely re-equipped. Afterwards the battalion was sent to Péronne, where it was placed in reserve before going into action.

The enemy's aviators had been thoroughly dominated, defeated continuously in combat and they began to appreciate the Hudibrastic saying :

He who fights and runs away
May live to fight another day,
But he who is in battle slain
Will never live to fight again.

The German airman's opinion of our airmen is well shown by the following incident related by a member of our Flying Corps :

"Did I tell you the Huns dropped a note yesterday, 'Please give your bloody Flying Corps a rest'? We give them no peace now, and we do offensive patrols up and down their lines."

Crude in form, but graphic.

The Germans had devoted much time to improving their second line of defence, which was threatened by the impending attack. One of their divisional orders of the early part of July which was found by our troops ran : "The conversion of villages into strong points is of the greatest importance. Such villages are Pozières, Contalmaison, Bazentin-le-Petit, Bazentin-le-Grand and Longueval." Contal-

maison was lost, but the other villages mentioned in the order were still held.

The working parties of soldiers had been strengthened by forced labour and French and Belgian men, and women too, had been compelled to work at defences from which their countrymen were to be shot down.

The first advance, although considerable in extent and still more considerable in the moral effect it had produced on the German soldiers, had had little or no influence on the average German citizen not in immediate contact with the fighting line. This was due to the always garbled and often mendacious accounts given in the German newspapers. Thus the *Kölnische Volkszeitung* of July 13 published the following remarks :

Notwithstanding that the battle was very severe— for the enemy attacked in very great superiority and the individual Englishman is a brave and resolute man—our relatively weak infantry has performed superhuman deeds and inflicted losses on the enemy which he will remember. . . . As is natural in a brave army, British losses in officers are also very great, but some educated ones who are able to form an idea of the war said "that cannot hinder us from making ever-renewed attempts to vanquish the Germans," for the hopes of their whole country are bound up with this thought.

Serious as every German became in spirit when we learnt that the armed millions of the Entente were rushing on us in storm attack on all fronts, that the

[*Official photograph.*

BRITISH ANTI-AIRCRAFT GUNS ON THE WESTERN FRONT.

ON A BOMBING EXPEDITION.

A French aeroplane photographed from another aeroplane while in full flight above the clouds.

Russians sought to overwhelm the weak places on our East front with their masses, that the Austrians had retired in Italy, and that the Anglo-French flood swelled up against us in the West, the course of events has hitherto shown that in this greatest, most mighty moment of the great war. our enemies' plans have been brought to naught by the stedfastness, joyful self-sacrifice, and conscious strength of our nation in arms. They fell on us simultaneously in order that we should not throw our troops like shuttles on threatened points —now East, now West. Things have gone all right without that. Imperishable is the heroism of these great days.

Lieutenant Alfred Dambitsch, who was wounded on the Somme, gave a description in the *Vossische Zeitung* of the Allies' tactics in their present offensive. He described the various weapons introduced during the war, such as liquid fire throwers, gas attacks, and submarines, and altogether gave a good idea from the German point of view of the British and French operations:

n this respect the present French and British offensive is the last word. The aim of any offensive in modern warfare is the destruction of the enemy. This is the object of the present offensive, the idea being to enclose us in a tactical ring by simultaneous bombardment with long-range guns from the front and the rear. Accordingly the greedy beast began eating at the back lines of the German front. First of all our third and second trenches were incessantly bombarded, mostly by heavy artillery, of which the enemy had concentrated unprecedented masses in the sector of attack. It was dug-outs which had to be battered down, so that at the moment of assault all the defenders, except a few survivors, and all the machine-guns might be buried. Our second and third trenches were bombarded in order to prevent our bringing up reserves. For the same reason all the communication trenches leading from the rear to the front position were kept under incessant fire. On the Somme every one of our columns had a good communication trench which led from the headquarters of the battalion to the front trench.

But the attack against our front from the rear extended still further. All the main and side roads and all the cross-roads were kept under fire so that approaching troops, munitions, supplies, and provisions had to pass through several lines of fire. Bombarding villages and places behind the front where the various reserves are supposed to be quartered is an old trick of the British and French, but this time the principle was carried out more consistently and recklessly than ever. All places up to a distance of 10 miles behind the front were brought under incessant heavy artillery bombardment, which often started actual fires, thanks to the incendiary shells used by the enemy.

The battering down of our advanced trenches was almost exclusively left to the heavy artillery and trench mortars, especially the latter. The French have made great improvements in this weapon lately. For the destruction of our trenches they exclusively employed those of the heaviest calibre, and they now throw their mines with greater accuracy and over longer ranges than formerly. Opposite my company not fewer than six mortars were placed. They were worked uninterruptedly, throwing hundreds of aerial torpedoes on our position from the first to the third trenches. They tore up our wire obstacles from the ground, poles and all, and threw them all over the place, crushing

LIEUT.-GENERAL C. W. JACOB, C.B.
In command of the Second Army Corps.

the dug-outs, if they fell on them, and damaging the trenches. In a very short time great portions of our trenches had been flattened out, partly burying their occupants. This fire lasted for seven days, and finally there came a gas attack, also of an improved kind.

Although the offensive was made by great masses of infantry and had been prepared with all the latest improvements of the science of war, the attempt to break our line completely failed. Our front is no longer in any danger. Though the attacks still continue we are prepared to meet them. Even to-day, when war is so largely a matter of mechanical contrivances, the old truth still holds good that in the long run it is always the men who are the deciding factor.

The deepest impression left on me was not a feeling of horror and terror in face of these gigantic forces of destruction, but an unceasing admiration for my own men. Young recruits who had just come into the field from home, fresh twenty-year old boys, behaved in this catastrophe ploughing and thundering as if they had spent all their life in such surroundings, and it is partly thanks to them that the older married men also stood the test so well.

July 13 had been uneventful, mainly given up to the preparations for the advance projected for next day. But there was considerable artillery activity on both sides and some infantry fighting by which we made appreciable advances at various points, in addition to which we captured some German howitzers with an appreciable supply of ammunition. South of Ypres and also of the La Bassée Canal raids on our trenches attempted by the enemy were easily driven back.

The strategic position on this date was as follows. The left wing of the Allies from Gommecourt southwards to the Ancre had made little progress. The centre, between the Ancre and the Somme, had carried the enemy's front-line and parts of his second-line position. South of the Somme the right wing of the Allied line formed by the French who were on the left bank of the river had pushed into the loop of the Somme and was almost at the gates of Péronne, thus menacing the communications of the Germans behind their line of trenches.

The Army Corps engaged at the beginning of the Battle of the Somme were stated in Chapter CLI., pages 489–90. Subsequently there were brought into front line the Second Army Corps (Lieut.-Gen. C. W. Jacob, C.B.); which ultimately took Thiépval, and, as will be seen later, the First Anzac Corps (Lieut.-Gen. Sir William R. Birdwood, K.C.S.I., K.C.M.G.).

The difficulties in the path of Haig and Foch will be the better appreciated when it is remembered that, under somewhat analogous circumstances, the Kaiser and Falkenhayn had failed

LIEUT.-GENERAL SIR WILLIAM R.
BIRDWOOD, K.C.S.I., K.C.M.G.
In command of the First Anzac Corps.

[*Official photograph.*

ANZACS ON THE WESTERN FRONT.
Within the Australian lines.

to pierce the Allied line in the First Battle of Flanders, although it had not been supported with any but the slightest trench work. More recently the Germans had failed before the elaborate defences of the French at Verdun. Yet the British and French, undismayed by the formidable character of the works they had to attack, proposed to pierce them, relying on the capacity of their troops and the greatly increased artillery at their disposal. By their efforts during the first twelve days of July considerable progress had been made, and they were now ready to continue the pressure forward to gain more ground towards the Thiépval-Longueval side.

The next step forward, therefore, was towards Contalmaison, the two Bazentins, Longueval, Delville Wood and Waterlot Farm.

The night of the 13th was very warm and calm. Clouds obscured the sky, but through them the moon and occasional stars were at times visible. Suddenly an arc of flame appeared on the horizon from Contalmaison Villa to Waterlot Farm. An answering ring of fire round our trenches was the immediate reply of the Germans, and the deafening combat of the two artilleries began.

The region of Ovillers—la Boisselle also was so dosed with shells as to give it the appearance of a volcano in eruption, while, far off on the right, a fainter curve of flame showed that the French artillerymen were busy.

About 3 a.m. on the 14th the moon set, and a faint light from the east crept over the battlefield. Half an hour later the illumination from the explosion of our shells somewhat died down. Our fire was being lifted and only the German artillery continued firing. The moment had come for the British movement, and the men leaped out of their trenches and moved steadily forward to assault the German position.

At 4 a.m. aeroplanes mounted into the air, and kite balloons ascended through the low hanging clouds.

Ten minutes later a red glow at the edge of Delville Wood, from which flames shot up, indicated that ammunition stores and "dumps" in Longueval had been set on fire. Dense clouds of smoke, rent in places by the blast of bursting shells, rolled over the ground.

As the Trônes Wood extended south of the British right it had, of course, to be taken. So long as it remained in German hands Longueval, if captured, could be attacked by

THE PIPERS AT LONGUEVAL.

From the Bernafay Wood and the trenches north and east of Montauban a body of Highlanders, preceded by pipers playing "The Campbells are Coming," crossed 1,200 yards of "No Man's Land."

the enemy from below, and it would also be difficult to reduce Waterlot Farm and Guillemont.

Out of the Bernafay Wood and from south and east of it the English infantry, which included men of Sussex, dashed forward. Machine-gun fire forced them to crawl forward on their hands and knees to approach the enemy line. In groups of two or three they slowly got to the edge of the tangled heap of felled trees which now constituted Trônes Wood and set about turning out its defenders. While thus engaged some of our men heard shouts in English from ahead of them. They came from a handful of West Kents who, with some Lewis guns, had been maintaining themselves on the eastern edge of the wood, which they had entered two days before. Separated from our lines by a barrage of shells, they and their captain had dug themselves in, captured 35 prisoners and put out of action some 150 Germans. Aided by this heroic band, our troops step by step drove the Germans from the whole wood, and by 9 p.m. Sir Douglas Haig was able to report that the Trônes Wood was at last entirely in our possession.

From the Bernafay Wood and the trenches north and east of Montauban a body of Highlanders, preceded by pipers playing " The Campbells are Coming," crossed the 1,200 yards of "No Man's Land." Under heavy shell and machine-gun fire, and amidst the smoke created by German smoke-bombs, they charged for the blazing wood-encircled ruins of the village. They were following, as it were, at the heels of a line of bursting shells discharged by the British gunners on the German first-line trenches in front of Longueval. What the shells had not accomplished, the bombs and bayonets of the Scots now achieved.

Forcing their way into the dug-outs, they accounted for most of the defenders who had escaped shrapnel and high explosive. The few who escaped ran off panic-stricken.

Our guns were now dealing with the second of the enemy's trenches ; then once more they lifted and the scene was repeated. One-third of this trench ran through Longueval itself, and the fighting which ensued was partly in the village. From a dug-out sprang a German officer, an axe in his hand. " I surrender," he cried in English to a kilted sergeant, at whom, however, he treacherously aimed a blow. The aim missed the head of the sergeant, who promptly bayoneted him. From one building

six mitrailleuses continued firing until it was entered and the Germans bombed. Down in the cellars of the house the Germans fought with the desperate courage of trapped animals.

Where the village joins on Delville Wood a redoubt with two field-guns and several machine-guns had been built. There the fighting was especially severe. Reinforcements were hurried through the enemy's barrage of shells, and, after their arrival, the Highlanders entrenched themselves on a line running eastward through the top of the village, across the south-west corner of Delville Wood, then south by the western edge of Waterlot Farm to Trônes Wood, where they connected up with the English infantry. The redoubt, with its field-guns, had not been captured, but a counterattack of the enemy had been repulsed.

Upon the Highlanders descended a very deluge of projectiles. An officer and his orderly were hit by the shrapnel. A few moments later four gas shells burst hard by the wounded men. The officer may be left to tell what followed :

I tried to move, but the shrap. had got me in the right thigh rather badly, and, apart from that, I felt all the sap trickling out of me as I breathed in the gas. It was like struggling against chloroform, and the last thing I remember was feeling that sleep and stillness were best. I should have slept all right, and been dead in a very few minutes. You'd never guess where I next found myself. I was wedged in the forked branches of a little tree, on the highest ground near, and on the ground below me was my orderly, unconscious, and bleeding a good deal from the flesh wounds in his arms and shoulders that he'd got from the same shrap. that hit the rest of us.

That little chap had carried me 300 yards, over the roughest sort of going, with any number of bullets flying round, and himself running blood from half a dozen flesh wounds. He'd been taught, you see, to make for high ground when gas was about, so before he fainted he'd planted me in that little tree. How he managed it I can't think, because I must be nearly twice his weight, and he's small all round—except in the matter of his heart. I guess that's something over standard in size and quality.

Yes, he's all right now, thank goodness. His wounds were none of them serious—splinters, you know, and he might have been doctored on the other side ; but I specially asked if he might come across with me, and he's here now, on this ship. I want to go and see his people with him when I can get about again ; and I mean to see his old employer, too, and let him know what sort of a man he's got in J——. He gave up a job in which he was earning £3 10s. a week, and joined up before the end of August, 1914. His grasp of the three R's is pretty weak. He tells me he never used to read even the papers, except to get a bit of news about coursing. He's got a wife and three kids at home, and when he joined he had to give up whippets that were more to him than his stable is to any owner of a string of racehorses.

We went out to France in May, 1915, and J—— has been once home on leave. All the rest of the time he's been in and out of trenches with me, and under fire most of the time. He's never known where his next meal's coming from, and an orderly of mine has a pretty thin time in the matter of sleep, I can tell you; for I'm up and down the trenches all night, and over the parapet a good deal, looking after wiring jobs and that sort of thing. That chap's carried his life in his hand all the time, and never known as much comfort in the last 14 months as the average working man in England gets every day of his life. He was due for leave before this Push, and indeed he was recalled from the railway station when leave was stopped. But nobody's ever heard him utter a word of complaint; two in the morning or two in the afternoon I've found him always the same smart, cheery, willing soldier, all the time, and always with eyes in the back of his head.

I wish you could tell the people here at home about men like J——. I tell you this New Army of ours is full of them. He hardly knew what I was talking about when I tried to thank him for what he had done for me and praised him a bit for his general behaviour. Honestly, you could see he wondered what I was getting at; half suspected I was chipping him. He was just doing his job. Of course, he does his job. That's the way he looks at it; that's the way all my lads look at it. Makes you think a bit, doesn't it, when you remember they none of them knew anything about soldiering a couple of years ago; and, mark you, nobody told J—— he was to enlist or ought to enlist.

I often used to wonder what our chaps thought out there, when they got hold of a newspaper, in billets, and read about conscientious objectors—and objectors who haven't any conscience. Queer position, isn't it, when you come to think of it? Mind, I'm not talking about the few genuine cranks, or whatever you call them. I'm talking about chaps who never believed in anything much, except the main chance, and having a good time.

And what about the exemptions? Why in the name of common justice should exemption be given to eligible men who have stayed in the background for 20 months, while men, often less eligible, have been

facing death to protect them all that time? These exemptions and able-bodied chaps going round after soft jobs in the rear—the toleration of them is an insult to men like my orderly; and the voluntarily enlisted New Armies are made up of his sort.

Towards nightfall the Highlanders stormed the redoubt, but the field-guns had been withdrawn by the Germans. Trônes Wood, Longueval and the southern outskirts of Delville Wood were won.

The two enemy trenches (converging outwards in the centre) between Longueval and Bazentin-le-Grand had, except in the middle, been stripped of their barbed-wire entanglements. A shallow road in front afforded some protection to the assailant. Our troops rapidly carried the eastern and western ends of the trenches. In the centre the uncut wire and six machine-guns held up the advance. The German garrison was now attacked by a Scottish regiment from the direction of Longueval. Our men dropped into the trenches and bombed the machine-guns; and soon the whole of the trenches from Longueval to Bazentin-le-Grand were occupied by the British.

Bazentin-le-Grand had in the last twenty minutes of the bombardment received no less than 2,000 shells. It had been pulverized, and the few Germans left offered little resistance to

Official Photograph.

A HIGHLAND REGIMENT ON ITS WAY TO THE TRENCHES.

[*Official Photographs.*

IN A FRONT-LINE TRENCH.
A Lewis gun in action.
Circle picture : Machine-gunners, wearing gas-
helmets, firing against a German trench.

the Irish attacking it. In a large cellar under
one farm a considerable number of German
wounded were taken. Some heavy howitzers
also were secured.

From Bazentin-le-Grand westwards a trench
zigzagged round the exterior of Bazentin-le-
Grand Wood to Bazentin-le-Petit. Two belts
of wire entanglements were in front of the trees.
A second trench, 150 yards back, with a wire-
entanglement before it, ran through the middle
of the Wood and in front of Bazentin-le-Petit.
But the British bombardment had obliterated
trenches and entanglements. At 4 a.m. our
troops on the right entered the Wood and began
to clear it of machine-gunners and snipers,
some of whom were ensconced in the tops of
trees. To their left, a little after 4 a.m., Irish
and other troops forced their way into Bazentin-
le-Petit, now reduced to a mass of battered
ruins.

A captain who was engaged in the capture of
this village gave the following picturesque
account of the fighting there :

I lost touch with my fellows, after I got peppered in
the thigh, in the beginning of the village fighting. But
my orderly stayed with me, and we did a bit of amateur

first aid. We dressed a bomber and two other fellows,
not of my battalion, in quite professional style. The
bomber still had seven bombs, and the others had rifles
and bayonets, and I had my revolver and trench dagger,
so as there was still a good bit of kick in us we started
on the prowl. The bomber was a sportsman. There was
one place where we could see a Boche machine-gun
section at work in the cellar of what had been a cottage.
There was nothing left but cellar then. The rest was
level with the ground. There must have been twelve or
fourteen Boches round that gun, bobbing up and down,
you understand, as they wanted cover. We crawled on
and on till we were no more than twenty paces on their
left flank, while they were blazing away like one o'clock,
quarter right, at our chaps. Our bomber was rather
badly wounded in his left shoulder, but he bowled well
with his right, I can tell you. He lobbed two beauties
right on the Boche typewriter. They seemed to put the
gun out of action all right, but for some reason I never
shall understand they only killed one man of the bunch
and wounded a couple of others. And just then four or

five more Boches came scuttling into that cellar from somewhere in rear, so there they were as thick as bees. Would they surrender? I thought I'd try them. "Come on, lad; we've got 'em!" I shouted; and, to the Boches, "Hands up!" Those Boches dropped their rifles as though their hands burned. Up went their hands, all except one chap, a sergeant, and he let fly at me. But I ducked. It was the funniest thing. The sergeant was a soldier, all right. He was cursing his men for all he was worth, and as he cursed the habit of discipline told, and the Boches picked up their rifles and stood on guard. Then the moment I showed up again down goes every rifle, up go all the hands, and the sergeant lets fly once more. They were like marionettes on wires, those Boches; up and down according as I showed my head. Only one real man in the lot, you see. But it seemed rough luck for him to have to be killed, because he was a man, so I gave the tip to my cripples; and we made a dash for that cellar, and while the rest of the bunch was bailed up by my orderly and the wounded bomber I fairly jumped on the sergeant. I didn't want him to notice my right leg was pretty helpless, so I embraced him round the neck with one arm and shoved his chin up with the other hand, while one of my cripples got his rifle; and so we got the bunch. They're not hard to handle now, once you can get them away from their N.C.O.'s. As for their officers, they seem to be busy taking care of number one and keeping well to the rear. I liked that sergeant, and he made a regular doctor's job of my leg for me, bandaged it most beautifully, and got two of his men to take it in turns carrying me on their backs on the way down to our dressing station.

By 5.30 a.m. the whole village was in our hands, and though a few ruins in the north of it were recovered temporarily by the enemy, by 9 a.m. the British had dug themselves in on a line which went through the cemetery east of the village to the cross-roads above Bazentin-le-Grand. During the afternoon they pushed up the open slope under shell and machine-gun fire and broke into High Wood, half of which they secured. This achievement was accompanied by another gallant deed unexampled in the western theatre of war since October, 1914.

A regiment of the Dragoon Guards and one of Deccan Horse had been ordered to follow up behind the assaulting infantry ready to take advantage of a sudden collapse of the German forces. In the late afternoon detachments of these regiments proceeded amidst the wild cheering of our infantry to the bottom of High Wood, and with sabre and lance charged the German infantry in some cornfields. The story of this extraordinary event, in which our horsemen were aided by machine-gun fire from our aircraft, may well be told by an officer of the Deccan Horse engaged in it:

At 6.30 we started our famous ride into the enemy country, every now and then coming under heavy shell fire—shrapnel and high explosive. No one can believe, without seeing, what a state the ground is in; there is not room for a table-cloth on any part of the ground there without some part of it touching a shell

[Official Photograph.

THE "FLYING PIG" ON THE SOMME.
Loading a Trench Mortar.

[*Official Photograph.*]

INDIAN CAVALRY AFTER THEIR CHARGE.

hole, so you can imagine the regiment galloping over it at full gallop, barbed wire—well cut by shell fire—old trenches, dead bodies, and every sort of *débris* lying in every direction. Words fail me to describe it. That was for about three miles ; then full tilt down a steep bank like the Haggard field, but steeper, into a very famous valley, where the shrapnel got worse, as we were spotted by one of their sausage balloons. This was soon driven down by the fire of our batteries, which just smothered it with shrapnel.

Here we went through our infantry, who cheered us madly as we galloped by, all wishing us luck. On we went, past the remains of guns and everything—tons of ammunition and abandoned material and dead Huns everywhere ; and we passed here an enormous gun they had left behind, so really I suppose it was we who took it. We were under cover here for half a mile, but suddenly, coming out of the valley, we had to turn sharp to the right up another little valley, and here we came under terrific, but rather inaccurate, machine-gun fire from two directions. I cannot tell you anything about casualties, but it was here my chestnut mare was killed. We went about a mile up this valley, and then got some cover under a bank—by " we " all this time I mean the regiment and our British regiment. Here we stopped for ten minutes, and then we got orders for our squadron to go on as advance guard in a certain direction.

It was now about 7.30 in the evening, and there were 24 aeroplanes hovering over us, and one monoplane came down to about 200 feet, and fired his machine-guns on the Huns just over us—going round and round—the finest sight I have ever seen. Well, we moved out under a heavy fire, and got on about half a mile. During this advance we rounded up eight prisoners, while between us and the British regiment, I suppose, we stuck with sword and lance about 40 of them—a glorious sight. Our men were splendid—and didn't want to take any prisoners, but these eight had chucked away their arms, so we couldn't very well do them in. They were simply terrified, and one clung on to my leg and kept calling ' Pity ! Pity ! " his eyes starting out of his head. Poor devil, I pitied him, and we sent him back to the regiment.

We dismounted in a little hollow then and went on foot through a damn good crop of wheat full of shell holes and dead Huns. Of course, we were creeping on our tummies all the way, as the fire was very hot. At last, after going a quarter of a mile, we got to the flat top of the hill, driving them before us. Here we had to stop, as the ground was being swept by rifle and machine-gun fire, and they were now shelling us heavily. We got our Hotchkiss guns into action, and set to work. By crawling slowly forward we got a field of fire, and could see the Huns plainly and a battery about half a mile ahead. We plugged a few here, and then it happened to get dark, and we had to retire about 300 yards to a better position and dig in for the night. This we did all right, the Huns making a feeble charge as we did it. I was alone at the time with a message, so I let fly six rounds at them with my revolver, and they all lay down ! However, it was not a healthy spot, and I had to crawl back, and rejoined the squadron. We got our horses, and came back and rejoined the regiment. One shell landed in the middle of us as we mounted ! These tin hats are damn good ! especially for shrapnel.

Well, we got back, and dug in like blazes. They made two weak attacks during the night, and shelled us all the time, and the star shells they sent up all night were like a firework display—a weird sight. One Boche crawled up to one of our listening posts in the dark, and we shot him, brought him in, but he died soon after. We hung on there till 4 o'clock, put up wire in front of us, and our battery helped us well. Infantry relieved us then ; they had just got up. You see, our job was to push on as far as we could and hold the line to give " the feet " time to get up. So we did our job all right.

We then rode back—" but not the six hundred.' We were treated to tear shells on the way back—awful sore on the eyes, and my good chestnut horse has both eyes bunged up to-day. Saw more wonderful sights coming back. We got water in the valley we started from, and then rode on back to this field, where we came first from our old camp. Terrible work to-day with the horses, and going through their kits. The divisional general came round last night and congratulated us.

Official Photograph.

WITH THE BRITISH ON THE SOMME.
Bringing in the wounded across No Man's Land.

WITH THE FRENCH ON THE SOMME.
The crater of a mine-explosion.

[*Official Photograph.*

RED CROSS MEN AT WORK.
Carrying in wounded near Thièpval.

and to-day we got congratulations from the Army Commander. Of course, we are all very bucked and proud. We slept sound last night, I can tell you, on the bare ground under the sky. Thank God, it is fine !

Meanwhile Bazentin-le-Petit Wood had been gained by the British. Through it ran the light railway line from Mametz Wood and three trenches. It was defended by numerous machine-guns and dug-outs, in one of which, 40 ft. below the ground, was the Colonel of the German 91st Regiment, who had sworn to "stay in the wood to hold it to the last." Between the wood and the British a trench ran from 50 to 75 yards in front of the trees, protected by two wire entanglements. Our artillery had made short work of trench and wire and our troops, suffering from machine-guns in the vicinity of Contalmaison Villa, were speedily scrambling into the wood. Soon after 7 a.m. they were at the top of it. Three hundred prisoners, including the Colonel aforesaid, had been captured. He had realized his intention, but not in the way he hoped. From the wood the troops on the right entered the top of Bazentin-le-Petit, where 200 more prisoners were secured. Away on the left fierce struggles went on round Contalmaison Villa. At nightfall our men were north of it, and the sun set on a great victory for British arms. We had broken back the German second line of defence over a length of four miles and captured several strongly fortified localities.

As a young wounded officer who took part in the fighting of the 14th said :

We all knew it was France's Day, and I can't help thinking our chaps borrowed something from our French Allies on Friday, as a sort of tribute to the French nation. They showed a great deal of the sort of sparkling *élan*, the rushing dash and gallantry, which we have come to associate with the French troops ; and they backed it all the time with their own inimitable doggedness and steadily pushful indifference to enemy fire.

A young second lieutenant, who had his right forearm badly smashed by a bomb in the attack on Bazentin-le-Petit, most gallantly led his platoon in the storming of the German front trench there. A German bomb landed at his feet, a few yards in front of the Boche parapet, when his platoon sergeant and three of his men were close at his elbows. Without an instant's hesitation this young officer stooped, picked up the bomb, and flung it back at the Boche trench. It exploded when halfway between himself and the German trench, and a large fragment of the spring and casing returned, boomerang fashion, into the thrower's arm. But his action saved several lives. These details were extracted from the platoon sergeant, who had a bullet wound over the left knee. The officer himself was much too full of the exploits of his men to say much of his own part in the affair.

We're pretty keen on our French pals, he said, in our battalion. We were down at ——, you know, alongside the French, before ; and my fellows can parley-voo like one o'clock. Well, they all knew about "France's Day," you know ; and "La Belle France," and "Vive Français," were our cries on Friday. Must've puzzled the Boche quite a bit, you know. No doubt Master Boche did give a pretty hot reception to the first two platoons and mine. There weren't many men of mine reached their line unwounded. But the splendid thing was that, excepting a few—who'll never move again (the boy's voice dropped sadly here)—excepting a few the fellows who'd been hit came on with the others. Some of them got there, yelling, with as many as three separate bullet wounds ; and half of 'em at least jumped into that Boche trench without a weapon in their hands.

Then was the sight. I was out of it, so far as fighting went ; but I saw it all ; and never saw anything finer in my life. Never was such a splendid scrum ! They took no more notice of Boche bayonets than if they'd been the spray of the sea—you know, when you're running in at low tide, and it's a bit parky, just at first ; and you're all shouting like the devil, on kind of short breaths, because it's cold.

Well, as I say, they just jumped straight on to those Boches, and I tell you the Boches fought well. And —here's a point that struck me—the Germans fought well, without leadership. Devil a sign of an officer did I see. And I was in that line for a good many hours. No, I reckon their officers keep out of it all they can. Queer, isn't it ? I don't know what our men would make of it if we did that sort of thing.

To see those chaps of mine tackling the Boche with their bare hands was worth living for—or dying for. It was meat and drink to me. They just tore their men down ; and wrenched their own rifles from them. One big section commander of mine was just like a terrier with rats ; except that he didn't wait for killing. He was too busy. He went for his men like a blooming lamplighter ; smashed 'em down ; grabbed 'em by the slack of the breeches and the neck, and chucked 'em back over the parapet, to roll down into the remains of their own wire. "Fall in there ! Fall in ! " he kept yelling, and goodness alone knows what he meant by it. But he put them out of business all right, and I sort of rounded 'em up from the little shell-hole where I lay ; and in a way they did fall in, in a cluster, lying on the ground. They were docile enough ; mostly stunned ; and I'd my revolver in my left hand. And then my lads cleaned out the dug-outs, mostly using German bombs. We left nothing alive in that trench ; and I don't believe the Kaiser's got a platoon in all his Prussian Guard who could have lived in the face of those chaps of mine, with their bare hands, on Friday. It was a great do, was " France's Day," at Bazentin !

The 14th July was the Fête Day of the Republic, the hundred and twenty-seventh anniversary of the Fall of the Bastille, the typical bulwark of the Ancien Régime, as life-crushing a Government as that of Modern Prussia. This anniversary had ever been celebrated with considerable fervour since the institution of the Third Republic, and in Paris there had always been a great military spectacle. While the British and French Allied armies had been celebrating it by fresh victories on the field of battle, it was marked by a spectacular incident which distinguished it from all other past occasions. For the first time in history soldiers of other nations fresh from the battlefield took part in the ceremony, and their presence was rightly interpreted by the French people as a visible sign emphasizing the pledge of the Allied Powers to fight together until complete victory should have been gained over Teutonic tyranny ; to teach the German people for all time that treaties are sacred, not scraps of paper to be torn up at will ; that military brutality would be stamped out, and that the attempt to gain the hegemony of Europe would be replied to by crushing to the ground the statesmen and people who insolently dared to seek it.

[*Official photograph.*

BRITISH TROOPS AT WORK BEHIND A SMOKE ATTACK.

THE FRENCH NATIONAL FÊTE DAY, JULY 14, 1916.

The British contingent passing through the Place de la Concorde in Paris, headed by the band of the Scots Guards.

It was indeed a solemn occasion, which spoke in direct and unmistakable terms to the whole world. The troops were marshalled in alphabetical order in accordance with diplomatic usage, the Belgian guests leading, next the British (Grande Bretagne), followed by the Russian, and then the soldiers of France. A Belgian band came first, followed by their infantry, then the machine-guns with their ammunition carts and cyclists. Next came the Belgian standard, received with deep emotion by the crowd, closely followed by a troop of Belgian lancers, all alike received with sympathy. As the last of these filed past the sound of the pipes broke on the ear. It was the band of the Scots Guards with their stalwart pipers at the head. Behind them came the representatives of the British Empire from England, Scotland, India and the realms of Britain beyond the seas. Great was the welcome they received from the cheering crowd, from the enthusiastic girls who showered flowers on them or pressed them into their hands. Next came the Russians moving in sections of 16, the fine men making a great impression as they went by singing their marching songs. Last of all marched the home troops, the beloved representatives of the nation in arms, with their bands playing airs which all the people knew, the noble " Chant du départ," which particularly appeals to Republican France with its old memories, and the no less celebrated " Mourir pour la Patrie." They had a warm reception, which spoke straight from the hearts of the multitude and showed the love which France bears towards her soldiers. Towards the end of the French procession came representatives of the French colonial troops from Africa and Asia, and last of all the Fusiliers Marins, those gallant troops who had fought so bravely and lost so heavily at Ypres and Dixmude. Their bravery recalled the regiment to which Napoleon gave the proud title of " One against ten," and of them France might also say as the Emperor did of the 32nd : " I had no anxiety ; I knew the 32nd were there." The reception given to the " 75's " was also great, for the people felt how much they owed to the magnificent field guns which had played so great a part in the battles. Nor must it be forgotten that if the material was good, no less perfect was the scientific training which had enabled the French artillerymen to get such great results from their weapons. They had set an example in the handling of guns which had been followed by all Europe.

One of the most interesting scenes in Paris was the bestowal by the President of honours which had been earned on the battlefield by fallen heroes, and were handed to their bereaved relations, to each of whom a certificate was given.

The 14th of July was also kept as a day of ceremony in England and in the Dominions beyond the seas. Queen Alexandra, who was the Patroness of the Croix Rouge Française, Comité de Londres, had started a movement to raise funds for the benefit of French wounded. In a little paper called *France,* which appeared specially for the day only, the following message from Her Majesty was printed :

To that glorious nation of France which has endeared itself to all Britons I send a heartfelt message of friendship and sympathy.

This anniversary of the National Day of France is to be marked by a collection of offerings for her gallant wounded, the funds being administered by the Croix Rouge Française Comité de Londres, of which I am Patroness. I warmly commend this noble enterprise of mercy to the people of the whole Empire. May their generosity forge yet another link between the sister nations.

All over Great Britain collections and demonstrations were held ; the Mayors of Provincial Boroughs enthusiastically responded to the call of the Lord Mayor of London, the Treasurer of the Fund, and a widespread system of collection brought in large sums to the treasury.

In London the results exceeded all anticipations ; flags, favours mounted on swords as pins, souvenirs from the trenches, little articles manufactured by the French soldiers from pieces of German shells and relics of every description, were offered and were eagerly bought. Many were the stories of ladies who received in return for a small flag a folded slip of paper in which notes, and in some cases cheques, were enclosed. Between seven and eight million emblems were distributed from the chief depôt at Knightsbridge by voluntary assistants, many of whom used their own motor-cars. Altogether a large sum was collected, to which our Colonies contributed in no mean measure, the total exceeding £100,000.

The British Army, through Sir Douglas Haig, forwarded the following message to the French President :

The British Army, fighting by the side of the brave soldiers of France in the bitter struggle now proceeding, expresses on the occasion of this great anniversary its admiration for the results achieved by the French Army and its unshakable confidence in the speedy realization of our common hopes.

[Official Photograph.

CAPTURED GERMAN GUNS.

M. Poincaré replied :—

I thank you, my dear General, for the good wishes which you have expressed towards France, and beg you to convey to the brave British Army my lively admiration of the fine successes which it has just achieved and which only this morning have been so brilliantly extended. They have produced a deep impression on the hearts of all Frenchmen. Those of your magnificent troops who have to-day paraded in the streets of Paris, in company with those of our Allies, received throughout their march a striking proof of the public sentiment. I am glad to have this opportunity of sending you—to you personally and to your troops—my warm congratulations.

The Tsar sent President Poincaré a congratulatory telegram repeating his full confidence and good wishes for the victory of France and her glorious Army. The President replied thanking him for having authorized the magnificent Russian troops to take part in the National Fête. He added that France, like Russia, had an active and resolute confidence in the final success of the Allies.

Saturday the 15th was spent in consolidating and extending the British lines. Between Fricourt and Mametz the Germans were forced back to their third line of defence. Over 2,000 prisoners were taken in twenty-four hours. Our troops pushed forward to the outskirts of Pozières on the left and cleared the last of the Germans out of the Bazentin-le-Petit Wood, penetrated farther into the High Wood and captured the whole of the Waterlot Farm. In the Delville

Wood troops from South Africa greatly distinguished themselves. What they performed there between the 15th and 18th was told by the soldier-father, himself on the Headquarters Staff, of a South African soldier killed in the fighting :

The dead lying in Delville Wood, were still unburied when I was there (because burial was impossible under the fire going on). Men lie in layers. The South African heroes lie underneath.

I wonder whether history will do them justice. Will it tell how, ordered to take and hold the wood at all costs, they took it—and then began one of the most heroic defences known in the history of war ? For three days (July 15–18) they were subjected to continuous bombardment by guns of all calibres. They held on with very little food or water. Over and over again they were attacked by overwhelming enemy forces. The gallant fellows fell fast under the terrific bombardment and attacks, but not a man wavered.

Finding them immovable, the Germans, at last, on the 18th, concentrated a terrible bombardment for seven hours on what was left of these splendid men, and then about 5 or 6 p.m. launched an attack by three regiments, on the survivors. The front trench was attacked in front and on each flank. My son's trench was attacked from back and front.

Our gallant, splendid men, reduced to a mere skeleton of what they were, beat back the Brandenburgers. It was during this awful time that my dear boy fell. They died, our noble South Africans, but they held the wood ! Thank God, they held the wood ! and thank God they kept up the traditions of our race ! And my splendid boy helped. He took no inconsiderable part either.

I want our South Africans to get the credit they deserve. If you have any friends who can spread the news of what they did, let it be told. I resign my dear son, who was very, very dear to me, into the safe keeping of my Maker, who gave him to me. It is very hard to part with him, but I glory in his glorious end, my splendid, chivalrous boy; and if his example inspires others he will not have died in vain.

Use this letter as you like in order to let the world know what the South Africans did. I want these heroes to have some (they can never have all) of the honour due to their glorious memories. What a theme for some painter's brush or some poet's inspiration!

Enraged at their defeat by the British on the 14th, the German Higher Command endeavoured to counterbalance it by a victory over the French south of the Somme on July 15. Under cover of a heavy mist large reinforcements were brought to the left bank of the river, and La Maisonnette Farm and the village of Biaches were violently assaulted. Both were carried, but the French quickly organized counterattacks, and the Germans were deprived of their hard-won gains.

On the next day (July 16) there was a heavy bombardment on both sides all along the line. Our troops from the east, on a front of 1,200 yards, made their way to within 500 yards of the village of Pozières, while the Royal Fusiliers—recruited chiefly from the Stock Exchange, Lloyd's, the Baltic and Corn Exchange—drew nearer to Pozières from the south to south-west. Five more heavy howitzers and four 11 mm. (4·3 ins.) guns fell into our hands together with a large amount of war material. During the night our troops were engaged in consolidating our positions, covered by a detachment in High Wood, which was afterwards drawn back into the new trench line.

On July 17 the long defence of Ovillers-La Boisselle came to an end. Like Carency in the Battle of Artois (May, 1915), the village had been gradually isolated, and the Prussian Guards of the 3rd Reserve Division found themselves in sore straits. The barrages of shells prevented both food and ammunition from being brought up in any quantities to the defenders. Water was scarce, and the spirit of the hungry and thirsty garrison, now greatly reduced in numbers, was much broken. Sir Douglas Haig decided to use one of his northern divisions to complete the conquest.

At dawn a tremendous bombardment opened, when the guns lifted their rain of shells from the shattered heaps of masonry which now represented all that remained of the once flourishing village of Ovillers-La Boisselle, and the British infantry from their side advanced to the attack. The first line started out of the Ovillers Wood. From the vaulted cellars and from behind wrecked houses the machine-guns and infantry of the Prussian Guards turned a terrific fire on the assaulting troops. Men fell and were left behind, but ever onward moved the British infantry until their goal was reached. Once the Germans' front line was gained the Grenadiers set to work to bomb the dug-outs and destroy their occupants or force them to surrender. As progress was made the sudden cessation of all fire from the various

[Official Photograph.

CARTING AWAY A CAPTURED GERMAN GUN.

[Official Photograph.

SEARCHING PRISONERS.
To make quite certain that nothing dangerous is being concealed.

points showed they had been won. The fight
was a hard and prolonged one. One machine-
gun, snugly placed in a ruined cottage, managed
to maintain its fire after the rest had been
conquered. A gallant officer, whose arm had
been shattered by a bullet, led a party of his men
against and killed the gun's crew. He was
then led off to an ambulance, whistling "Tip-
perary." At about 10 a.m. all resistance was
over, and the worn-out remnant of the Prussian
Guards surrendered. In one of the cellars
25 Germans, who had exhausted even their
emergency rations and had not tasted food for
two days, were captured. Of the German
garrison in Ovillers-La Boisselle only 126
survivors remained. The entry to the village
by the Bapaume road was defended by two
strong field works. Round them alone were
strewn some 800 corpses. Some of the
captured had lost their reason, and many
were dying of enteric. "You English fight
like devils," remarked one German, " and
we gladly surrender to such men as you are."
A party of prisoners were placed under a subaltern's guard. Among them were two officers,
one of whom is said to have unpinned the Iron
Cross from his breast and offered it to the
subaltern.

"Take it for having done what we considered
to be impossible," said the German ; " I give
it to you." The subaltern shook his head, and
explained that it was not a custom of ours to
deprive prisoners of what they had won by their
own valour.

The following captured documents are of
interest as showing the very heavy casualties
which the enemy had suffered in the recent
fighting :

From a company of the 3rd Battalion 16th
Bavarian Infantry Regiment to battalion
commander :

Severe enemy artillery fire of all calibres up to 28 cm.
on company sector. Company strength, one officer,
12 men. Beg urgently speedy relief for the company.
What remains of the company is so exhausted that, in
case of an attack by the enemy, the few totally exhausted men cannot be counted on.

From another company of the same regiment :

Very heavy intense enemy fire on company sector.
The company has completely lost its fighting value.
The men left are so exhausted that they can no longer
be employed in fighting. If heavy artillery fire con-
tinues the company will soon be entirely exterminated.
Relief for the company is urgently requested.

From 2nd Battalion to 3rd Battalion 16th
Bavarian Infantry Regiment :

The battalion has just received orders from Lieut.-Col.
Kumml that it is placed under orders of the 3rd Battalion 16th Bavarian Regiment as sector reserve. Battalion consists at present time of three officers, two
non-commissioned officers, and 19 men.

In the local actions which took place on this
day we captured some more prisoners, and the
total of unwounded German prisoners taken by
the British since July 1 was 189 officers and
10,779 other ranks.

The German losses in artillery proved to be
even greater than at first reported.

[Official Photograph.

WOUNDED GERMANS.
Being assisted by British troops.

[*Official Photographs.*

GERMAN PRISONERS.

Lined up on the road after they were taken from
the German trenches. Smaller picture : Convey-
ing a wounded German on a stretcher.

The captured armament collected by our
troops now included 5 eight-inch howitzers,
3 six-inch howitzers, 4 six-inch guns, 5 other
heavy guns, 37 field guns, 30 trench howitzers,
66 machine-guns, and many thousands of rounds
of gun ammunition of all descriptions.

This was exclusive of many guns not then
brought in and of the numbers destroyed by
our artillery bombardment and abandoned by
the enemy.

Before passing on to the subsequent fighting
let the reader see Ovillers-La Boisselle through
the eyes of a *Times* correspondent who visited
the scene of carnage three weeks later :

As far as La Boisselle itself you can take your motor-
car along the main Albert-Bapaume road, though you
will have the road to yourself when you do it. La
Boisselle on the right of the road is nothing more than a
flat layer of pounded grey stones and mortar on the bare
face of the earth. Of anything like a village or individual buildings there is, of course, no semblance.
On the left of the road the ground dips steeply down
for 50 yards or so, then slowly rises to what is called
Ovillers-La Boisselle, because that was where a village
of that name stood until a few weeks ago. To-day, if
La Boisselle is almost obliterated, Ovillers-La Boisselle
is non-existent.

Standing on the edge of the white road in the glaring
sunshine, with the roar of our own guns behind one and
the other guns ahead, one feels onself the only landmark
in a waste. The whole earth's surface, before and
around, is torn with shell-holes and seamed with lines of
trenches, all white, because the soil here is chalk. Such
land as there is between, unscarred, is almost bare of
vegetation, with only here and there a thin coat of sickly
grass or a dusty tuft of cornflower, mallow, or white
camomile. Opposite, crowning the gentle slope before
you, a few ragged stumps, fragments of tree trunks
some 10 ft. high, with bits of splintered lower branches
sticking from them, stand gaunt against the sky and
mark where Ovillers used to be.

Heading for Ovillers, we—for an officer was with me—
left the road and went down across the torn and blasted
earth to the white line of what was once the German
front line trench. It is a trench no more. It was not
much of a trench by the time our guns had done with it
at the beginning of this battle. After that, it was
pounded day and night through all the desperate
fighting which went on for the possession of Ovillers.
Since then the enemy has devoted a certain number of
shells a day to knocking the poor remnants of it about
a little more. It is a futile occupation, because no one,
except an inquisitive visitor like myself, would dream
of walking along it. The parapet is mostly strewn all
over the ground. In places it is mixed with, and fills
up, the trench, so that you go on the level of the ground.
Then a few yards may be decently intact, so that, half-
choked with rubbish as it is, it gives you shelter, perhaps,
waist high. It, and the ground around, are littered
with equipment. Cartridges, used or unused, and
unexploded bombs and bits of shells, or whole shells,
"duds," are everywhere beneath your feet. In the

[Official photograph.

LONDON SCOTTISH MARCHING TO THE TRENCHES.

hot sun the chalk is intensely white and the heat beats back on you from the baked earth, and the air is thick with the dreadful smell which belongs to battlefields and with the buzzing of flies. It is truly a vile place.

At last you come to a parting of the way, where an old German sign still sticks up from the fire step of the trench, one hand of it pointing " Nach Pozieérs." You turn where it tells you and go on—in the trench or beside it, it does not matter—till you pass the ragged bits of tree trunks, and you are in Ovillers. You would not know it but for the tree fragments, and, when you look, you see that there is a quantity of broken brick and stone mixed up with the kneaded earth, and also you come to a hole in the ground which, being square and lined with brick, is obviously not a shell-hole, but must be a cellar which once had a house above it.

By this time I have seen a good deal of ruin, but I have talked to experts who have seen more than I, and they agree that Ovillers is more utterly destroyed than any other village in the battle area.

No village could be more destroyed, because there is nothing left but the cellar which I have mentioned and two or three others like it, mere holes in the ground and minus quantities, so far as they are buildings at all. Of superstructure to the earth there is none. One point there is which those who go there speak of as a place to take your bearings from—a sort of Greenwich in this sea of desolation—and it is called " The Church." Undoubtedly a church once was there, because the maps say so, and there is still one fragment of a wall which may have been part of a church, and by it two graves. Why these survive it is impossible to say. If it was not for them no spot in Ovillers above ground would be different from any other.

Underground it is different. You have already heard how it was estimated that the dug-outs here could hold, and did hold, 2,000 Germans. It is doubtless true. One fears from the smell that they hold many yet. We went down into several, though the entrances to most are battered in by shells, and groped about by the light of matches among the litter and the darkness. There is one great dug-out—I mentioned it from hearsay at the time—where eighty dead Germans were found, the place, it is supposed, having been used, in the last days of desperate fighting, as a kind of vault into which the dead were hurriedly thrown with the intention some time of wrecking the place or sealing it up, or otherwise making it into a tomb.

Another large dug-out there is which the Germans used as a dressing station. It is admirably constructed, and has, besides the main entrance from the trench, another opening for exit which gave upon a road where ran a tramway line by which the wounded could be taken from the very door of the dressing station back behind the lines.

On through Ovillers we went by the winding trenches, not knowing when we left the village behind any more than when we entered it. And here one does not climb out of the trench to look. One cannot put a periscope up without its being shot to bits. Close at hand the rifles spat continuously and machine-guns stuttered and growled, and we had trench mortars at work, which heaved projectiles into the air so slowly that you saw them sail majestically to where the enemy was hiding in his trenches, there to explode prodigiously. For short ranges they are as serious as any shell of their size from a great gun.

To our right, close by, we were assured, was Pozières, though I confess I saw nothing of it, and to our left, a little farther off, was Thiépval, which also, though I have seen it from other places, I did not see from here. And ahead was Mouquet Farm. And all around was heat, and noise, and an almost intolerable atmosphere.

During the night of the 17th and 18th further substantial progress was made on a 1,000 yards front of Ovillers-La Boisselle, six

[Official photograph.

A PATROL UNDER FIRE.
Crawling up towards the German trenches.

machine-guns and several prisoners being captured.

While the Prussian Guard prisoners were being removed from Ovillers-La Boisselle, our troops away to the east approached Pozières. They stormed a double line of trenches from Bazentin-le-Petit to the south-east of the village, a distance of 1,500 yards. The trenches when captured were found to be actually filled up with dead and wounded. From the upper part of High Wood, lying over the crest of the heights, and therefore directly under the fire of the German guns, our patrols were, however, withdrawn and our line straightened out between Pozières and Longueval, which could now be attacked from two sides.

South of the Somme, on Monday the 17th, it was the turn of the Germans to take the offensive. From midnight to the late afternoon battalion after battalion charged up the La Maisonnette Hill. Met by the *rafales* of the " 75 " guns and by withering machine-gun fire, the waves of Germans receded. In the morning some of the enemy penetrated into the east end of Biaches, from which, however, they were soon expelled by French bombers.

When the sun was setting, and during the night, the Germans renewed their attacks between Biaches and La Maisonnette Farm. They were unsuccessful at La Maisonnette, but some parties wound their way along the canal into houses at the eastern end of Biaches. They were driven out the next day.

Near Biaches there had been a savage struggle for the fortified work in front of the village called Biaches Fort. A battery of machine-guns, hidden cunningly in a marsh, prevented a frontal attack. Fire had not sufficed to drive out the defenders of the work, though it had been severely damaged, and sterner measures were needed. An infantry officer volunteered to capture it by surprise, along a communication trench which, he had found, led into the fort. With a small party consisting of himself, a sub-lieutenant, three non-commissioned officers, three dismounted cyclists and a bugler, he crept up the trench into the interior of the redoubt. The Germans when he arrived were underground. Hearing steps, some of them cautiously emerged from their cellars and dug-outs. They found the French in their midst. Before they could recover from their astonishment, the French captain, firing with his pistol at the leader, who fell in a heap, shouted " En avant ! " His men darted forward and the Germans above and below ground surrendered. Prisoners to the number of 114 and three machine-guns were taken. In a few minutes the gallant Frenchmen had secured a fort which for twenty-four hours had kept our Allies at this point in check.

The next morning (July 18) General Fayolle, before the Germans had recovered from the repulse of their six battalions on the slopes of La Maisonnette Hill, launched a fresh offensive north and south of the Somme. The French line now extended from Biaches and the La Maisonnette plateau through Barleux to Estrées. In the course of the forenoon five miles of German trenches from Barleux to Soyécourt were secured. North of the Somme, on a frontage of four miles from the point where the French joined up with the British south of the captured Trônes Wood, our Allies overran the German fortified area and reached the Combles-Cléry narrow-gauge railway.

Thick mist and incessant rain had interfered with the French, as they did with the British operations on the 18th. At 5.30 p.m. the enemy, preceded by clouds of poisonous gas and pioneers carrying *Flammenwerfer*, attacked the British positions in the vicinity of Longueval and Delville Wood, where they formed a salient. The attack was heralded by a heavy fire of shells of all kinds, and was delivered by a whole division. One column of the Germans made for the copse, two other columns for the sides of the salient. The north side and Longueval were lost by us and so was a part of the wood. The garrison of the Waterlot Farm, midway between Longueval and Guillemont, however, resisted the German pressure, and our artillery promptly played upon the Germans in Longueval and Delville Wood. Reinforcements were hurried up, and preparations made for the necessary counter-attacks. According to the German report, the Magdeburg 26th Infantry and the Altenburg Regiments had particularly distinguished themselves in these engagements, and we had lost 8 officers and 280 privates taken prisoners. The fighting went on through the night and into the next day. At 9.30 p.m. of the 19th Sir Douglas Haig reported that most of the ground lost in Longueval and Delville Wood had been recovered, and that a large body of Germans massed for another—the fourth—attack on Waterlot Farm had been dispersed by our fire.

South of the Somme that day the French seized some trenches south of Estrées and took about 60 prisoners.

The Battle of the Somme, it must always be remembered, was but part of the British operations against the Germans in France and Belgium. To remind the reader that the long line of trenches and redoubts from the east of Albert to the north of Ypres was constantly agitated by bombardments and local attack let us, at the risk of digression, relate an incident which happened south of Armentières on the 19th. At this point an Australian division, exposed to a shell fire heavier than any they had ever experienced in the Gallipoli Peninsula, followed up a heavy bombardment of the German position, which, however, had not succeeded in destroying or burying all the defenders' machine guns, by a determined attack, aided by a British division on their left. They carried the front line trenches, but were held up by those in the rear. Farther south—in the centre—the whole fortified area was stormed, and the Australians emerged into more or less open country. On the right their comrades had to cross a wide space between the front and rear lines of the system. The Germans here held a very strongly fortified salient. At places the Australians scrambled into the enemy's works, but the Germans by diverting streams of water into the captured spots made the position difficult to hold. After enduring a tremendous bombardment for 11 hours the order was given to retire. The British Engineers had constructed communication trenches along which this movement could be carried out. 200 prisoners and some machine-guns were captured, but our losses had been severe.

" I hope," had written a German soldier of the 190th Regiment, captured at Contalmaison, " this awful business will soon stop." A prayer which we may be sure was cordially re-echoed by many of his fellow-countrymen.

During the night of the 19th-20th our bombing parties made a substantial advance east of the Leipzig Redoubt, which was one of the main obstacles barring approach from the south to the Thiépval plateau. Away to the right beyond Pozières, in the vicinity of the Bois de Foureaux or High Wood, round Longueval, Waterlot Farm, Delville Wood, Guillemont, and thence to the banks of the Somme, a continuous fringe of exploding shells showed that the German artillery was bombarding the British and French positions, to which our gunners were not slow in replying.

The noise was deafening. The sky was lit up by the bursting shells. Sir Douglas Haig had replaced the Western and Eastern Divisions and the Highlanders by South-countrymen and Lowlanders, and the enemy artillery,

[Official Photograph.

CARRYING WOUNDED ON TO A HOSPITAL BARGE.

anticipating an attack, was raining down showers of projectiles on the spots where it was imagined our troops were assembled for the attack. The "Jack Johnsons," which had been but sparingly used by the Germans since the Battle of Ypres, were again in evidence. "They came over," said a Devonshire lad afterwards, relating his experiences, "as thick and fast as hand-grenades." Craters often 40 ft. across and half as deep were formed by the explosion of their shells.

West of this scene an occasional shell was flung into the captured Trônes and Bernafay Woods and against Montauban. The French "75's," the chatter of the machine-guns and a dropping rifle fire added to the sounds of preparation and showed that all arms were participating in it.

Meanwhile, in their dug-outs, staff officers, telephone in hand, waited for the news of what was happening to the north of the Bazentin-Longueval position, where our men were again topping the crest and descending into the High Wood, moving up the rising slope of ground between that and Delville Wood, while through the broken branches and over the fallen trunks a South African contingent was making its way northwards and eastwards. The northern

houses in Longueval, the High Wood, the intervening space and Delville Wood, with the village of Guillemont, just east of the Trônes Wood, had to be carried before our hold on the plateau would be secure.

The rain, which had impeded operations for so many days, had now ceased, but had left a dark and heavy atmosphere, through which our soldiers fought. Many of the Germans, the bonds of discipline being loosened in the night of fighting, scuttled back or surrendered, but enough remained to put up a strenuous fight.

At 5.30 a.m. General Fayolle, anxious to assist the British on his left and suspecting rightly that the German reserves were stationed north of Guillemont, launched from Hardecourt and its environs an attack on Hardecourt Hill towards Maurepas, and the narrow gauge Combies-Cléry line. The Germans, alarmed at the new and unexpected attack which threatened their flank, brought southward several regiments from the British front, too late, however, to prevent the French from capturing by 9 a.m. several trenches between Hardecourt Hill and the Somme and from crossing the railway at various points. Prisoners to the number of about 400 were taken by our Allies, whose

[*Official photograph.*

MEN OF THE LONDON RIFLE BRIGADE.
In a reserve trench, waiting to advance to the front line.

A MINE CRATER ON THE SOMME.

[*Official photograph.*]

attack had appreciably lightened the difficult task of the British.

The sun had by now dispersed the mist which had covered the field, when it first rose, and illuminated the whole battlefield. Over it there were still the intermittent clouds produced by shell explosions from the powerful artilleries of both sides firing with their utmost energy, while overhead were seen circling the aeroplanes, round which the numerous white puffs showed that they were the target for anti-aircraft guns. Our troops which had been continuously engaged in this part of the field were now withdrawn and replaced by others. Well and ardently had they fought, the men from the west and east of England and from Caledonia, and they were now to be given a rest, their places at the front being taken by fresher men.

As the day wore on Guillemont received special attention from our artillerymen, and so heavy was the fire that the place seemed actually to shrink away under it.

The destruction wrought by the Allies that day was not confined to the battlefield. Over the German lines, aeroplanes, flying singly, or in squadrons, attacked the railways, aerodromes, hutments and other objectives, dropping on them tons of explosives. About 6.15 p.m. four of our aeroplanes encountered four

Fokkers and two biplanes, and the fight went on for over half an hour. One Fokker was destroyed, a second badly damaged; the rest of the German machines fled. None of ours had been injured. Between 8 and 9 p.m. four more of our machines met eleven of the enemy's, which included L.V.G.'s,* Rolands and Fokkers. The leader of our patrol made for an L.V.G., which hastily retired from the scene, and then drove down a Fokker. Attacked by a Roland, he was equally successful, forcing it also to descend. Meanwhile a second machine put out of action another Roland. Two Fokkers, when about to attack, nearly collided and had to draw off. The third of the British pilots, at a lower altitude, also disposed of a Roland, which fell in a " spinning nose-dive," but his own engine being hit by a shot from a Fokker, he descended in a steep spiral. The fourth pilot dived to his rescue, engaged the pursuer at a height of 1,000 feet, and the Fokker was observed to fall to the ground in flames. Eventually all the hostile aeroplanes were dispersed. A French pilot the same day brought down a German machine east of Péronne. These successes more than counterbalanced the loss of the four British machines which since the 16th had failed to return to their aerodromes.

* The L.V.G. was a two-seater biplane.

FRENCH CAVALRY PATROLLING.

At 10.55 p.m. Sir Douglas Haig was able to report that north of the Bazentin-Longueval line we had advanced 1,000 yards; our front now ran from the bottom of the High Wood to Longueval, through the middle of Delville Wood, then turned south by Waterlot Farm to a point between Trônes Wood and Guillemont. Heavy fighting still continued in the northern outskirts of Longueval and in Delville Wood.

General Fayolle this day had also won a considerable success north of the Somme. To the south of the river the French on the 20th had not been idle. Our Allies had advanced in the preceding fighting almost up to the gates of Péronne; they were at the bottom of the loop of the Somme. To enlarge this pocket southwards towards Chaulnes and the railway Chaulnes-Péronne was the next step to be taken. From the western outskirts of Barleux to Estrées their line ran back almost at a right-angle. Consequently the troops south of the Somme below Péronne were in a dangerous salient. To drive its southern face southward and thus enlarge the salient was Foch's object.

The French Colonial troops were employed for the purpose, and in the morning of the 20th a terrific bombardment of the German positions south of Estrées opened. Their positions extended from Estrées through the park of Deniécourt, the château of which had been converted into a formidable underground fortress, to Soyécourt, defended by formidable trenches, to the Bois de l'Etoile and Hill 90, situated north-west of Vermand-Ovillers, near which was a redoubt on the road to Lihons. If the French could capture Vermand-Ovillers they would be within easy distance of the Chaulnes junction, where the Amiens-Péronne and Roye-Péronne railways met. As the Roye region was the pivot of the German right wing in this part of the theatre of operations, the importance of the Chaulnes junction is obvious.

When the bombardment ceased the coloured troops of the French advanced. The Soyécourt labyrinth, the Bois de l'Etoile and the redoubt on the Lihons road near Vermand-Ovillers Farm were carried. By nightfall Soyécourt was surrounded on three sides. Thirty officers and 2,870 privates, 3 guns, and 30 machine-guns had been captured. A German counter-attack near Soyécourt delivered in the late afternoon by a battalion was severely repulsed by the French artillery and machine-guns.

Such was the battle of the Somme, of July 20.

[*Official photograph.*

BRINGING UP THE 75's IN THE GREAT ADVANCE.

To deceive the German people and their friends outside Germany, the German Great General Staff issued the following fabrication :

On both sides of the Somme the enemy yesterday, as was expected, prepared to deliver a strong attack, but it failed.

After the strongest preparation on a front of about 25 miles, attacks were made south of Pozières and to the west of Vermandovillers.

More than 17 divisions, comprising more than 200,000 men, participated in these attacks.

The meagre result for the enemy is that the first line of a German Division along a front of about 1¼ miles south of Hardecourt was pressed back from the advanced trenches into the next line of trenches lying 800 yards to the rear, and the enemy divisions penetrated into a salient in the little wood of Vermandovillers.

On the whole of the remainder of this front the enemy's wild onslaughts were broken to pieces against the death-defying loyalty of our troops, with extraordinary losses for the enemy. So far 17 officers and 1,200 men have been captured.

That, so far as numbers were concerned, the battle was on the large scale customary to these operations may be admitted. Otherwise the German fiction bore no relation to actual fact. The Allies were not successful at every point, but they made considerable gains and suffered no reverses of any moment.

During the night of the 20th-21st the enemy, after an intense bombardment with gas shells, entered High Wood, and recovered the northern part of it. The next day (July 21) the battle continued spasmodically from the Leipzig Redoubt to the Delville Road. A German bombing attack against the northern edge of our position in the Redoubt failed. Taking advantage of the fine weather, our aeroplanes bombed important points behind the German lines, and in the evening there was a good deal of aerial fighting east of them. An official account of our aerial activity that day may here be quoted :

Much successful cooperation with artillery was carried out ; 92 targets were engaged with aeroplane observation and 25 with kite balloon. Several direct hits on gun emplacements were obtained, the ammunition in one continuing to explode for over half an hour.

One of our machines, engaged on photographic duty, was attacked by a Roland, which came level and then dived and attacked under the tail of our aeroplane. Our aeroplane side-slipped till level with the Roland, and then fired three drums into it at 40 yards. The Roland fell to the earth near Leuze Wood.

One of our aeroplanes, whilst on artillery patrol at 4,000 ft., saw eight hostile aircraft at a height of 9,000 ft. It climbed to this height and was joined by five of our fighting machines. At this juncture the enemy were joined by five L.V.G.'s and two Fokkers. All our machines attacked the somewhat scattered enemy formation. A section of three of our machines dived on to one party, from which one Fokker plunged to earth from a height of 7,000 ft., and two other machines were forced to land. Another machine was seen to fall out of control into a village, and yet another fell headlong to earth in a field. The fighting lasted over half-an-hour, when the remaining enemy machines flew off in twos and threes.

The total of hostile machines brought down on this day was six, and at least three more were driven down damaged.

South of the Amiens-Chaulnes railway, in the Maucourt region, the Germans tried to rush the French lines, but were repulsed with the bayonet.

Saturday, July 22, was a comparatively uneventful day. The Germans bombarded our lines with gas and lachrymatory shells, while we prepared for a fresh advance in which the Australians were destined to distinguish themselves. At Berlin the Higher Command affected to be supremely confident. " In the Somme sector," ran the *communiqué* issued that day, " after their defeat of the previous days . . . our enemies had to abandon their great united attacks." However, all Germans did not agree with their leaders. For example, a German officer, interviewed by the *Vossische Zeitung* of this date, is reported to have said :

The English fought very bravely, notwithstanding enormous losses. I don't know how great their reserves are, but upon this will depend the length of the offensive. Our positions were badly knocked about, but the dug-outs and shelters held out very well, which is lucky for us. Besides this, the higher command knew what to expect about the attacks, and had taken the necessary measures to resist them. Finally, rainy weather came at the right moment to help us.

Herr Max Osborn, writing for the same journal, observed :

We are shaken by a burning pain as new streams of German blood are flowing, and we recognize our powerlessness over what cannot be changed. After two years of war the angel of destruction is passing through the ranks of German arms with a fury and mercilessness as if the death dance of battles had only just begun. Germans are critical, clear-headed, and strong enough to look the truth in the face. Whilst the enemies suffer fearful losses, we do not blind our eyes to the new mourning which has come to us, nor over the seriousness of the fate of this decisive battle which is raging on all the fronts. We should be unworthy of the stupendous task we have to fulfil, and of the scarcely comprehensible sacrifices which our heroes make, if we were not able to understand the whole fury and burden of these weeks. We feel as two years ago the raging storm of the united power of the enemy.

It is now a question of not less than everything for the life or death of our nation. We stand differently now from what we did in August, 1914. Unexampled deeds of fame lie between, but still the concluding point has to be reached, and everything is in the balance of death or life.

Everything between the Somme and the Ancre was, indeed, " in the balance of death or life."

On the evening of Saturday, July 22, the British artillery increased its fire on the German lines from Pozières to Guillemont. Here the Australians were about to play an important part in the Battle of the Somme. The force engaged was the 1st Anzac Corps (Lieut.-Gen. Sir William R. Birdwood, K.C.S.I., K.C.M.G.).

" A large sector of the horizon," said Mr. C. E. W. Bean, the official Press Correspondent with the Australian Imperial Forces, " was lit

[*Official photograph.*]

LOADING A BIG GUN.

up not by single flashes, but by a continuous bank of quivering light." The sweet heliotrope scent of German tear-shells pervaded the air in the vicinity of Pozières. Shells containing poisonous gas whistled towards and over the British lines. Projectiles which burst high up and came down like flaming torches descended among the crouching Australians and Territorials. A torrent of our artillery fire was turned on Pozières, the fortified Windmill behind it, the lines of trenches before the village and the barbed-wire entanglements.

Suddenly, about midnight, the British guns lifted and the Australians rose to their feet. At once rockets rose into the air, and bursting lit up the 500 yards or so of crater-pitted ground between them and the first German trench. The Australians, in the glare of the rockets, under a rain of shrapnel, moved steadily and rapidly forward. On their left Territorials—mostly Londoners—made for the west end of the village. The first German trench had been recently dug ; it was shallow, and the enemy there offered little resistance. Digging themselves in, the Australians halted, while our guns played on the second trench, a deep and well-built one beyond the tramway running about the outskirts of the village. There the Germans put up a better fight, but were all bayoneted or taken prisoners.

Having improved the second trench, the Australians, crossing to others, made their way through clumps of woods and orchards into the village itself. Two redoubts were captured on the way. Meanwhile the Territorials had on the left got above Pozières and were attacking it from the north-west. From daybreak onward the work of clearing out the Germans from the ruins of the village went on. At 11.30 a.m. the Germans, strongly reinforced, counter-attacked. They had been doped with ether and charged like a troop of madmen. In a horrible hand-to-hand conflict weapons of every kind were employed and some of the Germans used spiked clubs which had been specially made for this warfare. Backwards and forwards swayed the infuriated combatants. But by 4 p.m. our troops gained the mastery and by nightfall three-quarters of Pozières was won.

Less successful was the attempt to storm Guillemont at the southern end of the sector. Several' barbed-wire entanglements covering the position had not been destroyed. Raked by machine-gun fire and charged by the German reserves, the British who had effected a lodgment in the village from the north were obliged to withdraw.

Between Pozières and Guillemont there had also been fierce encounters. At one moment our men had expelled the Germans entirely from Longueval, but by the afternoon they had regained a footing in the northern houses of the village. On the French front there had been an artillery duel, and south of Soyécourt a German attack had been repulsed.

On the 24th the battle for the ridges north of the Somme continued, but nothing decisive occurred. The Australians and the British made some progress in and around Pozières, where six German officers and 145 men were captured and the French south of the Somme carried at night some strongly fortified houses and a stretch of trench between Estrées and Vermand-Ovillers.

The next day (July 25) the situation changed. For a week no rain had fallen and the ground had dried, which was favourable to the Allies, still the atmospheric conditions had been bad for our artillery observers, whether in the forward observing positions or high above the ground in aircraft. For it was hazy and the smoke of battle lay heavy on the earth.

As a consequence, battery after battery of the heavy German guns which had been hastily dispatched to the Somme front were safely placed by their detachments in various suitable positions behind Flers, the next village which would have to be stormed on the road through Longueval to Bapaume. During the 26th the increased volume of shell fire from the German side plainly showed the British that more guns had been brought into action against them. At the same time the strong reinforcements of infantry which had also reached the German lines commenced a series of formidable counter-attacks. One of these in the afternoon was directed from the north-east against Pozières, most of which village was in the hands of the Australians or Territorials. The cemetery on the north-west side had been taken by our men, but to the north-east the complication of trenches in front of the summit known as the Windmill on the ridge behind Pozières still held out. To rescue their comrades still lurking in or near the village the Germans swept down on both sides of the Pozières-Bapaume road from the direction of the Windmill. It was a brave but fruitless attempt. Such charges, already preposterous at the First Battle of Ypres, had, in face of the gigantic accumulation of guns and shells, now become suicidal. Caught by a deluge of shrapnel, the Germans hesitated, halted, and then ran back, leaving behind them the ground littered with the dead and dying. Almost simultaneously with this charge, another in the region of Guillemont met with the same fate. At other points parties of our infantry progressed. To the south of Estrées the French reduced some strongly fortified houses and farther west expelled the enemy from trenches north of Vermand-Ovillers. The salients created by the Allies north and south of the Somme were being gradually flattened out.

Night fell but brought no rest to the combatants. There was no moon and the only light on the battlefield was that caused by explosions of the shells or the occasional lights and rockets thrown up. About 3 a.m. on the 26th the Germans, undeterred by their losses of the previous day, commenced a counter-attack on our position between Longueval and Pozières. A flight of rockets shot up and great patches of ground became visible, betraying the enemy's advance. At once the trench mortars on our side began to fire, and the sound of machine-guns and of rifle-firing was heard, while our batteries behind poured a devastating fire on the assaulting troops.

The attack was beaten back and a second also failed. When dawn broke, "No Man's Land" was heaped with ghastly results of the British fire.

It was on July 26 that Pozières was finally captured and the second phase of the Battle of the Somme ended. The Territorials and Australians had penetrated the main German line just below the Cemetery, where numerous prisoners were taken. Thence the British worked eastward along the trench to the Pozières-Bapaume road and advanced against the positions guarding the high ground, north-east of the village. Most of the prisoners captured belonged to the 22nd Regiment, brought down from the Ypres region, and to the 157th Regiment.

Every building, every copse, wood, declivity in the ground had been utilized by the German engineers for defensive purposes, and vast underground dwellings had been constructed to house the garrisons in safety. Ample supplies of arms and ammunition were at hand for their troops and careful arrangements had been made to bring a powerful fire on the works themselves in case they should fall into the hands of the British; in short, the whole resources of military art had been exhausted to render this position impregnable. But, battered to pieces so far as the above-ground constructions were concerned, the nerve-shattered garrison had been unable to resist the determined assaults of the British and Australians. The process of clearing out the dug-outs was, as an officer remarked, something like drawing a badger. But it was done, and Pozières remained in the hands of our gallant troops.

Since July 1 some 24 square miles had been seized by the British. They had advanced eastward on an average 7,000 yards on a front averaging between 9,000 and 10,000 yards.

[*Official photograph.*

A VIEW OF POZIÈRES AFTER THE BRITISH ATTACK.

CHAPTER CLXV.

THE BATTLE OF THE SOMME (III.).

The Capture of Pozières—Delville Wood and Longueval—The Capture of Delville Wood—Sir Hubert Gough and the Fifth Army—Sir Douglas Haig's Plans—Cooperation with the French—Gains and Losses—Fighting about Guillemont—End of the Second Year of War—The Thiépval Salient attacked on August 4—The King's Visit to the Somme Battlefields—Wet Weather—British and French Advances, August 18–19—Position on August 22—The German Losses.

CHAPTER CLIV. brought the narrative of the Battle of the Somme up to the end, on July 25, of what may be called the Pozières phase. It will be remembered that the Australians played a very important part, and it may be well to give here an Australian account of the gallant conduct of their own men. Admirable in every way, it drew from the British Division acting with them a message saying that they were proud to fight by their side. The following description of the great engagement was addressed to the High Commissioner for the Commonwealth :—

On the night of July 22, our field artillery lashed down its shrapnel upon the German front line in the open before the village. A few minutes later this fire lifted and the Australian attack was launched.

The Germans had opened in one part with a machine-gun before that final burst of shrapnel, and they opened again immediately after. But there would have been no possibility of stopping that charge with a fire twenty times as heavy. The difficulty was not to get the men forward, but to hold them. With a complicated night attack to be carried through it was necessary to keep the men well in hand.

The first trench was a wretchedly shallow affair in places. Most of the Germans in it were dead—some of them had been lying there for days. The artillery in the meantime had lifted on to the German trenches farther back. Later they lifted to a farther position yet. The Australian infantry dashed at once from the first position captured across intervening space over the tramway and into the trees.

It was here that the first real difficulty arose along parts of the line. Some sections of it found in front of them the trench which they were looking for—an excellent deep trench which had survived the bombardment. Other sections found no recognizable trench at all, but a maze ot shell craters and tumbled rubbish

or a simple ditch reduced to white powder. Parties went on through the trees into the village searching for the position and pushed so close to the fringe of their own shell-fire that some were wounded by it. However, where they found no trench they started to dig one as best they could. Shortly after the bombardment shifted a little farther, and a third attack came through and swept in most parts right up to the position which the troops had been ordered to take up.

As daylight gradually spread over that bleached surface Australians could occasionally be seen walking about in the trees and through the part of the village they had been ordered to take. The position was being rapidly "consolidated." . . . That night, after dark, the Australians pushed across the road through the village. By morning the position had been improved, so that nearly the whole village was secure against sudden attack.

In the heart of the village itself there was little more actual hand-to-hand fighting. All that happened there was that from the time when the first day broke and found the Pozières position practically ours, the enemy turned his guns on to it. Hour after hour—day and night—with increasing intensity as the days went on, he rained heavy shell into the area. It was the sight of the battlefield for miles around—that reeking village. Now he would send them crashing in on a line south of the road—eight heavy shells at a time, minute after minute, followed up by burst upon burst of shrapnel. Now he would place a curtain straight across this valley or that till the sky and landscape were blotted out, except for fleeting glimpses seen as through a lift of fog. Gas shell, musty with chloroform, sweet-scented tear shell that made your eyes run with water, high bursting shrapnel with black smoke and a vicious high explosive rattle behind its heavy pellets, ugly green bursts the colour of a fat silkworm, huge black clouds from the high explosive of his 5·9's. Day and night the men worked through it, fighting this horrid machinery far over the horizon as if they were fighting Germans hand-to-hand—building up whatever it battered down ; buried some of them not once but again and again and again. What is a barrage against such troops ? They went through it as you would go through a summer shower—too

GERMAN GUN WRECKED AT POZIÈRES.

proud to bend their heads, many of them, because their mates were looking. I am telling you of things I have seen. As one of the best of their officers said to me, "I have to walk about as if I liked it—what else can you do when your own men teach you to ?" The same thought struck me not once but twenty times.

On Tuesday morning, July 25, the shelling of the day before rose to a higher note and then suddenly slackened. The German was attacking. It was only a few of the infantry who even saw him. The attack came in lines at fairly wide intervals up the reverse slope of the hill behind Pozières Windmill. Before it reached the crest it came under the sudden barrage of our own shrapnel. The German lines swerved away up the hill. The excited infantry on the extreme right could see Germans crawling over as quickly as they could from one shell crater to another, grey-backs hopping from hole to hole. Our guns blazed away hard, but most of our infantry never got the chance it was thirsting for. Our artillery beat back that attack before it was over the crest, and the Germans broke and ran. Again the enemy's artillery was turned on. Pozières was pounded more furiously than before, until, by 4 in the afternoon, it seemed to

onlookers scarcely possible that humanity could have endured such an ordeal. The place could be picked out for miles by pillars of red and black dust towering like a Broken Hill duststorm. Then Germans were seen to be coming on again exactly as in the morning. Again our artillery descended upon them like a hailstorm, and nothing came of the attack.

During all this time, in spite of the shelling, the troops were slowly working forwards through Pozières. Every day saw fresh ground gained. A great part of the men who were working through it had had no more than two or three hours sleep since Saturday—some of them none at all, only fierce, hard work all the time.

This is a good description of the heroic struggle.

July 26 was not marked by any important engagement, though two strong trenches to the west of Pozières were taken by Territorial troops, and some prisoners, including five officers, were captured : the day was generally spent in consolidating the position won. The French, too, were engaged on similar work.

The next day saw a recrudescence of the struggle and some fierce contests took place. Our line here ran through the lower part of Delville Wood and of Longueval, whence it turned south. There had been heavy fighting about these parts for the past 10 days, and on both fronts our men had made progress, but in each instance the Germans had been able to cling on to part of their defences, notwithstanding the terrible artillery fire which had been brought to bear on them, sheltering to a great extent in their dug-outs. It will be

LONGUEVAL.

remembered that Delville Wood had actually been overrun by us on July 15, and part of the defences of Longueval occupied, that the enemy had counter-attacked on the evening of the 18th and, after a severe artillery fire during the night, had, on the 19th, succeeded in regaining a footing in the wood and also in the northern portion of Longueval. For the next week there had been fierce artillery bombardment and the tide of battle ebbed and flowed. But we never altogether lost our foothold.

It was in Delville Wood that the South name and had become a mass of broken timber. Yet this offered, perhaps, even more difficulty to the movement of our troops than if all the trees had been upright, for the interlaced and matted mass of broken trunks and branches formed an extremely difficult obstacle while enough trees remained standing to afford fair cover from view for the defenders. In addition, the heavy shells of both sides had turned the surface of the ground into a series of pitfalls made by the craters of explosion. Over all were the ghastly sights of the unburied dead lying

A HEAVY HOWITZER IN ACTION ON THE SOMME.

African Brigade distinguished themselves by their bravery and tenacity so as to elicit commendation from the General commanding them. South Africa might justly be proud of the achievements of her representatives with the British Expeditionary Force.

Throughout the night of July 26–27 a crushing fire of shells had been directed against that portion of the Delville Wood to which the Germans still clung, and hand-to-hand encounters took place frequently. The "Devil's Wood," as our men not inappropriately called it, considering the horrible scenes which took place there, was some 159 acres in extent. It had almost ceased to be a wood in anything but about, torn to pieces by explosions of shells or bombs and bearing but small resemblance to the living beings they had once been. Such was the field of battle on which Briton and German strove for mastery.

Slowly but surely our men pushed on, the guns preparing the way by a curtain fire about 75 yards ahead of our attacking line.

It speaks volumes for the ability of our gunners that they should have been able to carry on this advancing curtain of crashing shells continuously and without injury to our following infantry. "It was queer," said a soldier who had been through the attack, " to see the shells bursting in front of one; the line

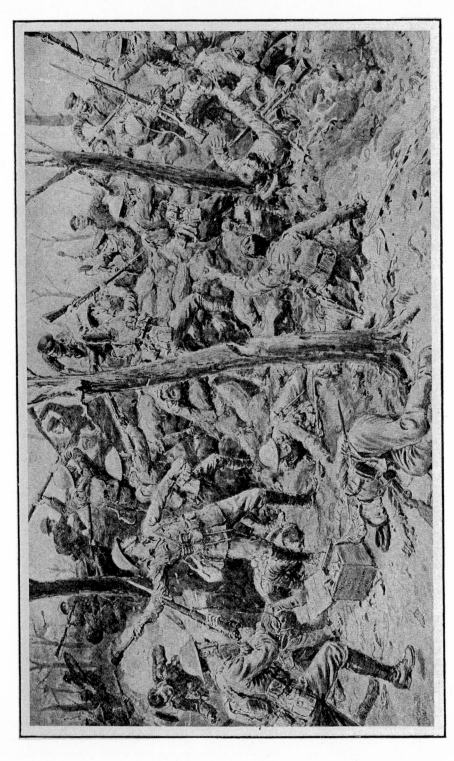

THE DEFENCE OF DELVILLE WOOD BY THE SOUTH AFRICANS.

was just about 75 yards ahead of us, flinging up the ground and smashing everything. It was wonderful how the gunners kept it just ahead of us."*

To the artillery, indeed, a great share of the success of the British arms was due. The enemy's positions had been subjected to such a fire as had surpassed all previous efforts. From June 27 onwards, said a correspondent of *The Morning Post* (on the authority of an artillery officer), we had fired an average of half a million of shells *per diem*. This, of course, was spread over the whole position of the enemy, highly concentrated against the parts to be assaulted, less against others.

On July 27 our cannonade was so fierce as to surpass all previous efforts, and yet, although it might have been thought impossible for men to have lived under it, there was still a sufficient number of German infantry left, and there were still sufficient of their machine-guns in place, to afford a considerable degree of resistance to the advance of our troops.

It will be realized that under these circumstances progress was slow: but assuredly it was certain. This was not only due to the artillery, but also to the excellent way in

[Official Photo.

SUMMER-TIME IN PICARDY.

which the bombers acted with the rifle-carrying infantry, and to the way in which no effort was spared to bring up machine-guns to support the latter. It is true that this bold action sometimes resulted in the loss of a machine-gun if the infantry were driven back, but that was only a small set-off to the advantage gained generally by bold handling of these weapons.

* From the *Daily Telegraph*, July 31.

On one occasion a party of Germans were seen carrying a machine-gun across a drive in the Delville Wood. One of our men moved out to a point whence he could bring a Lewis gun (which can be fired from the shoulder)

[Official Photo.

MAMETZ CHURCH.

to bear on the enemy, and completely wiped out the whole party. With some of his comrades he smashed the German machine-gun and then returned. The next day the same men pushed farther into the wood, but their weapon became jammed owing to a rough tumble over the broken wood; it was rendered useless and abandoned.

It was not alone physical difficulties which made our rate of advance slow. Every yard of progress on our part was met by a corresponding counter-attack, made often in the massed form to which our troops were now accustomed, and this was especially the case when we had won through to the edge of the wood. For us then it was the old problem how to advance from such a position over the open ground to the next hostile line. It was exactly this task which was imposed upon the enemy in his endeavours to regain the ground he had lost; he had to advance over a space without shelter to reach his objective. Every device was employed; interspersed with the shrapnel and high explosive fire were mingled gusts of poison and lachrymatory shells. But secure in their masks our men were undismayed, and held firmly to the ground they had won so bravely. The thick German columns formed admirable targets for our gunners. "You could see the Germans coming towards you in great waves of grey," said an officer present at the engagement.

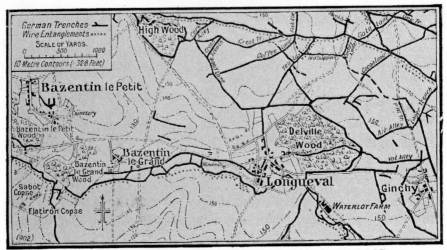

MAP ILLUSTRATING THE CAPTURE OF DELVILLE WOOD.

B t our infantry was ready for them, ready to ply them with machine-gun and rifle fire, ready to cover them with bombs. It was no case of coming to handy strokes, for of the multitude only individuals arrived anywhere near our line. It was mainly the artillery which stopped them, mowing them down so that they lay in long swathes, cutting deep lines through the solid columns, as shell after shell struck them full. The attack at last came to a standstill. Several times was the effort renewed, and each time in vain. Three fresh regiments, which one after another came on with great bravery, were almost annihilated, and when the few survivors straggled back to their trenches the ground between the two hostile lines was covered with the bodies of the dead and wounded. As our troops advanced, bombing here, bayoneting there, with an accompaniment of rifle shots and machine-gun fire, they gathered by the way many prisoners who had been hiding for safety in shell-craters or behind any available cover to guard themselves from the terrible artillery fire. Finally our men won their way to the extreme limit of the wood to the east and north-east, and commenced to consolidate their position.

They had also strengthened their hold on Longueval by seizing a portion of the northern end, and, advancing beyond it, had taken the orchard just on the outskirts of the village towards the north-west. It was a gain of some importance, as fire from it swept the valley which led upwards behind Bazentin-le-Grand towards Bazentin-le-Petit. We also took a redoubt, known to our soldiers as the Machine-

gun House, which protected, with a flanking fire, this part of the Delville Wood position. Creeping up under what cover was available, several of our officers led forward parties of bombers. These managed to get within heaving range, and then threw bomb after bomb into the work, killing nearly all the machine-gun detachments and capturing their weapons.

By the fall of night Delville Wood was entirely captured except for a small point in the northern end. We had inflicted very heavy losses on the enemy, while our own were, considering the magnitude of the success, comparatively slight. This, as we have seen, was largely due to the part played by our guns.

A subaltern, who arrived home in a Red Cross ship, after being wounded in Delville Wood, told an interviewer that there were "some real brave things" done at the end of that great fight. "They can't give D.C.M.'s to everyone, you know," he said, "but honestly, all those men earned it, just as well as any of the chaps who get it. What I am thinking about is the lot of things that nobody at all ever knows about; not even a man's own mates." And he told this story :—

We had to fall back a bit once, from a shallow trench at the top, after we'd been in it, and thought we'd got it. Well, we fell back for, oh, it must've been 10 minutes, the time I mean, and a lot more Boches came up along those communicating saps, and it almost looked once as though we would'nt get it back again. I got my dose in the trench, you know. When I saw our men all falling back I tried like the devil to get out. I was in quite a deep bit, and I nearly broke blood vessels trying to get out ; but it was no go. My shoulder was giving me hell, and the right arm would not work at all. Well, you know I'd rather have been sent West altogether. I always did feel I'd rather anything than be taken by the Boches. I had my revolver, of course ; but I'm not much good with my left hand. Ten to one they'd have got me alive. I could see over the edge, and I was cursing my luck when I saw a chap deliberately stop, turn round and look at me, and sort of weigh up his chances; and then go on again. He was falling back with the rest of our lot, you know.

Just then a Boche machine-gun opened as it seemed right alongside me. It was really just round the big traverse. "That settles it," I thought. "I'm done now." And it did settle it, too. That chap I'd seen, who'd evidently decided once that it wasn't good enough, he altered his mind when the typewriter began. Down on his hands and knees he went, and scuttled all the way back to where I was, like a lizard. He fairly gasped at me; no breath, you know. "On my back, sir," says he. And, somehow, he hauled me out, and slung me over his back.

I fell off three separate times, while he was scrambling down the slope with me, and three separate times he stopped, in all that fire, and fixed me up again. And then I felt him crumble up under me, and at the same time I got—this, through the left arm.

I rolled clear, and looked at his face. I'll never forget his face, but he had no coat or cap, and I didn't know his battalion. His forehead was laid open, and bleeding fast. I dragged him behind a stump, and laid him with his head on my haversack. Then I scrambled out to find a stretcher-bearer for him. But I got caught up in our advance then. You know what it is. And I went on, thinking I'd find my man after. Glad I went, in a way, because I had three bombs a wounded corporal gave me, and it was easy lobbing them with my left, at close quarters. By gad, I lobbed 'em all right; nearly lobbed myself to Kingdom come, too.

BRITISH BOMBERS ATTACKING THROUGH POISON GAS.
The German smoke-helmet has a round chemical filter, much larger than the nozzle of the British type.

But those bombs did their job all right before we cleared the trench. It was hours after before I could get a man to help me look for that good chap who'd dragged me out; and we never found him, never a sign of him. But to do what he did; thinking it out, too, in all that hell; why, many a chap's got the V.C. for no more than that, I think.

Yes, and there were dozens of things like that, in Delville alone, and the same all along the front, right through the push.*

Men like these were grand fighters, worthy of the noblest and best traditions of our fighting men.

It is interesting here to note the views of a German Commander, as to the main lesson of the fighting on the Somme, expressed to Mr. Cyril Brown, a correspondent of the *New York Times* :

Artillery! Artillery! Artillery! The side that can put most ammunition into the other fellow's face, and whose infantry can throw its hand grenades best, will gain ground. But artillery plays the main rôle in this battle. At the start when it was necessary to lay a barrier of fire on the enemy lines one battery had to cover a front segment of 800 yards. Now I have a battery for every hundred yards of the curtain fire.

To this it may be justly replied, in the language of one of Reuter's correspondents :—

This may possibly be true, for it is certain that the Germans have hurried up every available gun to this part of the front. But what the German Commander-

---

* *Morning Post*, August 2.

in-Chief omitted to say is that he is in an infinitely worse position in regard to being able effectively to emplace his artillery than ho was at the beginning of the British offensive. This is so conspicuously a war of artillery that, as has been said, the gain of a few yards, giving command of a ridge and observation, may make all the difference between dominance and untenability.

We have been steadily gaining ground that should be valuable for artillery work. The ponderous process of creeping forward is always going on, which means that the German artillery must either be always slowly withdrawing or courting destruction. As an artillery officer put it to me yesterday, in discussing the effects of Friday's and Saturday's fighting, the time is rapidly approaching when the German gunners from Beaumont Hamel to Bapaume must choose between Scylla and Charybdis : they must either stop and be knocked out, or get out. For we are fighting a great winning battle of position.

This means that as we progress over the Thiépval-Morval ridge the ground slopes down towards the Germans and this gives us the advantage of command.

The German General also went on to say, in reply to a question put by him as to whether the British showed signs of weakening :

No. The English are tough. One must be just to one's enemies. One must see them as they are. The English have not lost hope of success as yet. Despite their very heavy losses, which are known to me, they come back again and again. They are stubborn foes. One has to give them credit for trying again and again to break through my front. The English soldier is a worthy, excellent soldier, but his newer leadership is not on the heights.

The last few words are quite typically Prussian—*i.e.*, proof positive of the inability of

[*Official photograph.*

TRENCH PERISCOPE IN USE.

[*Official photograph.*

GETTING A HEAVY GUN INTO POSITION.

the race ever to judge their opponents fairly. Of course, the German General knew nothing whatever about the actual work of the leaders of the British Army; he had never been within miles of them. He admitted that in the western theatre of war there had been no scope for strategy. "It is all tactics now," to quote his exact words. But he surely must have remembered what his compatriot May pointed out in his celebrated pamphlet, *Die Preussische Infanterie in 1866*, that, in front-line fighting, above all in attack, there is but little room for anyone between the General and the actual troop-leaders, a dictum of which the truth has been proved in all subsequent wars. If this be the case, then it is a fair inference that if the British infantry beat the Germans, as the logic of facts proved that they had, some part of this result must be due to their leaders. Incidentally, it would also seem that the German subordinate leaders had shown themselves inferior to ours, unless the German general was prepared to admit that his troops were so hopelessly inferior to the British that even their company leaders could do but little with them.

The loss of Pozières the Commander-in-

Chief ascribed to an unlucky combination. "Somebody blundered," he said. A certain new formation had let itself be surprised by the enemy. Whether the blunder was due to the Generals, the regimental officers or the men, the German Commander did not say.

While the fighting had been going on in Delville Wood the attack on Longueval had also been progressing. There, too, the struggle had been in progress since the middle of the month, and the Scottish troops, who had hung on in spite of heavy losses from the continuous fire to which they had been exposed, had behaved with the greatest gallantry. They had been relieved by others who made some further progress, while English and Scots had combined to take Waterlot Farm and then secured a line back towards Trônes Wood. But the whole of Longueval was not yet ours. The Orchard had been won in this day's fighting (July 27); the northern end of the village, however, still gave a foothold to the Germans at the end of the day, though considerable progress had been made towards the desired goal.

South of the Somme the French made some progress to the east of Estrées and there was

RUSSIANS IN CHAMPAGNE.
Mounting a machine gun on a parapet.

a fairly lively fusillade in the outskirts of Soyécourt.

The chief event on this side was the enemy's effort to assume the initiative and create a diversion from the Somme fighting by attacks upon the centre of the western front north of the Aisne, at Ville-au-Bois, and in Champagne west of Prosnes. The latter attack was the more important. Delivered on a front about one mile wide, it gave the Germans no permanent advantage. For a time they succeeded in occupying a few trenches, but a counter-attack dislodged them without great difficulty.

The Germans made a small raid on our trenches just to the west of the Ypres-Pilkem road, but were at once counter-attacked and driven back. We also raided the German trenches farther to the south, after a preliminary bombardment. Here the enemy was first met outside his own wire and forced to retire with a loss of some 30 killed. Our troops, following up the retreating Germans, then pushed through into their trenches, where they found many casualties among the defenders caused by our artillery fire.

Both British and French airplanes did good work in locating the German batteries and newly constructed works. Owing to the clouds and mist our machines had to fly low and two of them did not return.

At 12.30 p.m., at another part of the line,

four bombing airplanes, armed with heavy bombs, set out to attack an important railway centre on the enemy's lines of communications where large quantities of ammunition had recently been reported. East of the line clouds were below 5,000 feet, which considerably favoured the expedition. The machines arrived over their objective between 2 and 2.30 p.m., and all four descended to heights of from 2,000 feet to 4,000 feet to drop their bombs. The station, which was crowded with rolling stock, and the sheds, containing ammunition, were attacked. Both were hit and fires were seen by our pilots to be started at four different points. The expedition was practically unmolested by anti-aircraft guns or hostile airplanes, and all our machines returned safely and landed on their home aerodrome within four minutes of one another.

On July 28, after severe fighting, the British drove the last remnants of the German garrison, which seems to have been furnished by the 5th Brandenburg Division, out of Delville Wood, and took prisoners 3 officers and 158 men. Twice did the enemy direct heavy counter-attacks against the British newly won positions, but on both occasions they were driven back. This day also saw the completion of the conquest of Longueval Village. Thus the German position here was completely conquered.

During the whole day there was considerable artillery action on both sides. In the Champagne the auxiliary Russian corps employed there penetrated into a German trench and brought away German prisoners. Little more than a hundred years before their countrymen had been acting with the Prussians against the French in the same country.

It was the right wing of the British Fifth Army, under Sir Hubert Gough, which had been brought up the Albert-Bapaume road into and through Pozières, while the left wing of the Fourth Army, under Sir Henry Rawlinson, was now on the crest of the main ridge between Pozières and Delville Wood. But the enemy still retained most of High Wood, from which he was not finally ejected until September 15; he also made desperate efforts to recover Delville Wood, and during the night of July 28–29 two violent but unsuccessful attacks were made on it. On Saturday the 29th the hand-to-hand struggle north and north-east of Pozières, in the neighbourhood of High Wood, and in the outskirts of Longueval, continued without intermission, and the British, despite the increased artillery fire from the German batteries, made some

slight progress. The northern portion of Longueval and its orchards were carried by our men, and the German trenches entered at a few points. Three enemy aeroplanes were destroyed and a kite balloon set on fire. South of the Somme, between Vermand-Ovillers and Lihons, the French rifle fire dispersed two strong German detachments endeavouring to reach the lines of our Allies, and French aeroplanes made a retaliatory attack during the night, dropping 40 bombs of 120 kilos on enemy stations in the Noyon district.

Pozières had been won by Sir Hubert Gough on July 25 and 26, but Thiépval, the strongly defended plateau between Thiépval and the Ancre, with the village fortresses of Courcelette north and Martinpuich south of the Albert-Bapaume road, were still in the possession of the Germans. Sir Douglas Haig therefore decided that it would be preferable for Sir Hubert Gough, who formed still the left of the attack, to confine himself to a "steady, methodical, step by step advance," while Sir Henry Rawlinson, in conjunction with the French north of the Somme, endeavoured to extend farther eastwards from Delville Wood.

THE REMAINS OF DELVILLE WOOD.

Maltz Horn Farm was now the spot where the British joined on to the French, but it was arranged that in the advance northward, in order to bring up the British right, the

GEN. SIR HUBERT DE LA P. GOUGH, K.C.B.
In command of the Fifth Army.

French should cooperate so as to prolong the line of battle to the east and do away with the objectionable salient which existed when our line ran back south from Delville Wood towards Maltz Horn Farm, and which was a source of danger. It was agreed that, advancing up the Combles Valley, the British right should move on Morval, the French left on Sailly-Sallisel. If the joint advance were successful, the Thiépval position, Martinpuich, and High Wood could be turned from the east.

To understand the next step taken by Sir Douglas Haig it is necessary to have some knowledge of the configuration of the ground in front of Sir Henry Rawlinson's centre and right and of the French left.

From Delville Wood the main plateau extends for 4,000 yards east-north-east to Lesbœufs and Morval, and for about the same distance south-eastwards to the woods of Bouleaux and Leuze. These woods were some 1,000 yards west of the considerable village of Combles, another village fortress below Leuze Wood in a valley, at the northern head of which were Morval on the west and Sailly-Sallisel on the east.

The high ground on each side of the Combles Valley sweeps the slopes of the ridge on the opposite side.

Pivoting on Delville Wood, Sir Henry Rawlinson was to swing his centre and right wing from the line Delville Wood-Maltz Horn Farm to the line Delville Wood-Morval, the French the meanwhile advancing simultaneously between Maltz Horn Farm and the Somme on Sailly-Sallisel. The capture of Morval and Sailly-Sallisel would inevitably result in the isolation and capture of Combles, and of most of the main ridge west of the Tortille, a tributary of the Somme, which enters that river two miles below Péronne.

To reach their objective, Morval, the British had to take, first, Guillemont, Falfemont Farm south of it, and the wood of Leuze, due east of Guillemont, and next Ginchy, and the wood of Bouleaux between Ginchy and Morval. From the former village the crest of the high ground runs northwards for 2,000 yards, and

LIEUT.-GENERAL THE EARL OF CAVAN, K.P., C.B.
In command of the 14th Army Corps.

then eastwards in a long spur for nearly 4,000 yards. Morval is at the eastern extremity of the spur and its garrison had a wide field of view and fire in every direction. A broad and deep branch of the Combles Valley separated Morval from Leuze Wood.

Between Sailly-Sallisel and the French line at the end of July lay the strongly fortified villages of Maurepas, Clery-sur-Somme, Le Forest, Rancourt and Fregicourt, and several woods and strongly entrenched positions. If the troops crossed the Péronne-Bapaume road and were on the eastern side of the Combles Valley, they would find themselves enfiladed by the Germans concealed in the fortress and wood of St. Pierre-Vaast.

During the night of July 29-30 the Allied guns were busy and a German ammunition depot near Courcelette was exploded by them. Feint attacks were made by the Canadians in two places south of Ypres and by the Royal Munster Fusiliers in the Loos salient, where a couple of raids by the Germans near the Hohenzollern Redoubt were easily repulsed.

At 4 a.m., Sunday, July 30, the bombardment preliminary to the battle between Delville Wood and the Somme opened, and the inhabitants of Amiens, 20 miles away, were awakened by the thunder of the Allied artillery, which steadily increased in intensity up to 6 a.m. The weather was of the sultriest, and the roads, where they still existed in the fighting area, were ankle deep in dust. The moment the bombardment ceased troops advanced from their entrenched positions in Delville Wood, amid the ruins of Longueval and Waterlot Farm and across the space between it and Maltz Horn Farm. In the centre the attack was successful. A battalion carried Guillemont and was preparing to debouch from the village when news came that the advance on Ginchy and Falfemont Farm had failed. For some hours our men held on to Guillemont

and were then withdrawn. About 250 German prisoners had been taken.

The day's fighting on the British front had

LIEUT.-GEN. SIR JULIAN BYNG, K.C.B
In command of Canadian Army Corps.

to some extent, justified the Order of the Day issued by the Kaiser a few hours later :

To the leaders and to the troops of the First Army I express from the bottom of my heart my deep appreciation and my Imperial gratitude for their splendid achievement in warding off the Anglo-French mass attacks of July 30th. They have accomplished, with German faithfulness, what I and their country expected of them. God help them further.

In the " further " fighting the Germans were destined to want all the help which they

A SUPPLY DUMP IN THE REAR.   *[Official photograph.*

[Canadian Official photograph.

SHELLING THE GERMAN TRENCHES NEAR COURCELETTE.

could get, and if mere mortals may judge events it does not seem that the Deity helped them. The German official *communiqué* of July 31 was as follows :

The British continued their operations near Pozières and Longueval yesterday, and they led up to a new great Anglo-French attack in the morning, undertaken by at least six divisions, between Longueval and the Somme.

The attack between Pozières and Longueval during the day was frustrated by our fire and did not materialize till the evening. This was also made by very strong forces.

The enemy was repulsed everywhere with heavy casualties and did not gain an inch of ground.

Wherever fighting at close quarters developed it resulted entirely in our favour.

In a dashing assault by our Bavarian and Saxon Reserves and our brave Schleswig-Holstein troops we captured 12 officers, 769 men, and 13 machine guns.

South of the Somme there were artillery engagements.

This report was in flagrant contradiction with the British *communiqué* issued at 11.12 p.m. on the 30th. "In the neighbourhood of Pozières," it ran, "the day has been spent in strengthening the ground gained during the last week, and there has been no infantry fighting in that area to-day." The

advance in the Longueval region, too, did not begin in the evening, but in the morning.

"The enemy," said the German bulletin, "was repulsed everywhere." Let us see what had really happened between Maltz Horn Farm and the Somme.

After a tremendous bombardment, to which the German artillery replied violently but ineffectually, our gallant Allies in the morning carried the whole system of enemy trenches for a depth varying from about 300 to 800 yards. They reached the outskirts of Maurepas, captured the remnants of the wood north of the station of Hem, the quarry near it, also Monacu Farm on the road from Hem to Clery-sur-Somme. During the afternoon Monacu Farm, whose square, grey-roofed tower had up till then escaped destruction, was attacked again and again by the Germans, moving along the edge of the thick green wood in the marshes on the right bank of the Somme. Though the enemy advanced bravely, he was shattered by the French guns and rifles, and by sunset

[Official Photograph.

STRETCHER BEARERS IN NO MAN'S LAND.

Monacu Farm, its tower now in ruins, remained in the possession of the French.

During the night the German assaults on the farm and the Hem Wood were renewed. The French guns on the south bank of the Somme enfiladed the charging masses and inflicted heavy losses on them. Monacu Farm was for a time recaptured by the Germans, but it was speedily recovered by the French. South of the Somme a German trench between Estrées and Belloy-en-Santerre and 60 prisoners were captured in the course of the next day, the 31st.

Meantime the British, under cover of night,

bombs were dropped on the German communications and billets; a train was blown up, an ammunition depôt fired, and an airplane resting on the ground destroyed. The enemy air squadrons ventured to engage ours; several were damaged, but at nightfall three of our own were missing. A *Times* correspondent enables us to understand the feelings of the officers responsible for the planning of those aerial raids:

It is immensely interesting to watch a squadron starting off on some distant and daring enterprise, but vastly more thrilling to see them come home. It is during the time that his men are away that the commanding

[*Official Photograph.*

INTERIOR OF SIGNAL EXCHANGE DURING THE BATTLE.

had been strengthening the positions gained by them near Guillemont, and had advanced their posts at some points on the plateau, north of Bazentin-le-Petit. The summer heat of this day was, however, so fierce as to restrain active movements, so that there was comparative quiet along the battle-front. Vast clouds of dust raised by the motor-lorries added to the discomfort of the soldiers working manfully in a sweltering atmosphere. The combined dust and haze impeded aerial observations for artillery purposes, but without preventing the Royal Flying Corps that day doing a good deal of useful work in the shape of several bombing raids. Seven tons of

officer has the most anxious time that he has to go through. I have shared, in minor degree, the anxiety of such a vigil.

They had gone, very cheerfully and with almost no words said, on a long and dangerous flight over the enemy's territory. A large flight of our fighting machines soaring in the sunlight, into and beyond the clouds, is a sight more beautiful than any flock of birds that fly. They had all disappeared into the distant blue, and nothing then remained but to wait. Would they attain their end? And if they did, how many would come back? It is nervous work waiting, even for an accidental outsider. For the commander who has sent them on their errand it is trying to a degree.

At last they came—one singly, and, after some minutes, another and then another and another, till at last the tale was complete. They had all come home safely, and they had done what they had been sent to do—as the way of our airmen is—down to the last detail.

Arrived at their destination, they had dropped down from the dizzy heights at which, on such an errand, they fly, and then methodically, one after another, they had done their work. From that height an airman's trained eye can watch the course of his bomb in clear weather until it actually strikes the ground. So they had seen them fall; they had seen them strike the railway trucks and station and the depôt where the stores were kept. Each had had his object and each had found it. They had seen the bombs—explosive and incendiary—strike true, they had seen the wreckage and the smoke and the flames and they knew that their work had been thorough. And only the last had been fired at.

At less than 2,500 feet an anti-aircraft gun should have little trouble in finding an airplane. Perhaps the men with the "Archies" were having their after-luncheon nap—the day was very hot. So all our machines but one had dropped their bombs—not hurriedly, but with precision—before the enemy's guns spoke—and then they spoke harmlessly

"Oh, yes; they came pretty near," the pilot of the last machine said casually; "nothing unusual." For these men to have the shells exploding "pretty near"

about their ears is a daily incident. They merely report it, saying they were fired at by a gun at such-and-such a place, much as if they said that they had lunched there.

On Tuesday, August 1, the enemy, whose artillery, like our own, had been very active during the preceding night, attacked the British trenches north of Bazentin-le-Petit and was repulsed. To cover his discomfiture he claimed to have beaten off a British assault near High Wood. At the same time the Germans alleged that a French advance at Maurepas, "carried out by eight waves of attackers," had been completely defeated, and that in the evening a French attack at Monacu Farm had been utterly repulsed "after violent fighting." As the French did not take the offensive, but victoriously beat off several counter-attacks during the day, and as Monacu Farm was not assaulted, but continued to be held by the French, the German statements were entirely without foundation. Perhaps the imaginary success was claimed in celebration of the second anniversary of the outbreak of war.

The next day (August 2) the Chief of the German Army Command painted a picture of the battle of the Somme for the German people :

Since the beginning of the Anglo-French offensive on the Somme sector—called in England "The Great

[*Official photograph.*

SERVING OUT WATER TO GERMAN PRISONERS.
Inset : German Trench near Estrées.

[*Official photograph.*

BRITISH SOLDIERS TOSSING CIGARETTES TO GERMAN PRISONERS.

Sweep "—a month has now elapsed, during which, according to earlier announcements by our enemies, an encircling movement was to be completed at all costs. It will now be useful to examine briefly what has been achieved.

Though on a front of about 28 kilometres (15½ miles) they have driven a wedge of about four kilometres (2½ miles) depth, they themselves will not assert, after their experiences of July 20, 22, 24, and 30, that the German line has been shaken at any point.

This success cost the English, according to careful estimates, a loss of at least 230,000 men.

For an estimate of the French losses in this fighting no definite basis is at our disposal, but, as they had to bear the brunt of the battle, their losses must also be heavy, in spite of their greater military skill.

The total losses of our enemies must, therefore, amount to about 350,000, while ours, though regrettable, cannot be compared with theirs so far as numbers are concerned.

The truth was better stated by General Joffre in his Army Order of August 1 :

Your third year of war begins. For two years you have borne without flinching the weight of an unrelenting struggle. You have brought to nought all the plans of the enemy. You beat them on the Marne, stopped them on the Yser, and defeated them in Artois and Champagne while they were vainly seeking victory on the Russian plains.

Then, by your victorious stand in the five months' battle, you have shattered the German striving before Verdun. Thanks to your stubborn valour the Armies of our Allies have been able to forge weapons the weight of which our foes are to-day feeling upon all fronts. The moment is at hand when, under our common pressure, German military power will collapse.

Soldiers of France, you may be proud of the work already accomplished. You are resolved to carry it through to the end. Victory is certain.

Sir Douglas Haig, too, was no less confident. He said :

Great Britain, which has sealed on the battlefield an eternal *entente* with France, will range herself to the end beside her noble Ally in the attainment of the necessary reparation for the unjust aggression of the Germanic Empire.

To Great Britain's services General Roques, the French Minister of War, replying to a letter of Mr. Lloyd George, bore ungrudging tribute :

I greet your soldiers, our gallant brothers in arms, who have hastened from all parts of the British Empire for the defence of civilization against the Germanic hordes and are formed in Armies whose powerful organization, effected in so short a time, will remain in history a subject of admiration. In the battles which they are waging at our sides your splendid soldiers daily give us a proof of their unshakable firmness and heroism. The soldiers of the Republic are proud to have such comrades and greet with enthusiasm their brilliant successes.

Decisive battles are raging. At the hour chosen by the Allies, in complete unity of action, we are attacking the enemy, who will soon see his dream of domination vanish and will totter on all fronts. Powerfully organized for these battles, abundantly provided with all the means and materials which they lacked at the beginning, and deeply conscious of the *rôle* they are playing at this moment in the world for the triumph of right and justice, your Armies and ours, with those of our faithful Allies, will continue without cessation this struggle, which will, perhaps, still be long and fierce, but which will bring victory to our glorious flags.

On August 2 a light breeze tempered the great heat. The air remained hazy, but did not prevent our artillery, in cooperation with the Royal Flying Corps, from destroying seven gun emplacements, six ammunition dumps near Grandcourt, two miles north-east

of Thiépval, another ammunition depôt at Courcelette, and several other emplacements. A few hostile airplanes crossed our lines, but were speedily driven back, one being brought down and another injured. The French chaser-planes were still more successful. Sergeant Chainat brought down his seventh and eighth German machines, and 14 other enemy airplanes were seriously damaged. North of the Somme the French stormed a work between Monacu Farm and Hem Wood. One hundred German corpses were found in it, and four mitrailleuses were taken. Several German attacks against Monacu Farm, delivered after sunset, were repulsed, and the new positions between the farm and Hem Wood were put in a proper state of defence.

In the Estrées region south of the river a German trench north-west of Deniécourt and some prisoners were captured. Two counter-attacks by the enemy for the recovery of the lost position were repulsed.

August 3 was the sixteenth day on which no rain had fallen, and the heat continued to be very trying to the opposing soldieries. All through the night the German artillery had been pounding our line from Maltz Horn Farm to Longueval, the village of Pozières and points in the background, such as Fricourt, Bécourt, and what had once been Mametz

Wood, but was now little more than a confused heap of timber with a few upstanding tree stumps. At dawn the enemy fire slackened, but later the Germans intermittently maintained a barrage west and south-west of Pozières, Longueval, Mametz and Caterpillar Woods. Under the cover of darkness four strong German detachments moved on Delville Wood. Their approach was detected, but no notice was taken of it until they were within close range. Then they were greeted with machine-gun and rifle fire and with bombs. They quickly turned back, leaving heaps of dead and wounded behind them. We, in our turn, took the offensive on the 3rd and gained some ground north of Bazentin-le-Petit by a bombing attack, and there was severe fighting round Pozières and farther west. Our heavy guns, which had also been actively engaged through the night, drove the enemy by their fire of high-explosive shell from a strong point between Pozières and Thiépval. The Germans scuttled back from it across the open, and were mowed down by the shrapnel of the British field artillery. It was an admirable example of the combined use of heavy and field artillery.

North of the Somme battlefield, in the Loos salient, German and British trench mortars were engaged in a brisk exchange of projectiles, and we bombarded the enemy's lines near the

Hohenzollern Redoubt, while the German guns shelled villages near Arras and Armentières and exploded a small mine near Souchez. The French during the night had dropped projectiles from their airplanes on the stations of Ham and Noyon, and on the 3rd, French airplanes brought down four enemy machines, one near Guillemont, two near Maurepas, and a fourth in the Barleux region. Sub-Lieutenant Guynemer was responsible for the last. It swelled his bag of German aeroplanes to twelve. South of the Somme a German attack south of Estrées was beaten off.

It will be remembered that, according to Sir Douglas Haig's plan, Sir Hubert Gough was to make "a steady, methodical step-by-step advance." On August 4 it was decided to attack the Thiépval salient, which formed a strongly prepared fortress jutting out towards our fronts. The assault was to be made from the south side, between Ovillers-la Boisselle and Pozières. About Pozières the highest ground is just above and north-eastward of the village along the Albert-Bapaume road. There we had already bitten into the German second line system of trenches just east of the top

of the village. On a front of some 3,000 yards westward from this point to another point almost due north of Ovillers-la Boisselle Sir Hubert Gough made preparations for an advance. From Pozières Australian troops with Englishmen from Surrey on their left in the open, and beyond this Sussex and then Kentish regiments, were to push forward. Opposite to them in two parallel lines of trenches, in intermediate and support trenches, in deep dug-outs and redoubts, lay hidden detachments of the German 17th and 18th Reserve Divisions of the 9th Reserve Corps, reinforced by units of the 11th Prussian Corps and by Ersatz Battalions. Behind the German defences above Ovillers-la Boisselle stood out the ruins of Mouquet (called by our men "Moo-Cow") Farm, fringed by shattered trees. It was another of those formidable forts with which the British had become so familiar.

All through the previous day (Thursday, August 3) our guns ceaselessly rained shells on the selected objective. Barbed wire entanglements were torn to pieces, and shell craters and tumbled earth replaced the clean-cut trenches. Courcelette and Martinpuich, in which the

[*French official photograph*

FRENCH SOLDIERS HARVESTING IN PICARDY.

German reserves were hidden, began visibly to crumble away.

Towards dusk the crescent moon rose, while distant cornfields were still red in the rays of the disappearing sun. Darkness set in, and the Germans, alarmed by the violence of our gun-fire, discharged coruscations of brilliant lights in the direction of the British trenches. At great risk men jumped up and kicked off the burning projectiles. Bouquets of gas shells descended in the British lines and masks had to be donned. About 9 p.m., when there was still some twilight left, our troops leapt forward. On the left the Kentish soldiers' immediate objective was a trench running diagonally across the ground in front of Mouquet Farm. The ground in front of it had been recon-

noitred before the attack began by the colonel in command, accompanied by one of his captains. He now led his men against the trench, or what was left of it. With bomb and bayonet it was rapidly cleared. Many of the enemy surrendered, others fled from the farm or took refuge in the numerous dug-outs. Some of these were more than usually elaborate. One of them was a veritable two-storey subterranean villa. It consisted of six rooms, a kitchen and signalling station. The upper rooms were 15 feet, the lower 30 feet, beneath the surface. Beautiful tapestries, handsome carpets, comfortable furniture, cupboards full of wine, spirits, liqueurs and cigars, female apparel, revealed the tastes of its occupants. Water and electric light were laid on. In another dug-out there were camp beds for 120 soldiers.

The Germans rallied, and bombing parties from Mouquet Farm advanced against our men, but were cut down by a young officer with a Lewis gun.

To the right of the Kentish troops the men of Sussex and Surrey carried all before them, while the Australians from Pozières burst

[*Official photographs.*]

THE BATTERED REMAINS OF FRICOURT.
Inset : Martinpuich Church.

[*Official photographs.*

A GERMAN TRENCH.
Inset : German dug-out.

through the German lines and captured the crest of the ridge above Courcelette and Martinpuich. In places we had gained as much as 600 yards in depth.

Of the incidents which occurred some may be related.

Before the enemy parapet was reached a soldier, wounded in the knee, fell into a crater, where he rested with his feet in the air. When the stretcher-bearers arrived they found him singing at the top of his voice, " Send shot and shell." The leader of a bombing party was twice blown off the steps descending into a trench. He picked himself up, took possession of an enemy bomb store and, at the head of his men, used the bombs to such effect that the trench was quickly his. A patrol which had got ahead of the line found itself isolated and fired at on both flanks. One of the men, silhouetted against flares and Verey lights doubled back to report his comrades' position. He was told that the patrol was to retire. He returned safely to it, and with a Lewis gun covered its retreat, killing some 50 of the enemy.

During the night of the 4th–5th the enemy delivered a series of counter-attacks, employing, among other weapons, the horrible flamethrowers, but their efforts to recover the lost position were unavailing.* Opposed by the

* The effect of the burning liquid was to saturate and set on fire the clothing of the men it hit. That the results gained by this brutal weapon were of no military value was indicated by the following report of an officer : —" Its effect may be very easily exaggerated. When you see it for the first time it rather gives you the jumps. It looks like a big gas jet coming towards you, and your natural instinct is to jump back and get out of the way. A man who thinks nothing of a shell or a bullet may not like the prospect of being scorched or roasted by fire. But in my experience the effective range of the *flammenwerfer* is very limited, and the man who manipulates it as often as not is shot or bombed by our fellows. They call it devil's fire, but when they recover from their first fright they care for it as little as they do—well, say for the devil himself. The actual cases of burning by devil's fire have been very few." There was, however, evidence to show that at first the *flammenwerfer* did produce considerable effects, and it is certain that these were obtained at the cost of great torture to the men hit.

THE GERMAN FLAME-THROWER.

advanced on the German trenches south-east of Estrées.

Monday, August 7, was more eventful. After a heavy bombardment the enemy between 4 and 5 a.m. once more attacked our new lines north and north-east of Pozières. For two days he had been bombarding this position fiercely. Suddenly the guns lifted and a comparatively fresh regiment rushed for a trench held by Australians. The latter and those near them were not to be caught napping. Headed by an officer who had won the V.C. in Gallipoli, they captured all who reached the trench and caught the remainder while retiring with so heavy a fire that " No Man's Land " was soon strewn with German bodies. A party of the Australians were, however, isolated. They remained fighting for five hours, when, their leader being wounded, they asked for relief. At 8.50 a.m., and again at 4 p.m., further assaults were delivered and failed. During the

fire of our guns and mitrailleuses, the attacks were shattered one after another, and daybreak revealed the usual result of the ill-conceived assaults—hecatombs of dead and dying on the ground in front of our trenches. The counter-attacks had been accompanied by an extraordinary fire of artillery, which was continued on the 5th. Nor were our gunners backward in the duel. They exploded ammunition reserves in Courcelette and Miraumont north of it and in the valley of the Ancre, besides wrecking ten gun emplacements, while Guillemont and High Wood also received especial attention. On the French front there was some fighting in the air, two enemy machines being wrecked.

On Sunday, August 6, the weather was less hazy, and in conjunction with the aeroplanes our artillery put out of action a number of the enemy guns. Early in the morning the Germans twice attacked in the area north-west of Pozières ; in the afternoon we progressed along the trenches east of Pozières in the direction of Martinpuich. The *flammenwerfer* enabled the foe to enter one of the trenches captured by us, but later it was almost entirely recovered. For the French the day was comparatively quiet, but south of the Somme they

[Official photograph.

PUTTING-UP A FIELD TELEGRAPH.

night the Australians in the face of shrapnel and machine-gun fire stormed some German trenches. Part of the troops missed their way, with the result that only a fraction of the attackers reached their objective. They were led by a young Tasmanian officer,

rear. The Tasmanian dragged a prisoner with him to a spot where Germans were waving a white cloth. They surrendered, and he went next to the end of the trench still held by the enemy and bombed him for an hour. After receiving two orders to retire, he

ENEMIES IN THE SAME TRENCH.
French soldiers in the foreground are divided from the Germans in the distance
only by sandbag traverses.

who ran along the trench with a revolver, shooting German after German. Refilling his revolver he killed four more. A German then threw a bomb at him, but he was fortunately not injured. The bomber was at once shot, and his companions bolted to the

withdrew with his prisoners. "There is no reason, as far as I can see," Lord Kitchener had said on January 11, 1910, at Melbourne, " why the national forces of Australia should not make their standard of efficiency on a par with, if not higher than, those of the military Powers

[Official photograph.

AWAITING THEIR TURN IN THE TRENCHES.

of Europe and elsewhere." That judgment had been proved to be correct in Gallipoli, in Flanders, and in Picardy.

While the Germans were taking the offensive against Sir Hubert Gough, Sir Henry Rawlinson resumed his in the Guillemont region. During the night of the 7th-8th the British advanced between Longueval and Maltz Horn Farm. The troops on the extreme right carried the trenches in their way and pushed on to the high ground due south of Guillemont; but their neighbours got hung up in the darkness. The centre, on the other hand, traversed the German lines and entered Guillemont itself. They worked through the ruins to the south-eastern corner and dug themselves in. Separated from their supports by the enemy in the east of Guillemont and unsupported by their comrades on their right who had been hung up, they were isolated. In the course of the 8th some made their way back. Others were killed or taken prisoners. North of Guillemont some ground was gained, and a machine-gun position near the railway station taken. But our men were not able to capture the ridge, and, as the ground to the south of Guillemont was dominated by the garrison of this village and by the Germans on the plateau and in the woods to the north, it had become evident that Guillemont could not be captured as an isolated enterprise without very heavy loss. Arrangements were therefore made with the French for a series of combined attacks to be delivered in progressive stages against Maurepas, Falfemont Farm, Guillemont, Leuze Wood, and Ginchy. The French at the end of the afternoon of the 7th had prepared for this by carrying a line of trenches between the Hem Wood and the Somme east of Monacu Farm. They had captured 120 prisoners and 12 machine guns. By this success they threatened the flank of the Maurepas-Combles-Sailly-Sallisel position. South of the river their artillery had destroyed enemy batteries in the region of Lihons, while their aeroplanes had wrecked two German captive balloons and brought down several machines. During the 8th our Allies assisted Sir Henry Rawlinson by advancing east of Hill 139, north of Hardecourt, and seizing a small wood and a trench north of the Hem Wood. Two counter-attacks by the enemy east of Monacu Farm were beaten off, and 230 prisoners, including two officers, taken.

On August 16 it was announced that the King had just returned from a week's visit to his Army. His Majesty arrived in France on Tuesday, August 8, and after his formal reception by French officers of high rank and by a guard of honour of the North Staffordshire Regiment, three-quarters of whom were men convalescent from wounds, he went to Sir Douglas Haig's headquarters, where the situation was fully discussed and the details of his Majesty's tour mapped out. With his characteristic energy every hour of his time was fully employed, and thus he was able to make a thorough inspection of the forces. From front to rear he saw everything there was to be seen—men and material, trenches and the avenues of supply to them, sick and wounded, and the organizations which look after them. Many of his soldiers were spoken to, many hundred thousands of them saw him. He visited them at rest in their billets, reposing from their arduous work at the front, and also in the advanced line within sound of the guns, ready to attack.

The King saw General Joffre and General Foch, who had been commanding the French advance on the Somme, and gave the G.C.M.G. to General Fayolle and General Balfourier, besides investing other officers with the C.B. or C.M.G. and giving twelve D.S.O.'s to French officers. He also pinned the V.C. on the breast of Private A. H. Proctor, of a Territorial Battalion of the Liverpool Regiment.

On Sunday the 12th the King visited the left of the Line and attended Divine Service, and then went on to see the King and Queen of the Belgians, and distributed the Distinguished Service Order and the Military Cross to Belgian officers and the Distinguished Conduct Medal to Belgian soldiers. To the Queen he gave the Royal Red Cross in token of his appreciation of the excellent work she had done in the military hospitals.

Before his excursion to left of the line the King had gone to the immediate front of battle on the 9th, and he had been taken to a position from which a front view of the opposing trench lines was to be had. From it a wide expanse of country, from Souchez on the left, by La Folie Farm, and Neuville St. Vaast to Arras on the right, was clearly visible, while immediately in his front was the Vimy Ridge where so much severe fighting had previously taken place. To reach this view point, it was necessary to pass through ruined villages and along a road which had been recently shelled and which was well within reach of hostile guns.

On August 10 the King visited the actual scene of the Somme fighting. He was on ground

WOUNDED SOLDIERS WATCHING A TRANSPORT COLUMN.

[Official Photograph.

THE KING ON THE BATTLEFIELD NEAR POZIÈRES.

which was more or less frequently under fire of the Germans, whose shells were often placed not only on the section where he was but also on the country behind it. Leaving their motor-cars at a point near our old front trenches (see coloured map which forms frontispiece of Vol. IX.) the King and his staff walked over the ground on which some of the fiercest fighting of the early days of July took place. The position as it was at the time when our forward movement began was explained to him and then the party went over what had been the intervening space between the hostile lines before the British advance, but which was now included within our own occupation. It was a desolate and horrifying sight. The whole surface was pitted with shell holes or by the craters of mines, while scattered about were broken fragments of war material—sandbags, wire entanglements, timber which had served to shore up trenches, scraps of uniform, and the thousand and one things which the terrible fire had twisted and turned out of shape till their original purpose could be with difficulty discerned.

Next the King visited some of the captured German trenches. Here he could see the thorough way in which our artillery had done the work of destruction, parapets levelled with the ground, wire entanglements torn to frag-ments. One of the German dug-outs was visited. The King then returned to a position behind the British line which afforded a fair view of the area of actual conflict. Mametz was immediately below him, Contalmaison behind it and higher up, Fricourt on the left, and Thiépval beyond on the spur which forms the south side of the Ancre Valley. Rather more to east but on the same long ridge of high ground was Pozières, which we had taken little over a fortnight before and which was now being actively shelled by its late possessors. The King could also see Montauban, and part of Bernafay and Trônes Wood, and more to the north above the latter Longueval and some indication of Delville Wood, names which will be for ever associated with the deathless courage of his troops.

It is easy to understand how much the soldiers appreciated the King coming up to the front into the area of danger. On his way home the King's way led through miles of delighted soldiers; at every village and camp he was given a great reception. He passed through the Headquarters of the Anzac troops, and here he stopped to express his high appreciation of the glorious work his troops had done. Once more he was greeted with hearty cheers, as he was again when he encountered an Australian brigade on its way back from the front to a well-earned rest behind the lines. The brigade was halted when it learned the King was coming, and when he reached them and drove slowly by the cheering was tremendous.

After a week of strenuous work the King returned to England, having first issued the following Order to his troops :—

OFFICERS, N.C.O.'S AND MEN.

It has been a great pleasure and satisfac-tion to me to be with my Armies during the past week. I have been able to judge for myself of their splendid condition for war and of the spirit of cheerful confidence which animates all ranks, united in loyal coopera-tion to their Chiefs and to one another.

Since my last visit to the front there has been almost uninterrupted fighting on parts of our line. The offensive recently begun has since been resolutely maintained by day and by night. I have had opportunities of visiting some of the scenes of the later desperate struggles, and of appreciating, to a slight extent, the demands made upon your courage and physical endurance in order to assail and capture positions pre-pared during the past two years and stoutly defended to the last.

I have realized not only the splendid work which has been done in immediate touch with the enemy—in the air, under ground, as well as on the ground—but also the vast organizations behind the fighting line, honour-able alike to the genius of the initiators and to the heart and hand of the workers. Every-where there is proof that all, men and women, are playing their part, and I rejoice to think their noble efforts are being heartily seconded by all classes at home.

The happy relations maintained by my Armies and those of our French Allies were equally noticeable between my troops and the inhabitants of the districts in which they are quartered, and from whom they have received a cordial welcome ever since their first arrival in France.

Do not think that I and your fellow-countrymen forget the heavy sacrifices which the Armies have made, and the bravery and endurance they have displayed during the past two years of bitter conflict. These

[Official Photographs.

THE KING'S TOUR.

Mine Craters on either side.

Inset: Making friends with peasants.

sacrifices have not been in vain; the arms of the Allies will never be laid down until our cause has triumphed.

I return home more than ever proud of you.

May God guide you to victory.

In two days (August 7 and 8) the French had secured the whole line of German trenches on a front of 3¾ miles to a depth of 350 to 500 yards. It was an excellent adjunct to the forward movement of Sir Hubert Gough between Ovillers-la Boisselle and Pozières. The latter's line on the 8th, it should be added, was vainly attacked by the enemy in two places. On the

eastern portion of the Leipzig salient, south of Thiépval, German bombers approached our trenches. They were easily repulsed. North-west of Pozières, four attacks supported by *flammenwerfer* were delivered by the Germans, but they only managed to seize about 50 yards of our trench. It was but a small set off to the heavy loss sustained by them.

To appreciate what was being achieved by Sir Hubert Gough's right wing we must remember the difficulties encountered by it. The southern face of the Thiépval plateau was a bare surface pitted all over with a perfect network of craters caused by our high-explosive shell, the only variant to this destruction being a few isolated tree trunks. On the west there was a steepish dip; but from Ovillers-la Boisselle to Mouquet Farm the rise in 3,000 yards was only 30 feet. Every foot of ground on this natural glacis was exposed to the fire of the field artillery in Thiépval and the heavy guns and howitzers hidden in or in the out-skirts of Courcelette and Grandcourt and the rifle and machine-gun fire of the Germans. The glacis itself was intersected by a skilful network of trenches of the most carefully constructed kind, flanked by machine-guns in the caponier-like protrusions such as have been already described.*

On Wednesday, August 9, north-west of Pozières—in the region above described—the Australians advanced their lines 200 yards on a frontage of 600 yards, and north of Pozières they bombed enemy trenches and captured 25 prisoners.

The fighting from Guillemont to the Somme continued, the Germans in the night of August 8–9 counter-attacking north of the Hem Wood. They were repulsed with loss except at one point where they gained a footing, from which they were soon ejected by our men on the 9th. Between the Hem Wood and the river the Germans bombarded the French organizations with large calibre shells. South of the river they attacked between Lihons and the Chaulnes railway. They temporarily gained a footing at one point, but were thrust out with the bayonet. Several enemy guns were destroyed by our artillery, and some of his

* See Vol. IX., p. 483.

THE KING VISITS A GERMAN TRENCH.

[*Official photographs.*

THE KING ON THE BATTLEFIELD WITH SIR HENRY RAWLINSON AND GENERAL CONGREVE.

magazines exploded. A train was set on fire by our airmen.

The day was signalized by another experiment in devilry made by the Germans. Shrapnel imbedded in phosphorus which burned the flesh were fired at the Australians. This was quite useless from a military point of view, and did nothing but add torture to the wounds. The night before in the Ypres salient there had been a German gas attack, which was ineffectual.

The spell of dry weather now came to an end, and welcome showers fell on the night of August 9. The next day, Thursday, in the afternoon, two regiments of fresh German troops were mustered in the quarries and gully behind Mouquet Farm. Soon after 5 p.m. they topped the ridge behind the Pozières windmill and charged down on the Australians. The charge was preceded by a heavy shell fire, but ran into a barrage from our guns behind our lines. Under shrapnel, high-explosive and machine-gun fire the waves thinned visibly. Only a few of the bravest reached our lines, where they were promptly laid by the heels. In the region of Hem Wood the French, through rainy and foggy weather, continued to progress during the night of the

9th–10th, and south of the Somme a German reconnaissance accompanied by bearers of *flammenwerfer* was repulsed west of Vermand-Ovillers.

Another step preliminary to the advance on Sailly-Sallisel was taken by the French on August 11. The portion of the enemy's trenches north of the Somme between the Hardecourt region and the river opposite Buscourt was the objective, it being intended to bring the French front up to that point on the south of the Somme. The third line of the enemy, four miles or so long, consisted of three and, in some places, four trenches, and was liberally provided with redoubts and dugouts. In the morning of the 11th the French seized a wood half a mile north of Maurepas, on the ridge commanding the valley up which ran the Péronne-Combles railway. A few hours later they gained a quarry and two little woods north of the Hem Wood. The two attacks, which resulted in the capture of 150 unwounded prisoners and 10 machine-guns, had been preceded by a severe bombardment. A counter-attack by the enemy on the quarry at 9 p.m. was repulsed with heavy loss. The next day our Allies pushed on to assault the main German position. Their advance parties

[*Canadian official photograph.*

TESTING THE TELEPHONE OF A KITE BALLOON BEFORE ASCENDING.

[*Canadian official photograph.*

AN OFFICIAL PHOTOGRAPHER AT WORK ON THE FIELD OF BATTLE.

penetrated into the Hem Wood and east of the station of Hem, where a great many German corpses were discovered; the southern part of Maurepas and the cemetery were carried, and the French front extended eastwards to a depth of from 660 to 1,100 yards. North of the road from Maurepas to Clery-sur-Somme and the crest line of the ridge west of Clery village, unwounded prisoners numbering over a thousand and 30 machine-guns were secured by this brilliant action. A counter-attack by the Germans failed under French fire, and they were unable to recover the church or cemetery of Maurepas. The same day south of the Somme the enemy tried to assault La Maisonnette, but the attacking waves of men were caught by the French barrage and literally swept away. When night fell our Allies were victorious at all points. In the Estrées region they had also executed numerous destructive bombardments on the hostile organizations.

Nor had the British been inactive. On the night of the 10th-11th they had progressed north of Bazentin-le-Petit. At 5.45 a.m. on the 11th they had repulsed a determined counter-attack and north-west of Pozières they had continued to advance. Late in the day the Germans delivered desperate charges against the Australians north of Pozières.

They were defeated with heavy loss. These successes must have rejoiced the heart of President Poincaré, who on the 12th had visited the British Headquarters Staff, and inspected the ground which had been conquered east of Albert. Thence he proceeded to the Somme, where he met General Joffre.

On Sunday, August 13, rain fell in plenty. During the preceding night we had pushed forward south of Guillemont. North-west of Bazentin-le-Petit, we forced our way up Munster Alley and broke into the new German line running due west of High Wood on a front of between 600 and 700 yards to a depth of 500 yards, while Sir Hubert Gough on a curve approximately a mile in length brought his front to within about 200 yards of Mouquet Farm. A part of the captured German trenches was, however, in the night recovered by the enemy.

Large numbers of Germans observed by an aeroplane to be concentrating north of Pozières were dispersed by artillery fire.

North of the Somme battlefield raids were carried out on the Vimy ridge, in the region of Calonne and east of Armentières. Mines were fired by the British south of the Hulluch quarries, and north of Neuve-Chapelle, and by the Germans a mine was exploded south of

[Official Photograph.

WOUNDED GERMANS AT A BRITISH ADVANCED DRESSING STATION.

Souchez. The Royal Flying Corps had on the 12th sent out a squadron of 68 machines, which, with a loss of three, bombed airship sheds at Brussels and Namur and railway stations and sidings at Mons, Namur, and Courtrai.

On the 14th and 15th there was little to record. Sir Hubert Gough's troops, however, recovered nearly the whole of the trenches on the southern face of the Thiépval salient north-west of Pozières, abandoned on the 13th; During the night of the 14th-15th we also forced an entry into the enemy's lines near Mouquet Farm.

The next day, Wednesday, August 16, Sir Henry Rawlinson commenced to carry out Sir Douglas Haig's plan for the advance on Combles and Morval. The French, after intense artillery preparation, in the afternoon captured 1,650 yards of German trenches north of Maurepas, and at certain places reached the Guillemont-Maurepas road. To the south of Maurepas, on a front of a mile and a quarter, they pushed forward some 600 yards, and cleared the enemy out of their positions east of the Maurepas-Clery road. Numbers of prisoners were taken and heavy losses inflicted on the enemy. South of the Somme our

Allies stormed a powerfully organized trench system on a front of 1,300 yards south of Belloy-en-Santerre. We, in our turn, at the same time captured 300 yards of trench west of High Wood, and advanced our line west and south-west of Guillemont. Here there was a deep wooded ravine, some 550 yards in length, which started from just below Angle Wood and ran north-west towards Maltz Horn Farm. The ravine had been stormed by the French and our business was to seize a trench going north-eastwards from the top end of the ravine. This was successfully accomplished and another mesh added to the net being cast round Guillemont.

While we took the offensive in this quarter soon after sunset on the 16th, early on the morning of the 17th a violent attack was delivered by the enemy against our position north-west of Pozières on a broad front. Six waves of infantry advanced, but, coming under our artillery and machine-gun fires, they were driven off, suffering severe losses. Two advances from Martinpuich were also repulsed, and north-west of Bazentin-le-Petit we captured 100 yards of trench. The French on the 18th repulsed several counter-attacks south-east of Maurepas.

At noon on Friday, August 18, the continuous roll of our heavy artillery announced that a battle along the whole semicircle from Ovillers-la Boiselle to the Somme was about to begin. After a tremendous bombardment of the enemy's trenches and works the Allied infantry delivered their attack all along the line, at 3 p.m. on the right and soon after 5 p.m. on the left. The French between Maurepas and the Somme extended their positions farther east of the Maurepas-Clery road. They captured the Calvary Hill, south-east of Maurepas, and expelled the enemy from several ruins in the village.

North of Maurepas the British cleared out a labyrinth of trenches at the head of the Maltz Horn Farm ravine and joined hands with the French who had taken Angle Wood copse on the eastern side of it. The quarry on the southern outskirts of Guillemont was stormed by South Midland troops. Two waves of German infantry, which were seen to be mustering for a counter-attack by an aeroplane, were promptly dispersed by shrapnel. During the night the survivors received reinforcements and returned once more to the charge, but the quarry on the western side of Guillemont remained in our possession.

Above Guillemont the British from Waterlot Farm and Delville Wood advanced their line half way to Ginchy, and captured 211 prisoners. The ground in this region was a maze of trenches and the performance of the English county regiments engaged here was particularly creditable.

On the west of Delville Wood the British line was pushed forward some distance north of the orchards, and we gained a footing in High Wood. Between High Wood and the Albert-Bapaume road our men approached closer to Martinpuich.

Sir Hubert Gough had been equally successful. His troops had drawn nearer to Thiépval, had seized points on both sides of Mouquet Farm, and gained the quarry 300 yards south of the latter. Hundreds of prisoners, some of them of the 29th Prussian Regiment, were taken.

Such was the battle of Friday, August 18. The account of it transmitted on Saturday to the German people ran as follows :

Our brave troops, in self-sacrificing perseverance, yesterday resisted victoriously the gigantic efforts of our allied enemies. In the afternoon, after an artillery preparation which increased to the utmost violence, the British and French masses attacked almost simultaneously north of the Somme on a front of about

[*French official photograph.*

M. POINCARÉ (in light coloured uniform) AND GENERAL JOFFRE AT THE FRONT.

20 kilometres (12½ miles) long between Ovillers and Clery. The battle raged far into the night.

At several points the enemy penetrated our advanced line, but was ejected from both sides of Guillemont, which is firmly in our hands. The enemy occupied portions of the trenches.

Between Guillemont and Maurepas during the night we shortened the salient of our line a little, according to plan.

The enemy paid for his unsuccessful efforts with the bloodiest sacrifices.

The Prussian Guard and the Rhenish, Bavarian, Saxon and Wurtemburg troops firmly maintain their positions.

During the night of August 18–19 the enemy had delivered several very determined counter-attacks, but except in the Guillemont-

we have captured some hundreds of yards of enemy trench.

East and south-east of Mouquet Farm we have advanced our line by some 300 yards.

Between Ovillers and Thiépval we have pushed forward on a front of over half a mile.

As a result of these operations several hundred prisoners have been taken by us.

In the course of Saturday the German confined themselves to shelling our positions, though there were some attacks by bombers after dark. We made a further advance on both sides of the Albert-Bapaume road for some 300 yards north-east of the Pozières windmill, the ruins of which still stood up

[*French official photograph.*

DRIVING A MINE.

Maltz Horn Farm area, where he regained a little ground, these were everywhere repulsed. At 3.7 p.m. on August 19 the British Headquarters telegraphed the facts, so far as the British were concerned, facts which may be contrasted with the fiction of the German Staff above quoted:

From High Wood to the point where we join up with the French we have advanced our line over a frontage of more than two miles for a distance varying between 200 yards and 600 yards.

We now hold the western outskirts of Guillemont and a line thence northwards to midway between Delville Wood and Ginchy; also the orchards north of Longueval.

Between High Wood and the Albert-Bapaume road

above ground. The situation at 11.45 p.m. was, according to the British Headquarters, this:

As a result of these operations we have captured the ridge south-east of, and overlooking, Thiépval and the northern slopes of the high ground north of Pozières, from which we get an extensive view of the east and north-east.

We are holding the western edge of High Wood and the trenches made by the enemy extending for some half mile to the west of the wood.

We have advanced our line half way to Ginchy and to the edge of Guillemont, where we now hold the outskirts of the village, including the railway station and the quarry, which is of considerable military importance.

The number of prisoners passed back up to 4 p.m. to-day as the result of these operations is 16 officers and 780 other ranks.

The *Times* Correspondent reported on the fighting as follows:

Among troops which had done conspicuously well in the fighting have been some battalions of the Warwicks; they fought with the greatest dash and determination and accomplished very gallantly a difficult and important undertaking. Very early in this battle battalions of the

furiously from a bomb-stop—a small barricade hurriedly erected to check the operations of hostile bombers—against a party of Boches who were dodging behind a traverse and throwing explosives at our men. The company commander is an expert rifle shot, and in order that he might fire as many rounds as possible within a given time he employed two of his men as loaders—just as if he had been engaged in a grouse-drive and the bomb-

[*Official photograph*

A MINE EXPLOSION.
Inset : Crater left by a mine explosion.

same regiment did very well indeed, and they have every right to be proud of themselves.

Mention ought also to be made, in another connexion, of the Suffolks, and of the heroism which they showed at a critical moment in another stage of this battle. It would be absurd, in such splendid fighting as has been done here, to say that any one regiment or class of troops had done better than any other. But none certainly have a finer record than the Suffolks.

Yet, when one talks in this way, the names of a score of other English regiments leap immediately to one's mind and shame one. Lancashire, Yorkshire, Stafford, Leicester, and Lincoln; Middlesex, Berkshire, Bedford, Essex, and Kent; Hampshire, Gloucester, Sussex, Wilts, Devon, and Somerset; Durham, Northumberland, Shropshire, Northampton, Cheshire . . . one must call the roll of the English counties if one would praise all who have behaved in a way for which all praise is too faint. Territorials, Kitchener's Army, and Derby Recruits, Infantry, Light Infantry, and Fusiliers—there is no drawing the line anywhere. All have shared alike, and there is glory enough to go round and to spare.

It may be well here to record a typical example of German treachery (from a report in the *Morning Post* of August 25) which took place on the 18th:—

A German rushed forward with his arms in the air in token of surrender. Then, when he got near to the Warwicks, who were preparing to accept him as a prisoner, he suddenly produced a couple of bombs from some receptacle in his uniform and hurled them at the men who were advancing towards him. "What did you do?" I inquired of a sergeant. "Well, sir," came the reply, "he bolted away back, but we eased him up with three bayonets."

The following incidents from the same source are also interesting:—

One of the many heroic episodes of the attack concerns a captain who borrowed rifles from his men and fired

stop was a butt. He killed and wounded a number of the enemy, and ultimately forced them to retreat. The Warwicks advanced so fast that the Germans fled from dug-outs, leaving half-consumed meals behind them. In one instance a party of our men descended into a luxuriously-equipped "funk hole" and finished off a meal of coffee and sausages which some Boche officers had been partaking of when they suddenly decided to "bolt for it." One soldier finished a half-smoked cigar and another had the good fortune to find an unbroken box of cigars as a souvenir. Obviously there is no shortage of the good things of life at the German front, whatever may be the condition of the people who still dwell in the Fatherland.

The French from the Maltz Horn Farm ravine to the outskirts of Clery-sur-Somme had on the night of the 18th-19th beaten off several violent assaults with machine-gun fire and grenades. All that the Germans succeeded in gaining to counter-balance their losses was a small section of trench north of Maurepas. It was recovered the next day, Sunday the 20th, and our Allies also carried a wood strongly organized by the Germans between Guillemont and Maurepas. At noon and later the British repulsed several attacks delivered against the new line established half a mile from the western corner of High Wood;

a little to the west, north of Bazentin-le-Petit, we also made some further progress.

Thus by August 20 the Allies had seized a large part of the ridge in the semi-circle from Thiépval to the Somme. They were on the heights above Thiépval and Bapaume, and approaching the Bapaume-Péronne highway. Their leaders had decided that only the barest details of the fighting on the 18th and 19th and the preceding days should be published, but the reader must not forget that the battle between the Ancre and Lihons was one of the greatest and most important, forming as it did a considerable step towards the final capture of the dominating ground. Both British and French were assaulting fortified positions compared with which those of the Turks at Plevna or Kuropatkin at Liao-Yang and Mukden were insignificant. It was impossible to manœuvre against the enemy's flanks and the battle had to be won by driving wedges into the German lines, and capturing the salients thus created. The wonder was not that progress was slow but that any progress was made. When it is remembered that most of the men at Sir Douglas Haig's disposal had been a few months before civilians unacquainted with the rudiments of war and that the oppo-

nents of the British were the soldiers of a nation in arms which had been trained from childhood to consider war and the training for war as the highest objects of existence, one is lost in admiration at the British achievements.

Not less astonishing were the feats performed by our French Allies. At the opening of the war they had not been so ready for the fray as their cunningly organized opponents. In August 1914 the French Army had sustained defeats. Yet two years later we find them attacking the enemy with that confidence which the latter had displayed when, in overwhelming numbers, he had driven Lanrezac from his unfortified position on the Meuse and Sambre. The men of the Argonne, the Champagne and Picardy had shown they were true to the traditions of Jena, Auerstedt and Friedland.

Seeing the vital importance to them of retaining the Thiépval salient and preventing the British and French from seizing the whole summit of the ridge which commanded the Bapaume-Péronne road, it was not to be expected that the Germans after their defeats on the 18th, 19th and 20th would be content with a passive defensive. Their military teachers since Frederick the Great had always

[*Official photograph.*

SOME OF THE LEICESTERS BACK FROM THE BATTLE.

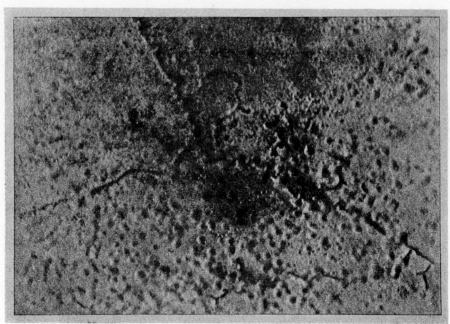

[Photographed from an Aeroplane.

SHELL-PITTED GROUND ON THE SOMME FRONT.

insisted that the best method of defence was counter-attack. About noon on Sunday, August 20, they advanced against half a mile of our trenches west of High Wood. If they could maintain themselves in the angle where Sir Hubert Gough's and Sir Henry Rawlinson's lines met they could bring a flanking fire to bear upon the British pressing their way up the southern face of the Thiépval salient, and also those moving on Ginchy. Here and there the enemy entered the British trenches, but were promptly driven out again. On Monday, the 21st, the same experiment was repeated by the Germans in the same region. A tornado of shells was launched on our men in High Wood at 1.30 a.m., and subsequently three bombing attacks were made. All were repulsed. North-west of High Wood some of our covering parties withdrew before strong forces of the enemy, but when the latter pursued they were brought up short by fire from positions west of the wood. The Germans also bombarded the Pozières region and the area north-east of Contalmaison with gas shells, and made an ineffectual attack near Mouquet Farm. South of Thiépval our guns caused a conflagration in one of the enemy's batteries, which burned fiercely for some time, and they also forced a hostile balloon to descend. Meanwhile the French in the wood between Guille-

mont and Maurepas had taken six field guns, and their aeroplanes had brought down two German machines, one south of Estrées and the other near Berny.

On Tuesday, August 22, while the French were south of the Somme, seizing trenches south-east of Estrées and east of Soyécourt and, north of the Somme, advancing into the outskirts of Clery and capturing prisoners north of Maurepas, Sir Hubert Gough gave the Germans another demonstration of the power of the British artillery and the cool courage of the British infantry. The blow this time was aimed at the south-western end of the Thiépval salient. As already narrated, we had taken the Leipzig Redoubt north of Ovillers-la Boisselle. Between the redoubt and the few shattered trees beyond the ridge which marked the position of the ruins of Thiépval, extended tier after tier of German trenches. Away to the right a valley rose up to Mouquet Farm. Our men had to storm the trenches and to cross the bullet-swept valley.

The weather was bright and cool, perfect for aeroplane and artillery observation. During the afternoon our 9·2 howitzers methodically shelled the enemy trenches and dug-outs, but there was little else to indicate that one of the most frightful bombardments ever delivered was imminent. About one shot in three fell full in

CAPTURED GERMAN GUN NEAR HIGH WOOD.

the front line of the Germans. Half of the rest hit fairly the communication trenches. "It was pretty shooting," says an eye-witness, "closer on its target from three miles away than the average man would get with a cricket ball from 30 yards." At intervals other guns joined the howitzers in their deadly work. Giant spurts of sand and smoke, brown and grey-black, intermingled, mounted upwards, while explosions of white shrapnel smoke aided the grim preparatory action now in hand. Then suddenly the fire gained tenfold in intensity; the real work of annihilation had begun. What next happened may be left to the pen of Mr. Beach Thomas, the correspondent of *The Daily Mail*:

I had grown tired of looking and listening and expecting, when the heavens opened. It was as if someone, as in the legend, had unbarred the cave of the thunder and the winds. You could not, of course, distinguish one gun, one battery, from another; but there was just a single standard of comparison or contrast to keep one sane. Two sorts of noise conflicted. Which was louder : the honk and whinney of the shell, splitting the air, or the joint explosions from the gun and from the shell ? The nature of the effect was that the thinner, nearer, shrewder noise of the split atmosphere seemed to be laid on the top of the general thud. One copied the other.

The shrapnel and the high explosive, bursting over the German trenches, gave a similar impression in the domain of sight. The wicked lightning of the shrapnel, bursting extremely low, topped the heavy smoke and earthy columns from the heavy shells. For a few seconds I could distinguish separate hits : a shrapnel, that raked an alley, a heavy shell that struck a parapet ; but such distinctions were soon wiped out. The valley, "the shooting gallery," running towards Mouquet, even the line of scarred trees that stand for Thiépval, were lost in smoke ; and in front a mass of fumes and dust moved like a great cumulus cloud before the western wind, and as it moved it was ever renewed at the base.

To another correspondent—the *Times* correspondent—the bombardment was no less unprecedented :

In the course of my life I have seen many gigantic things, like typhoons and prairie fires and forest fires and most of the great volcanoes of the world, and some battles, and the fall of Antwerp. But merely as a spectacle, for the splendour and the power of it, I doubt if anything ever resembled what went on then for the next 20 minutes. The young officer beside me sat muttering "Oh, my God ! Oh, my God ! " For me, I wished to shriek, to bite my fingers, to do I knew not what. And all one could do was to drum one's heels on the ground and gasp.

How many guns we had at work I do not know, and could not tell if I knew. Hundreds—thousands—millions—I do not know. But they began all at once, breaking suddenly on the sunlit silence. In 10 seconds hundreds of shells had plunged upon that one devoted spot of earth. In 20 seconds it seemed that there must have been thousands. Hurricanes, whirlwinds, thunderstorms, and gigantic conflagrations ; bring them all together and concentrate them on all in a ring of a few acres, and you will have only a suggestion of what went on immediately before our eyes. One almost sobbed from sheer exaltation ; for the overmastering sensation was astonishment at the power of it—at the power of British artillery and the splendour of its accuracy. I

do not think that one shell dropped three yards on this side of the German trenches ; and I do not think there was one stretch of 10 square yards on and beyond the trenches, over all the area attacked, on which a dozen shells did not fall in as many seconds.

Of course, it was a small area. We could concentrate here on less than 1,000 yards the guns which ordinarily have charge of miles of enemy front. So terrific was it that, above all the roar of the explosions, the sound of the shells passing overhead filled the ears with a shrieking louder than any wind. As for the ground where the shells fell, it simply was not. Rent and torn in every direction, it heaved itself into the air, not in spurts or bursts, but universally in one great duststorm. There was no ground, no trench, no brown earth or green ; nothing but chaos, swirling and incredible, until the smoke grew and blotted even chaos out.

And still the hail went on. At last the order for the advance was given, the artillery fire was lifted and became a barrage behind the enemy's trenches. Our men left their own trenches and ran forward to the edge of the whirlwind of fire, smoke, dust and heaving ground which receded before them up the slopes of the ridge. So well had the gunners performed their task that the Germans scarcely offered any resistance. With less than 100 casualties we had taken positions fondly believed to be impregnable, and a couple of hundred prisoners to boot.

The same evening the Australians gained a little more ground near Pozières, and we brought our line closer to Courcelette. Between Martinpuich and Bazentin we had gained another hundred yards of trenches. In Guillemont the fighting with the Wurtembergers continued, and south of that village we penetrated the enemy's lines and captured a machine-gun.

The gains made were substantial and had been won with surprisingly small losses—a proof that the tactical methods employed were thoroughly suited to the situation and a happy augury for the future. So complete was the command of our guns over the ground behind his front trenches that the enemy found it very difficult to bring up reinforcements, and experienced considerable losses in doing so. "The enemy's losses," wrote the *Times* correspondent, "in killed and prisoners alone were about five times our total casualties, including even the lightest flesh wound. If their wounded were no more than equal to their killed and missing— a most improbable thing—their losses were ten times as big as ours. Nor does this make any allowance for what may have been done—and it must have been much—by our artillery fire when it lifted to beyond the trenches which we took."

The terrible conditions in the German lines when reinforcements reached them were well

[*Official Photograph.*

GERMAN TRENCH NEAR THIÉPVAL.

exemplified in a letter written on August 10 by a German officer of the 133rd Infantry Regiment : *

The relief yesterday (he wrote) is incredible. The route taken—Ligny, Warlencourt, Pys, Courcelette—on the way to the trenches was very dangerous. During the first part the thunder of the guns was very disagreeable, and the second part was very unsafe. Heavy shells fell right and left of the road. Mounted troops, cars, field kitchens, infantry in column of route, were all enveloped in an impenetrable cloud of dust. From Courcelette to our position in the line we relieved across the open. If the enemy had only noticed that what a target he would have had !

Our position was, of course, quite different from what we had been told. Our company alone relieved a whole battalion. We had been told we were to relieve a company of 50 men weakened by casualties. The men we relieved had no idea where the enemy was, how far he was, or if any of our troops were in front of us. We got no idea of our supposed position until six o'clock this evening.

* From the *Daily Telegraph.*

To-night I am taking my platoon out to form a covering party. My men and I are to lie in shell holes in part of an old demolished trench of ours. The English are 400 metres away. The Windmill is over the hill. The hundreds of dead bodies make the air terrible, and there are flies in thousands. About 300 metres from us is a deserted artillery position. We shall have to look to it to-night not to get taken prisoners by the English. We have no dug-outs. We dig a hole in the side of a shell-hole, and lie and get rheumatism. We get nothing to eat or drink. . . . The ceaseless roar of the guns is driving us mad. Many of the men are knocked up.

From another man, in the 3rd battalion of the 124th Regiment, there is a letter which pays a doleful tribute to our flying men :

I am on sentry duty, and it is a very hard job, for I dare not move. Overhead are the English airmen and in front of us the English observers with telescopes, and as soon as they perceive anything twenty-four "cigars" arrive at once, and larger than one cares to see—you understand what I mean. The country round me looks frightful. Many dead bodies belonging to both sides lie around.

THE BATTLE OF THE SOMME (IV.).

POSITION ON AUGUST 22—GERMAN "MORAL"—FIGHTING OF AUGUST 24—WILTS AND WORCESTERS AT THIÉPVAL—FRENCH GAINS—GERMAN COUNTER-ATTACKS—ALLIED OFFENSIVE OF SEPT. 3-6—FEINTS ON THE ANCRE—THE MAIN ATTACK—THE FALL OF GUILLEMONT—THE FRENCH OPERATIONS —GENERAL MICHELER'S ARMY—SEPTEMBER 9—THE IRISH AT GINCHY—HEAVY GERMAN LOSSES—FRENCH SUCCESSES ON SEPTEMBER 12—THIÉPVAL AND THE "WUNDERWERK"—SEPTEMBER 14—FRANCO-BRITISH COOPERATION AND PREPARATIONS—POSITION ON SEPTEMBER 15.

THE events of the Battle of the Somme up to the evening of August 22 have been already related in Chapters CLI., CLIV. and CLXV. We had made considerable progress, but the country had still to be reached over which manœuvre battles might be fought unhindered by entrenchments prepared months beforehand, and where the Allies might fairly hope that the superior *moral* of their troops would ensure the defeat of the enemy. As early as July 30 the Germans had begun to appreciate the dangers which would arise if their lines were pierced between the Ancre and the Somme. An Order of the Day of that date, signed by the German General in command, had run as follows :

Within a short space of time we must be prepared for violent attacks on the part of the enemy. The decisive battle of the war is now being fought on the fields of the Somme. It must be impressed on every officer and man up at the front line that the fate of our country is at stake in this struggle. By ceaseless vigilance and self-sacrificing courage the enemy must be prevented from gaining another inch of ground. His attacks must break against a wall of German breasts.

The German General was right ; the glorious retreat from Mons and the fighting on the Marne had shown that in open country the British and French Armies were superior to his troops. A letter written by a prisoner of the German XIIIth Corps shows how the battle of the Somme was regarded by the German rank and

file, and the straits to which the foe was reduced. "We are, indeed, no longer men, but as it were half-living creatures." Other prisoners confirmed the statement and showed that previous battles compared with that on the Somme were "child's play." One slightly wounded German, who before the war had been manager in the grill-room of a well-known London hotel, and who had fought against the Russians on the Eastern Front, observed : "I suppose they will send me back to England under circumstances very different from those in which I left London more than two years ago. Well, I am quite ready for the change—anything to be out of the awful hell in which I have lived here." "Here" was Delville Wood. "At first," he remarked, "I was confident that we must win—everybody thought so. But we had not reckoned on your fleet, which I know has got us by the throat. . . . We cannot win. Neither," he added, with affected hopefulness, "I think, can you and your Allies. It is true that it is we, and not you, who are now on the defensive ; but we are far from being exhausted, and I think that before long you will have to make terms with us. If you don't, and it's going to be a fight to the finish, then all I can say is God help everybody ! " These statements, which might be supported by many others, showed how greatly the *moral* of the Germans had been affected. On the other

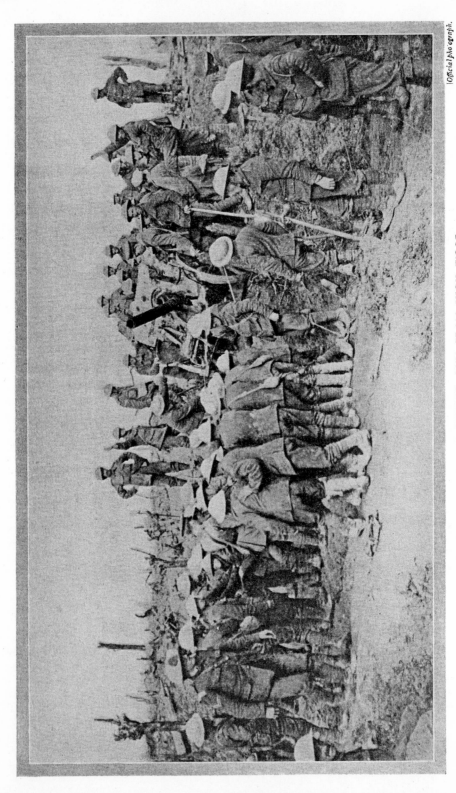

[Official photograph.

BRINGING BACK A CAPTURED GUN FROM HIGH WOOD.

hand, our soldiers were full of confidence and
elated by their successes.

At 9 p.m., on August 22, a desperate effort
was made by the enemy to recover the trenches
wrested from him south of Thiépval. The
waves of German infantry reached and entered
them in places, but their success was short-
lived. Counter-attacks promptly disposed of
all who had penetrated, or drove the survivors
back. A second assault at 1 a.m., on the
night of the 22nd-23rd, was equally futile.
Our artillery and infantry fire wrought terrible
execution among the charging lines which were
lit up by the light of their own flares. Both
attempts resulted in heavy losses to the enemy,
without any gain.

While these operations were in progress the
German artillery kept up a severe fire against
High Wood and Bazentin-le-Petit. The German aeroplanes in the evening had shown
unwonted activity. They had been engaged
by our airmen, and at least four machines
destroyed. Others were driven down badly
damaged, or pursued to their aerodromes, while
ours suffered no casualties. An aerial reconnaissance was completely successful, and

[Official photograph.

A TRENCH NEAR THIÉPVAL.

bombing raids were carried out by us against
sundry points of importance.

During the 23rd we resumed the offensive
south of Thiépval and secured 200 yards of
German trench, straightening our line and
improving our position in this region. The
counter-battery work of our guns was this day
very effective. The enemy's artillery in three
different areas was silenced, and it was reported that a score of direct hits had been
made. Our gunners had some time since

overtaken and were now outclassing in accuracy
the enemy's, and the German ammunition
showed signs of deterioration, as the percentage
of blind shells discharged by the hostile artillery
was steadily rising. "Duds," as our men

[Official photograph.

A GERMAN "DUD" LANDS IN A
TRENCH NEAR THIÉPVAL.

called them, were, however, not always a disadvantage when they came from our own guns.
One of our officers, when ascending the parapet
of a German trench, felt a shell from a British
gun drop immediately behind him. Fortunately
it did not explode, but the shock of impact on
the ground lifted him over the parapet on to a
German, whom he speedily took prisoner !

As the sun was sinking, the sky, which for
four days had been bright and cloudless,
became overcast, and a steady rain commenced
to fall. At 8.45 p.m. the German batteries
concentrated their fire on the ground gained
by us between Guillemont Station and the
quarry, the capture of which has been already
recounted. When the gun-fire lifted, a body
of infantry advanced with the greatest determination and reached the British parapet. A
sharp and fierce struggle ensued, and then, as
was usual in hand-to-hand combats, the
enemy broke, leaving behind him many dead
and wounded.

At 12.30 a.m. on Thursday, August 24, the
German artillery repeated the bombardment,
but no infantry assault materialized. In the
course of the same day, on the battlefield of
Loos, a German raid was repulsed by us near
the celebrated Hohenzollern Redoubt, and
north-west of La Bassée some of our troops
successfully entered the enemy's trenches.

Meanwhile, north of the Somme the German
guns had violently bombarded the French
front lines and communication trenches north

and south of Maurepas, while south of the river, after intense artillery preparation, the enemy had launched attacks against the troops of our Allies in and south-east of Soyécourt Wood. They were all repulsed. Adjutant Dorme on the 23rd brought down his fifth and sixth German aeroplanes. The former fell in the direction of Moislains, north-east of Péronne, the latter in the region of Marche-le-Pot, north-west of Chaulnes. Four other enemy machines were severely damaged by French

found on the person of, a prisoner of the German 125th Regiment captured about this date.* "During the day," he wrote, "one hardly dares to be seen in the trench owing to the British aeroplanes, which fly so low that it is a wonder they do not come and pull us out of our trenches." Forgetful of the glowing pictures painted by his superiors of the exploits of German airmen, he indulged in some bitter reflections. "Nothing is to be seen," he grumbled, "of our German hero airmen, and

THE SITE OF THIÉPVAL.

[*Official photograph.*]

machine-gun fire, and another was destroyed near Roye.

The events of the 23rd, above described, naturally did not figure in the German *communiqué* of the 24th. That veracious document deserves to be quoted :

North of the Somme yesterday the fresh efforts of the enemy during the evening and night failed.

The British attacks were again directed against the salient between Thiépval and Pozières and our positions at Guillemont.

At Maurepas, especially to the south of that village, strong enemy forces were repulsed after fighting which was at some points severe.

On Thursday, August 24, the weather again turned fine, and the aerial supremacy of the Allies was once more pronounced. What our command of the air, coupled as it was with so marked a superiority of our artillery, meant to the enemy, and how it affected his *moral* may be gathered from the diary kept by, and

yet their ratio is supposed to be 81 to 29 ! The fact that the British are one thousand times more daring is, however, never mentioned. One can hardly calculate how much additional loss of life and strain on the nerves this costs us. I often feel doubtful," he added, "regarding the final issue of our good cause when such bad fighters are here to champion it."

The weather conditions being so favourable, it was decided by the Allied Commanders to make three new thrusts into the German lines, one on the left towards Thiépval, the second in the centre at Delville Wood, and the third on the right in the Maurepas region. The advance between Authuille Wood and Mouquet Farm on Thiépval was entrusted by Sir

* *Morning Post,* August 28.

[*Official photograph.*]

THE WILTSHIRE MEN GOING TO THE FRONT.

Hubert Gough to the Wilts and Worcesters. In the reduction of the position still retained by the enemy on the upper eastern fringes of Delville Wood, units of the Rifle Brigade were to take part. The French were to capture the last ruins in Maurepas, to which the Germans were clinging, and to extend their line northwards to the Clery-Combles railway, southwards to Hill 121. Opposing the Wilts and Worcesters were detachments of the Prussian Guard; while the 5th Bavarian Reserve Division and the 1st Division of the Prussian Guard, commanded by the Kaiser's second son, Prince Eitel Friedrich, confronted the troops of our gallant Allies. To save the Thiépval salient, to prevent the British from Delville Wood reaching the summit of the ridge over which ran the Longueval-Flers-Ligny-Tilloy-Bapaume road, to check any eastward movement along the ridge on Ginchy and Combles and to stop the forward movement of the French through Maurepas on Combles, the Germans had concentrated every available battery and man. Their guns, though in numbers inferior to those of the Allies, were numerous. The front of battle was the 8-mile line which ran from Authuille to Maurepas.

Between the Wilts and Worcesters and the village of Thiépval, hidden by the tree-crowned ridge, lay a long trench which had been named by the enemy after their idol, Hindenburg. Into this, protected by a maze

[*Official photograph.*]

MEN OF THE WILTSHIRE REGIMENT ADVANCING TO THE ATTACK.

WORCESTERS RESTING IN A HARVEST FIELD.   [*Official Photograph.*

of trenches, there ran back, at its western end, a perfectly straight trench. Another trench the " Koenigstrasse," itself joined by another, commemorated the recovery of Lemberg. Where the Koenigstrasse met the Lemberg trench there were strong redoubts. Our troops, ensconced behind their parapets, had to cross 300 yards of sloping, open ground. Towards the right a glimpse could be obtained of the ruins of Mouquet Farm. Away on the left was the shattered wood of Authuille.

Under the blazing autumnal sun officers and men were posted in the trenches, smoking pipes and cigarettes, and watching the huge shells bursting from time to time above their heads. The novelty of the shells had worn off, and they attracted little attention. " Worse than the rats are these infernal flies," a lieutenant was heard to say, as he tried to puff them off with tobacco smoke. A breeze blowing from left to right slightly mitigated the stifling heat. Nothing betrayed to the foe that an assault in this area was imminent. He for his part was grimly silent. Now and then, however, a head cautiously thrust above the parapet, and rapidly withdrawn, showed that the Hindenburg trench was still tenanted. But for the rush through the air and explosion of an occasional shell, there was nothing which showed visibly the preparations for the struggle about to begin.

The hours passed by, and the sun was reaching the western horizon, when suddenly the whole scene was transformed with lightning-like rapidity. In a moment, volley after volley of heavy shells was poured forth from our batteries against the devoted sector to be assaulted. The noise from the guns was deafening, and was echoed by that of the exploding shells as they burst on the German lines, throwing up into the air clouds of smoke mingled with earth from the parapets which they struck. Blown slowly eastward by the light breeze which rent the mist here and there asunder, there were revealed masses of timbers and the shattered bodies of the German soldiers who had held their front trenches thrown up into the air. Ever and anon a projectile would reach a shell store and blow it up with a mighty crash, accompanied by flames which lit up the neighbourhood like lurid lightning.

" Magnificent, splendid," was the cry of a French officer who saw the display. " How grand are your guns." Above the rushing shells and beyond the smoke of their explosions flew our aeroplanes watching and signalling back the effect of our gun-fire. Regardless of the bursting shrapnel fired at them by the anti-aircraft guns, the white puffs of which could be seen surrounding our gallant airmen, the latter swept backwards and forwards as they calmly carried out their observation duties.

Ten minutes was the time allowed for the intensive bombardment of the Hindenburg, Koenigstrasse, and Lemberg trenches. By this time the German artillery, roused to a perception of what was about to happen, had got to work, and was pounding our front line trenches and placing barrages in front and behind them. The order was now given to the Wilts and Worcesters, and wave after wave of them dashed forward. On approaching the Hindenburg trench a gap of some 50 yards separated Worcesters from Wilts. Into this gap pressed groups of Prussian Guards, and a fierce bombing and bayonet struggle took place. The Prussians were killed, wounded, or taken prisoners. One of the Wilts officers—an expert shot—snatched up a rifle and shot five of the enemy bombers dead. A sergeant of the same regiment ran along the top of the parapet of the trench bombing the Germans in it. Some of the Prussians issued from their dug-outs and, refusing to surrender, put up a plucky but unavailing fight. On the left the maze of trenches was cleared, snipers and Lewis guns silencing the machine gunners, and the redoubts at the junction of the Koenigstrasse and Lemberg trenches were rushed. Altogether it was, in the characteristic language

of the soldiers engaged, "a very fine and a very pretty show." We had penetrated to a depth of 300 yards on a front of a little under half a mile, and were within 650 yards of the southern outskirts of Thiépval itself. Over 200 prisoners had been taken. How many of the Prussian Guard lay dead and wounded in the torn and twisted ground captured was not ascertained. Our losses, on the other hand, were relatively insignificant. "We evacuated portions of our advanced trench north of Ovillers, which were completely destroyed," was the comment of the German Higher Command on this action. To cover this admission of defeat, it was stated in the German *communiqué* of the 25th that "repeated Anglo-French attacks were delivered simultaneously yesterday evening on our (the German) entire front from Thiépval to the Somme," and that between "Thiépval and the Foureaux (High) Wood the enemy attacks collapsed with great loss."

In the "sector Longueval-Delville Wood," the German *communiqué* admitted that the Germans had suffered a reverse, which was a mild expression for what had really happened. The enemy garrison holding the northern and eastern fringes of the wood and the adjacent orchards was disposed in three lines of trenches, all strengthened with redoubts and provided

[*Official photograph.*

WORCESTERS GOING TO THE FRONT.

HEAVY WORK ON A MUDDY ROAD.

with dug-outs. The foremost trench was well within the wood, and to reach it broken tree-trunks and craters had to be crossed. The second trench was on the edge of the wood—shallow and lightly held. It served only as a support to the first. The third was very formidable. Though the Germans had not had time to construct their deep dug-outs for the infantry, they had connected with trenches a number of dug-outs formerly occupied by the gunners of the batteries which, in the early stages of the Battle of the Somme, had fired over Delville Wood at our troops advancing up the ridges. At the extreme eastern angle of the wood was a strong redoubt garrisoned by some 50 men. Unlike the Prussian Guard at Thiépval, the Germans anticipated an attack in this quarter. Before the time fixed for it, our troops were subjected to a very heavy bombardment of 8 in. and 5.9 in. shells. This did not, however, succeed in deterring us from delivering the blow. It was preceded by a hurricane of shells of all calibres which churned up the edges of the wood and wrecked the German positions in the open. When the guns were supposed to have done their work, the British left their trenches, and advanced against the enemy's position. On the left or

LONDON GUNNERS LOADING A HEAVY GUN.

western side of the wood progress was delayed, when the open country was reached, by an enfilading machine gun. An officer with a small group of his men hastily built a barricade which received the stream of bullets, and our troops on the right coming up soon put it out of action. Then the advance continued some 500 yards along and on both sides of the Longueval-Flers-Bapaume road to the summit of the ridge, whence they looked down on the village of Flers, our machine guns greatly assisting the operation. It was reckoned that we had sprinkled the ground north of the

actual arrangement of the four companies of the battalion, which may be regarded as typical of the method usually employed by our infantry on such occasions.

We have just finished our "act" in a part of the so-called "Great Push," and, as perhaps you already guess, I am still alive! I will tell you a little about it.

For the last fortnight we have been working day and night in preparation for an offensive of our own. I and my two platoons were to be in the fourth line, two companies going over first, then one company, and then mine in reserve to come in for all the shelling and dig communications up to the front line. There was to be a bombardment, and at 5.45 we were to go over.

At 3 p.m. we were all in our places; all knew exactly

GERMAN PRISONERS, GRAVE AND GAY.

wood with no less than 999,500 bullets on that day, an expenditure of ammunition which five years before would have been regarded as impossible and foolish.

The attack on the left had met with little resistance. On the right, in the direction of Ginchy, the fight went on after sunset, and well into the next day, until the redoubt at the north-eastern angle of the wood and the other posts of the enemy were in our possession. Thus the way from this point to Combles *via* Ginchy was opened. Of the nature of the fighting a vivid idea is given by an officer's letter. It is, moreover, valuable as showing the

their own job, and all waited for the minutes to go by. Quarter to four came at last, and our heavies started. Immediately the German lines became a mass of earth, bits of trees being tossed about in the air like the foam on giant waves—in fact, it looked for all the world like a heavy sea, only the waves were of earth. When the last 10 minutes came, intense fire was started. The ground rocked and swayed in the frightful din and force of explosions, and every one was deaf and dazed by the roar.

Finally, after what seemed years of waiting, 5.45 came, and I stood up and watched the two first companies go over, all strolling perfectly in line, all calmly smoking, while the few German survivors ran out like men demented, with hands up, yelling for mercy with the usual cry of "Kamerad, Kamerad!" Then the Huns started to barrage our old front line in which I and my two platoons were crouching. Shells fell all round us. Two or three times I was completely deafened, saw yellow

HAND-TO-HAND FIGHTING.

and red, got knocked down by the concussion, and still didn't get hit.

My time came, and we went on to do our job of digging, right in the middle of all the shelling. I got the men started and then just waited to get blown to bits. I saw shells falling amongst small groups of men, and sometimes German prisoners; sometimes our men were simply scattering to pieces in the air. Then a curious thing happened. All of a sudden rapid rifle fire and machine-gun fire opened into us, and I gave the order to drop tools, fix bayonets, and get into position to meet an attack, or, if necessary, to attack. I thought our front line had been broken, but couldn't be certain what had happened, for everything was smoke and flying earth with trees falling and being blown skywards.

I gave the order to crawl forward towards the firing, and then I saw that about 30 Germans with a machine-

gun was pushed over the crater's edge and wiped out the gun team.* In addition to our successes in the Thiépval and Delville Wood regions, our airmen had engaged and driven down damaged a number of enemy aeroplanes, and several trains had been hit on the German lines of communication.

While Sir Henry Rawlinson's troops were slowly debouching from Delville Wood on Flers and Ginchy, the French, after a two-days' bombardment of terrific intensity, attacked on August 24, at 5 p.m., the Germans who still

[*Official photograph.*

A TRENCH COUNCIL: TWO GENERALS AND THEIR STAFFS AT THE FRONT.

gun had, after surrendering, taken up their arms again, and were firing at us. I felt something burn my neck, but took no notice. We crawled steadily forward and then started throwing bombs. Again I felt something burn my back and I shot the German who had fired at me. About three minutes later the Germans surrendered to me, and although I was going to order my men to kill them all for their treachery, I thought better of it, got hold of their captain, and got some information out of him in French, and then sent them back under escort.

Two companies of the enemy, from the direction of Ginchy, counter-attacked during the night (24th-25th), but were driven back by machine-gun fire. The Lewis gun was proving invaluable. For example, the Germans had a machine gun concealed in a crater. It held up the advance at this point until a Lewis

lurked in part of Maurepas and the trenches north and south of the village. The left wing of the assaulting infantry, assisted by a British demonstration south of Guillemont, swarmed over the Maurepas-Ginchy road and penetrated to the north of the Clery-Combles railway. In the centre the Germans were cleared from the ruins still defended by them in Maurepas and from two lines of trenches in the open ground beyond. South-east of Maurepas our Allies got astride of Hill 121. The First Division of the Prussian Guard had,

---

* The Lewis gun can be fired from the shoulder—*i.e.*, it is a one-man weapon. The Maxim cannot be so employed.

THE FRENCH ATTACK ON MAUREPAS: PASSING A BARBED-WIRE FENCE.

under the eyes of Prince Eitel Friedrich, suffered a bloody reverse. Eight field guns, 10
machine-guns, and some 600 prisoners had
been captured, and the French line had been
advanced 200 yards on a front of a mile and a
quarter. At 8 p.m. the French dug themselves in and awaited counter-attacks. One
came during the night. As the western side
of Hill 121 commanded Maurepas, it was
natural that the Germans should make every
effort to recover it. The enemy's masses
advanced boldly, but under the shell and
machine-gun fire were unable to attain their
object. Reluctantly the German Higher Command had to content itself by circulating
another false statement : "The village of
Maurepas," it admitted, "is at present in
French hands, but between Maurepas and the
Somme the French attack met with no success."
Hill 121 *is* between Maurepas and the Somme.

So cowed was the enemy by his experiences
on the 24th that, apart from some fighting in
the neighbourhood of Delville Wood, no
attempt was made to recover the lost positions
till late on the 25th, when at 7 p.m. the German
batteries bombarded the British first-line
trenches along the greater portion of our front
south of the Ancre until early in the morning
of Saturday, August 26, and at 7.45 p.m. the
Prussian Guards were thrown in two waves at
the Wilts and Worcesters. The attack was
pressed with determination, but repulsed with
heavy loss to the foe. We, on the other hand,
made further progress to the east of Mouquet
Farm, and also along the Courcelette-Thiépval
road. At the right extremity of our line the
British trenches west of Guillemont, between
the Quarries and the Montauban-Guillemont
road, were ineffectually attacked. At 10 p.m.
a German reconnaissance in the direction of

Hill 121 was dispersed. The British counter-
batteries that day, the 25th, destroyed or
damaged many of the enemy's positions, and
the French artillery, as usual, had been active
with good effect.

On Saturday, August 26, the fighting continued round Mouquet Farm, and in the
evening we captured 200 yards of German
trench north of Bazentin-le-Petit, and a
machine-gun. The weather had again become
bad, and the Allied operations were consequently hindered. A heavy storm overtook
eight of our aeroplanes, and five machines did
not return to their aerodrome.

On Sunday, August 27, there was considerable
artillery activity on both sides, and we gained
some ground north-west of Ginchy. This
period of relative rest was, according to the
German *communiqués*, one of constant fighting,
in which, according to their own account, the
Germans were successful. Thus the *communiqué*
of August 27 was to the following effect :

North of the Somme, yesterday morning and during the
night, the British, after strong artillery preparations,
made repeated attacks south of Thiépval and north-west
of Pozières, which were repulsed partially, after bitter
hand-to-hand fights. We captured one officer and 60
men.

Advances north of Bazentin-le-Petit and grenade
fighting at the Foureaux Wood were also unsuccessful
for the enemy.

In the Maurepas-Clery sector the French, after a violent artillery fire and the use of flame throwers, brought
up strong forces to an unsuccessful attack. North of
Clery we repulsed parties which had penetrated there.

South of the Somme grenade attacks west of Vermandovillers were repulsed.

On Monday, August 28, in spite of the vile
weather, we gained a little ground eastward of
Delville Wood, and some minor enterprises
near Mouquet Farm were successful. Our
long-range guns hit troops and wagons in different places between Miraumont and Bapaume.
The next day, Tuesday, August 29, in the

afternoon a heavy storm burst, but nevertheless we continued to gain ground between the
western outskirts of Guillemont and Ginchy.
Between Delville Wood and High Wood hostile
defences were captured, and south-east of
Thiépval further progress was made and a
machine-gun captured. An attack by the
enemy near Pozières windmill was dispersed,
and during the night of the 29th-30th, West
Australians and men from New South Wales
went at a run over the slippery clay and
entered Mouquet Farm, and trenches north-east
of it. There was some close hand-to-hand
fighting, after which our men returned to their
own lines. The bad weather continued on
the 30th, and the only incident of note was
our capture of a small salient south of Martinpuich, taking prisoners 4 officers and 120 men.
In the evening the rain ceased.

The importance of the British gains in High
Wood and Delville Wood was too well understood by the German leaders for them to
resign themselves patiently to the loss of that
sector, the key to the crest of the main ridge.
On Wednesday, August 30, every gun that
could be brought to bear on the British lines
between Bazentin-le-Petit and Longueval,
poured out shells throughout the day, and
towards evening an attack was launched on our
trenches in the vicinity of High Wood. Caught
by machine-gun, trench-mortar, and artillery
fire, the enemy's troops hesitated, and then

drew back into their shelters, leaving behind
them heaps of killed and wounded. Even
fresh troops could not stand such punishment.
That the spirit of many of the Germans on the
battlefield was shaken may be gathered from
a German regimental order dated the next
day, which was subsequently secured by us.

I must state with the greatest regret that the regiment
during this change of position, had to take notice of the
sad fact that the men of four of the companies, inspired by
shameful cowardice, left their companies on their own
initiative and did not move into line. To the hesitating
and fainthearted in the regiment I would say the following : " What the Englishman can do the German can do
also, or if, on the other hand, the Englishman really is a
better and superior being, he would be quite justified in
his aims as regards this war, namely, the extermination
of the German. There is a further point to be noted.
This is the first time we have been in the line on the
Somme, and, what is more, we are there at a time when
things are more calm. The English regiments opposing
us, as has been established, have been in the firing line
for the second, and in some cases even for the third time.
Heads up and play the man."

In another order, bearing the date of September 18, which was found in a captured dug-
out, there was the following passage :

Proofs are multiplying of men leaving the position
without permission or reporting, and hiding at the rear.
It is our duty, each at his post, to deal with this fact with
energy and success.

The next day, Thursday, August 31, after
an intense bombardment, no less than five
attacks were made on a front of some 3,000
yards between High Wood and Ginchy.
Four times the British, in their muddy, water-
logged trenches, beat off the Germans, but

THE FRENCH ATTACK ON MAUREPAS: CROSSING A DESERTED TRENCH.

their fifth charge was more successful. On the north-west of Delville Wood we were obliged to give ground, and our advanced posts

A LOOK-OUT.

beyond the north-east of this point were forced some distance back. At one part a few of the enemy penetrated into the wreckage. All, with the exception of 21, who were taken prisoners, were promptly killed.

The time had now come for a further advance against the German lines from Ginchy to Clery-sur-Somme, and, south of the Somme, from Barleux to Chilly. While the preparations for it were in progress, the British and French, except at one or two points along the front of battle, desisted from any infantry offensive. But on the night of Friday, September 1, we recovered the trenches north-west of Delville Wood taken from us by the enemy the

day before. On September 2, the only infantry action consisted of some bombing encounters.

During both days the British, French, and German artillery was active, and on Saturday the enemy's guns discharged large numbers of gas shells at our positions. South of Estrées the Germans recovered some trenches lost by them to our Allies on August 31.

There were also a considerable number of aerial combats. On September 1 a British airman encountered a squadron of twelve Rolands. It dived in amongst them, firing a drum of ammunition from its machine gun, and broke up their formation. Then the British pilot swiftly placed himself beneath the nearest enemy machine, and another drum was discharged at it from below. The Roland, badly damaged, plunged to earth,

[Official photographs.

NEAR DELVILLE WOOD: BRINGING UP STONE FOR REPAIR OF TRENCHES.

A WATER-LOGGED TRENCH.

south-east of Bapaume. Another company of hostile machines flew to avenge their comrade. The British aeroplane attacked one of the enemy's, which went down and landed in a

A STORM-TOSSED AEROPLANE LANDS UPSIDE DOWN.
In this accident, however, no one was hurt, nor was the machine badly damaged.

gap between two woods. After battling with the rest and expending all his ammunition, the lieutenant in charge of the British machine returned safely to his base. The same evening another lieutenant, single-handed, attacked a German group of eight aeroplanes in the air over Bapaume. One was sent spinning downwards to its destruction. On September 1 the French aeronauts accounted for four German machines, Adjutant Dorme bringing his " bag " up to eight, by emptying at close quarters his machine gun into a German aeroplane above Combles. It came crashing to the ground east of the village. On the other hand, the Germans claimed to have put out of action on Saturday six of the Allied aeroplanes.

Be that as it may, it is certain that on Saturday four more German aeroplanes were badly damaged in encounters with the French, and that, to distract the German commanders, numerous British and French bombarding squadrons crossed the German lines and dropped bombs. A naval aeroplane in the afternoon bombarded the shipbuilding yards at Hoboken, near Antwerp. The French squadrons once more visited the railway station of Metz-Sablons, throwing 86 120 mm. bombs on the buildings and railway trenches, and 60 bombs of the same size on military establishments north of Metz. Two hundred and ten bombs were allotted to the stations of Maizières-les-Metz, Conflans, Sedan, and Autun-

le-Roman, and to the cantonments and depôts at Guiscard, Ham, Monchy-Lagache, Nesle, and Athies. These raids were a fitting prelude to the great battle which was to be joined the next day, Sunday, September 3, between the Ancre and the region south of Chaulnes.

Up the roads leading to the hostile fronts streamed countless motor-lorries carrying ammunition and supplies. The main and light railways were full of trains. Concealment of our intentions from the Germans was impossible. They were aware that we were about to attack, and made their arrangements to meet us. Reinforcements from the Eastern and from other sections of the Western front were being brought by train or motors or were marching to the line Bapaume-Roye. In anticipation of the coming onslaught the German artillery on Saturday and throughout the night of September 2–3 hurled myriads of projectiles on spots, like the Trônes Wood, where they suspected that the British or French were concentrating the troops about to take part in a struggle which might prove to be decisive. Most, if not all, of the Prussian Guard had been brought up, and so dangerous did the German Higher Command consider the position to be that in the Guillemont region alone they massed the whole of the 2nd Bavarian Corps, and the 11th and 56th Divisions.

The first step of the new Allied offensive

[*Official photograph.*

MACHINE GUNNERS PREPARED FOR AN ATTACK UNDER COVER OF POISON-GAS.

was taken during Sunday, Monday, Tuesday and Wednesday, September 3, 4, 5 and 6. It was preceded by a bombardment even more severe than any which had preceded it. Feint attacks were also made on both sides of the Ancre and near Thiépval. Throughout the night of September 2-3 an almost continuous zone of fire seemed to stretch for 30 miles south of the Ancre. The horizon, to watchers in the background, appeared to be ablaze. When day broke the German lines were seen everywhere blotted out by the fumes from exploding shells, amid which could here and there be seen thrown up into the air the masses of timber, brick, and the various materials used by the Germans in constructing their defences. From behind the lines squadrons of aeroplanes rose and engaged one another above the dull and gas-laden atmosphere.

Dawn was breaking when the momentary cessation of our guns far off on the left beyond Thiépval indicated that Sir Hubert Gough's troops were advancing against the Germans north and south of the Ancre. As in the battle of July 1, Sir Douglas Haig had hoped by a demonstration against the northern face of the Thiépval salient to deceive the enemy's leaders as to his intentions. The position to be assaulted was indeed formidable. From the river-bed the ground rose on the left to the ridge, in a crease of which lies Beaumont Hamel, on the right to the Thiépval plateau.

Under Beaumont Hamel were huge caves filled with the German reserves, many of whom had also shelter in the trenches and dug-outs on the slopes of the Ancre Valley.

The destructive bombardment had wrecked the German parapets, filled in their trenches, blocked up the entrances to their dug-outs, and converted the ground to be traversed into a collection of pits formed by the craters of the exploding shells. The British north of the Ancre speedily crashed through the first and second German lines, sweeping away all opposition. But on the right, south of the Ancre, the attack was held up by shell fire, and soon the troops north of the river were enfiladed by machine-gun fire and artillery fire and counter-attacked. As the day wore on it was seen that no advantage would be gained by their remaining in the conquered area. They were slowly withdrawn, and the bombardment was once more renewed.

Almost simultaneously with the attack in this region, the Anzacs assaulted the southern face of the Thiépval salient at Mouquet Farm, now a waste of battered rubbish lying among broken tree-trunks. They were opposed by the Reserve Regiment of the 1st Division of the Prussian Guard. The struggle was of the most stubborn and bloody description. Through shrapnel and machine-gun fire the Anzac soldiers came to grips with the Kaiser's picked troops. Into one of the roomy underground villas a party of our men descended. It was apparently untenanted, and the Anzacs were leisurely appropriating some of the cigars left by the late occupants when a number of Germans entered and called upon them to surrender. " Surrender be d——d ! " was the reply. " Surrender yourselves ! " Bombs were flung at and by the intruders, and in the smoke-filled cavern the combatants swayed to and fro for several minutes. Finally the surviving Anzacs got the upper hand and emerged into the open, driving before them a few wounded and cowed prisoners. The result of the Mouquet Farm action was that at the end of it our troops were well beyond the ruins and on the high ground to the north-west, and were holding the position won. There they were ineffectually counter-attacked on the next day.

The actions on both banks of the Ancre and at Mouquet Farm in the early hours of September 3 were, as mentioned, feints on the part of the British. It was at noon that the main attacks of the British and French were delivered north and south of the Somme. The position held by Sir Henry Rawlinson's troops, who were facing east, ran from the east of Delville Wood southward to near Guillemont Station,

and thence by the quarry at the western edge of Guillemont to near the head of the ravine which runs westward from Angle Wood. Sir Henry's immediate objectives were Ginchy, Guillemont, and the German trenches from Guillemont through Wedge Wood—a small patch of trees—to the redoubt of Falfemont Farm which faced Angle Wood. Behind Falfemont Farm and east of Ginchy and Guillemont lay on high ground a long, narrow wood, Leuze Wood, the northern end of which was known as Bouleaux Wood. Here among the as yet untouched trees the German reserves were hidden. From the lower end of Leuze Wood a narrow spur 500 yards long extends south-westwards. Wedge Wood was in the valley on the Guillemont side, Falfemont Farm at the end of the spur. Beyond and below Leuze Wood in a deep wooded valley was Combles. To facilitate the French movements from Maurepas towards the heights east of Combles, Sir Henry Rawlinson at 9 a.m. had launched an attack against Falfemont Farm. Our troops reached the farm, but could not hold it. This strong outpost of the enemy was not taken till the morning of September 5.

While the Germans were clinging desperately to Falfemont Farm, the Irish, Londoners and

HEAVY FRENCH ARTILLERY AND MOTOR LORRIES ON THE WAY TO THE FRONT.

North Countrymen, at noon on Sunday, assaulted Guillemont and the fortified areas north and south of the ruined village, in which the only thoroughfare now discernible was the slightly depressed highway running through the centre of the shapeless heaps of masonry to Leuze Wood and Combles. This highway was crossed 500 yards east of Guillemont by a sunken road connecting Ginchy with Wedge Wood, and along the sunken road were rows of deep dug-outs, especially on the south-western and southern sides of the village. One wrecked and battered barn, all of Guillemont that remained, served to guide the British to their objective. Every other edifice in the village had long before been pounded into shapeless fragments, or resolved into dust. Expecting the attack, the German artillery had discharged at our front lines in the morning, among other projectiles, a large number of gas shells.

The garrison of Guillemont consisted of Prussian Guards and Hanoverians. They had been driven into their subterranean refuges by the storm of shells which preceded the British advance. Some of the defenders who ventured to show their heads were blinded by the smoke, dust and fumes. In such a murky atmosphere the periscope was useless. Nothing could be seen, and little heard but ear-splitting explosions. Then, accompanied by a wild burst of cheering and the shrill wailing of the war-pipes, waves of Irishmen burst over the northern section of Guillemont. The first, second, and third lines of the enemy were passed and the sunken road beyond reached in one rush. To the right of the Irish, Londoners and North Countrymen moved coolly forward at the heels of the advancing barrage of shells. The combination of Celtic and English troops was irresistible.

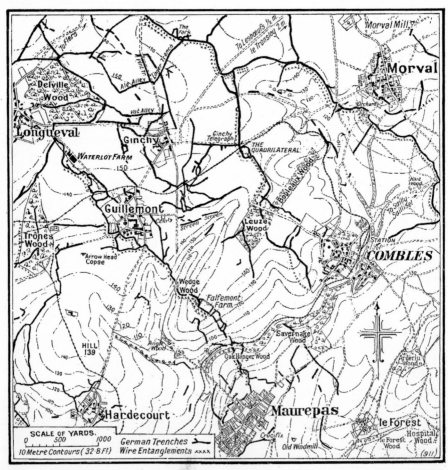

MAP ILLUSTRATING THE OPERATIONS AROUND GUILLEMONT AND GINCHY.

THE RUINED STATION AT GUILLEMONT

[*Official photograph.*]

Prussians and Hanoverians who had emerged from their holes and were firing at the backs of the Irish were taken in flank by platoons of an English battalion engaged in methodically rounding up the enemy in the quarry and southern section of Guillemont. A hollow road leading south-west from Guillemont was cleared of the Germans. There 150 corpses were afterwards counted and numbers of prisoners taken. The quarry north of it gave considerable trouble, as the defenders kept below ground until the assailants had passed, after which they emerged and fired at the backs of the British pressing eastwards. A detachment was speedily directed to storm the quarry, and soon cries of " Kamerad ! " and " Mercy ! " told that the task had been accomplished. Meanwhile from Guillemont station our men had swept round the northern edge of the village, and from Arrow Head copse to the south other British troops had pushed up to meet them. At last the village which had so long resisted us was taken, and, undeterred by machine-gun fire from Ginchy, Wedge Wood and Falfemont Farm, Irish and English pressed on, cleared out the Germans from their refuges along the sunken road, and dug themselves in. The German 73rd, 76th and 164th Regiments had ceased to exist. The headlong flight of some Hanoverians was bitterly commented on by a Prussian officer who, however,

had permitted himself to be taken prisoner : " They run well," he said to his captors, " they will be in Berlin before I am in England ! " Of the prisoners, some forced into the open by sulphur bombs were weeping. Six out of 43 occupants of a dug-out on the Ginchy-Wedge Wood road sobbed as they crawled into the presence of a bombing party, and begged for quarter. An officer—spectacled and elderly—went on his knees before a British sergeant. Many Germans offered watches and trinkets in the hope of saving their lives. But it was explained to them that British soldiers were not thieves.

The capture of Guillemont was succeeded by the seizure of Ginchy, and the systematic bombardment of Leuze Wood, but in the afternoon and evening the Germans counter-attacked at Ginchy and Guillemont. They succeeded in recovering the former, but were repulsed with terrible loss at Guillemont. Meanwhile north of Delville Wood and away to the north-west of it in High Wood we had gained ground. Rain again fell in the evening and impeded the advance.

The next day, Monday, September 4, Sir Henry Rawlinson's offensive was resumed. Through the night and the morning of the 4th the bombardment, now chiefly directed against Ginchy, Leuze and Wedge Woods and Falfemont Farm, had continued. The rain ceased and the sun shone on the battlefield. Ginchy was assaulted, and at 3 p.m. our troops from the sunken road charged into Wedge Wood, and carried it and the trench beyond it. Falfemont Farm—or rather its site—was also attacked from the north and south and momentarily taken. Suddenly a solid line of Prussian Guards emerged from Leuze Wood and charged over the high ground towards Wedge Wood and the farm which lay on the slope of the ridge opposite Angle Wood. As the oncoming infantry reached the edge of the ravine it was swept by shrapnel and riddled by machine-gun fire. After a desperate struggle Wedge Wood remained in our possession, but Falfemont Farm was reoccupied by the enemy. Meanwhile parties of our men from the sunken road had penetrated into Leuze Wood, and many hardly fought combats had taken place in the ruins of Ginchy.

On the morning of Tuesday, September 5, Falfemont Farm was taken, but the Germans were still entrenched in the greater part of Ginchy, where attack and counter-attack had succeeded one another in rapid succession. By the evening of the same day we held Leuze Wood firmly, and it was completely cleared of the Germans the next day. We had by then advanced on a front of two miles to an average depth of nearly one mile. We had disposed of thousands of the enemy, including large numbers of prisoners, and many machine-guns. Seldom had the tenacity of the British soldier been exhibited to greater advantage than in this four days' battle.

The battle of the Somme during this period was equally memorable in the annals of our gallant Ally. North of the river at noon on September 3, when the British were advancing against Guillemont, General Fayolle, after a tremendous bombardment, flung his infantry at the German trenches from the northern environs of Maurepas, to the western outskirts of Clery-sur-Somme (a length of 3¾ miles). The 2nd Bavarian Corps, stimulated by Hindenburg's recent visit, barred the way, but the onset of the *poilus* was irresistible. They drove the enemy up the eastern side of the Combles Valley almost to the northern edge of Combles; they stormed Le Forest and carried the German trenches between it and Clery-sur-Somme. They also in places crossed the Combles-Clery-sur-Somme road. The latter village was taken, and a German counter-attack south of Le Forest was caught under the fire of French batteries and completely dispersed. Two thousand unwounded prisoners, 14 guns, and 50 machine-guns were captured in this most successful action. During the night the French gains were consolidated, and the next day the advance was continued. The French forward movement east of Le Forest outflanked the Hôpital Farm and occupied the crest of the ridge to the west of the Bois Marrières. Several sorties from Combles were broken by machine-gun fire and by artillery barrages. Five hundred more prisoners and 10 machine-guns were brought in by the victors. During the night torrential rain hindered the operations, and the enemy took advantage of the lull to attempt a counter-attack. Debouching from the wood of Anderlu, north of Le Forest, he endeavoured to pierce the new French line between Combles and Le Forest; but the artillery and machine-guns soon stopped it. On Tuesday, September 5, the French reached the western border of Anderlu Wood, captured the Hôpital Farm and the Rainette Wood, entered the Marrières Wood, north-east of Clery-sur-Somme, and occupied the end of the ridge across which runs the road from Clery to Bouchavesnes. South of the Somme, Omiécourt, at the edge of the river bank, was taken and the southern brought into line with the northern sector. The Colonial troops carried the village at the point of the bayonet in 40 minutes. The remnant of the enemy's garrison endeavoured to escape but were stopped at the level crossing of the Bapaume-Péronne light railway and forced to surrender. By this time 24 heavy and 8 field guns, 2 bomb mortars, 2 trench guns, a depôt of 150 mm. shells, a captive balloon, and numerous machine-guns had been wrested from the Germans. During Wednesday, September 6, nothing of importance occurred on the French front north of the Somme, but in the night of the 6th–7th, violent counter-attacks were made on the French garrison in the trenches at Hôpital Farm. They were all stopped by artillery barrages.

Thus, by the evening of September 6, Sir Henry Rawlinson's right wing ran from the western edge of Ginchy through Leuze Wood to the edge of the ridge overlooking Combles, and the extremity of General Fayolle's left wing was across the Combles Valley, in the woods just south of the village. Thence the French line went south-westwards through

CAPTURE OF FALFEMONT FARM.

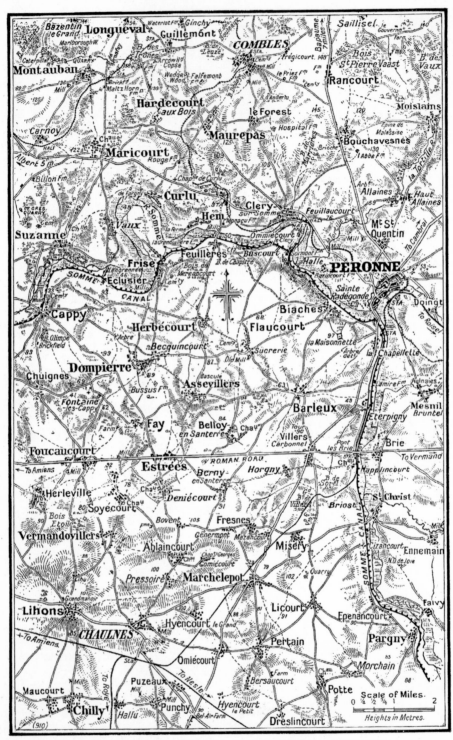

THE GROUND OVER WHICH THE FRENCH ADVANCED.

the wood of Anderlu by Hôpital Farm into the wood of Marrières. Thence it turned southwards and touched the Somme just east of Clery-sur-Somme. The reduction of Combles and the advance on Sailly-Saillisel would not long be delayed. Through Clery-sur-Somme the French Commander was also in a position to aim a blow at Mt. St. Quentin, the northern key to Péronne, and the Péronne-Bapaume highway.

While Sir Henry Rawlinson and General Fayolle were moving on Combles, the French

Somme, the French south-west of Barleux carried three trenches and advanced over a mile to the outskirts of Berny and Deniécourt. Farther south they secured Soyécourt, capturing a battalion, and also progressed farther in Vermandovillers, where there were sanguinary encounters in and around the church.

At 2 p.m. the new French Army, under General Micheler, came into action, but it was not till approaching 5 p.m. that a breach was made in the German lines slightly north of Chilly. Through it poured the victorious

AFTER THE CAPTURE OF GUILLEMONT: THE RETURN OF THE IRISH BRIGADE.

south of the Somme had not been idle. On Monday, September 4, Fayolle's right wing, in conjunction with a new French Army, deployed south of Vermandovillers, and delivered battle between Barleux and Chilly, a village south of Lihons, along a front of over 12 miles. Barleux, attacked since July, again and again had held out, and at the opening of the battle the French line ran from the west of Barleux south-westwards to Belloy-en-Santerre, then to the west of Soyécourt and through the north-western portion of Vermandovillers by the Soyécourt-Lihons road to the district west of Chilly. After a very severe bombardment analogous to those which had been such a feature of the recent fighting north of the

French infantry, and by 5 p.m. the enemy had retired to his second position, leaving behind him 1,200 prisoners and several guns and machine-guns. The whole of Chilly was abandoned to the French, who also seized Hill 86 and entered the western fringes of Chaulnes Wood. South of Chilly the French heavy artillery caught and dispersed enemy troops moving along the Liaucourt-Fouches road. During the day 2,700 prisoners had been captured south of the Somme, and the French had made an appreciable advance towards the Péronne-Roye high road. Six counter-attacks delivered by troops hurried up from the Roye region were beaten off, chiefly by shell fire, and the French were left to consolidate during the night their new positions, which turned out very wet. Several assaults in the neighbourhood of Belloy were repulsed, and 100 more prisoners secured.

Tuesday, September 5, was another successful day for our Allies in the operations south of the Somme. Massed charges of the Germans occurred at numerous points, notably between Barleux and Belloy and between Belloy and Soyécourt. They were made in vain, and the French, after inflicting heavy losses on the

and advanced as far as the southern projection of the park. The French were now across the Barleux-Chaulnes road, and their guns were able to dominate Barleux from the south as well as from the north. The northern portion of Vermandovillers was completely cleared of the enemy as far as the Vermandovillers-Estrées road, and the Etoile Wood was captured. South of Vermandovillers the troops of Micheler's Army expelled the Germans from the long plateau north of the Chilly-Hallu road

LIGHT RAILWAY BEHIND THE FRENCH LINES.

enemy, retained their hold on the ground they had captured. East of Soyécourt our Allies, driving the enemy before them, reached the north-western and southern borders of Deniécourt Park, which, with its chateau, had been strongly fortified, and between Soyécourt and Chilly they carried a salient and numerous works south of Vermandovillers. The total prisoners taken had now risen to 4,047, including 55 officers. Counter-attacks in the Berny-en-Santerre and Deniécourt regions were smashed by barrages.

On Wednesday, the 6th, in the afternoon, the right wing of General Fayolle's Army stormed German trenches south-east of Belloy, carried most of the village of Berny-en-Santerre

and attacked the enemy trenches on the eastern slopes at the foot of which ran the Chaulnes-Roye railway. Round the junction of the Amiens-St. Quentin and Roye-Chaulnes-Péronne railways the struggle raged till 6 p.m. The entrenchments here were particularly strong, but the French succeeded in storming them. At sunset our Allies were within a few hundred yards of Chaulnes station. Their artillery had crushed a sugar factory with munition depôts north of it, and east of Chilly the troops of a Saxon Division, hurried up from the Aisne front, had met with a bloody reverse. Later the Germans debouched from Horgny, and attacked again and again between Barleux and Berny: but artillery barrages prevented them from reaching the French lines. In the day's fighting 400 and more prisoners had been captured.

During the night of the 6th-7th 16 French bombarding aeroplanes dropped heavy bombs on Villecourt, a village on the Somme, between Péronne and Ham, on Athies, through which passes the Péronne-Ham highroad, and on Roisel, a station between Péronne and Cambrai, and the enemy vainly attacked the French between Berny and Chaulnes. Four times his artillery deluged the French positions south of Vermandovillers with high explosive and shrapnel shell, and after each bombardment the Germans in masses advanced to recover the ground lost by them in the course of the preceding days. At no point, however, were they successful. Two hundred more prisoners were captured, and on the 7th our Allies carried some more trenches east of Deniécourt.

Thus, between September 4 and 7, Generals Fayolle and Micheler south of the Somme had cut the Roye-Péronne railway, loosened the hold of the Germans on Chaulnes, and driven a wedge into the enemy's zone of fortifications between Chaulnes and Barleux. North of the Somme the French from Clery had moved nearer to Mont St. Quentin, which defended Péronne from an attack down the Bapaume-Péronne road and the guns on which protected the fortified village of Barleux. The left wing of General Fayolle now extended northwards from the east of Clery to the southern environs of Combles.

Across the Combles valley the right wing of Sir Henry Rawlinson on September 7 stretched from Falfemont Farm by the wood of Leuze to the western outskirts of Ginchy. Generals Fayolle and Micheler now suspended their offensive, while Sir Henry Rawlinson made preparations for the storming of Ginchy and the expulsion of the Germans between Ginchy and the Bois des Bouleaux, the long strip of woodland running north-eastwards out of the wood of Leuze. These preparations were made on the 7th and 8th, during which there was fighting—on the 8th—round Mouquet Farm, in High Wood and at Vermandovillers, where the French advanced and captured 50 prisoners.

In beautiful but misty weather Sir Henry Rawlinson struck his blow on Saturday, September 9, in the presence of the British Premier, Mr. Asquith, who had been spending

GENERAL FAYOLLE AND HIS CHIEF
OF THE STAFF.

some days in the Somme area. The troops detailed for the operation were drawn from Ireland and England. The line of battle ran from the north-east of Pozières by High Wood and Ginchy to Leuze Wood.

After the usual intense preliminary bombardment the troops at 4.45 p.m. went forward over their parapets. On the southern side of the Pozières-Bapaume road towards Martinpuich they carried a series of trenches and captured 62 unwounded prisoners. Soon after 9 p.m. the victors beat off a counter-attack, inflicting heavy losses. The attack in High Wood was also successful, our men advancing 300 yards on a 600 yards front. It was, however, the assaults on Ginchy and the ground from Ginchy to Leuze Wood which were the crowning triumph of the day.

Ginchy and the area south-east of it were defended by fresh troops, the 19th Bavarian Division supplying the garrison of the village, and troops of the 185th Division lining the trenches from Ginchy to the north-western end of Leuze Wood. At 4.45 p.m. the Irish

A PATROL IN CHAULNES WOOD.

made for Ginchy. The ruins—especially those of a farm near the centre of the village—bristled with machine-guns. This attack was graphically described by an officer who took part in it. He wrote :

We were in reserve. The front line was some 500 or 600 yards higher up the slope nearer Ginchy. We knew that a big attack was coming off that day, but did not think we should be called upon to take part. Accordingly, we settled down for the day, and most of the men slept. I felt quite at home, as I sat in the bottom of the deep trench, reading the papers I had received the previous day from home. I went through *The Times*, and was much interested in its *Japanese Supplement*, for the memories it brought back of many happy days in Dai Nippon were vivid ones.

It was about four o'clock in the afternoon when we first learned that we should have to take part in the attack on Ginchy. We were ordered to move up into the front line to reinforce ; none of us knew for a certainty whether we were going over the top or not, but everything seemed to point that way. Our shells bursting in the village of Ginchy made it belch forth smoke like a volcano. The Hun shells were bursting on the slope in front of us. The noise was deafening. I turned to my servant O'Brien, who has always been a cheery, optimistic soul, and said, " Well, O'Brien, how do you think we'll fare ? " and his answer was for once not encouraging. " We'll never come out alive, sir," was his answer. Happily we both came out alive.

It was at this moment, just as we were debouching on to the scragged front line of trench, that we beheld a scene which stirred and thrilled us to the depths of our souls. The great charge of the Irish had begun, and we had come up in the nick of time. Mere words must fail to convey anything like a true picture of the scene, but it is burned into the memory of all those who were there and saw it. Between the outer fringe of Ginchy and the front line of our own trenches is No Man's Land, a wilderness of pits so close together that

you could ride astraddle the partitions between any two of them. As you look half right, obliquely down along No Man's Land, you behold a great host of yellow-coated men rise out of the earth and surge forward and upward in a torrent—not in extended order, as you might expect, but in one mass. There seems to be no end to them. Just when you think the flood is subsiding, another wave comes surging up the bend towards Ginchy. We joined in on the left. There was no time for us any more than the others to get into extended order. We formed another stream converging on the others at the summit.

By this time we were all wildly excited. Our shouts and yells alone must have struck terror into the Huns, who were firing their machine-guns down the slope. But there was no wavering in the Irish host. We couldn't run. We advanced at a steady walking pace, stumbling here and there, but going ever onward and upward. That numbing dread had now left me completely. Like the others I was intoxicated with the glory of it all. I can remember shouting and bawling to the men of my platoon, who were only too eager to go on.

The Hun barrage had now been opened in earnest, and shells were falling here, there, and everywhere in No Man's Land. They were mostly dropping on our right, but they were coming nearer and nearer, as if a screen were being drawn across our front. I knew that it was a case of " Now or never," and stumbled on feverishly. We managed to get through the barrage in the nick of time, for it closed behind us, and after that we had no shells to fear in front of us.

I mention merely as an interesting fact in psychology how in a crisis of this sort one's mental faculties are sharpened. Instinct told us when the shells were coming gradually closer to crouch down in the holes until they had passed. Acquired knowledge, on the other hand—the knowledge instilled into one by lectures and books (of which I have only read one—namely, Haking's " Company Training ")—told us that it was safer in the long run to push ahead before the enemy got our range, and it was acquired knowledge that won.

And here another observation I should like to make by the way. I remember reading somewhere—I think it was in a book by Winston Churchill—that of the Battle of Omdurman the writer could recollect nothing in the way of noise. He had an acute visual recollection of all that went on about him, but his aural recollection was *nil*; he could only recall the scene as if it were a cinematograph picture. Curiously this was my own experience at Ginchy. The din must have been deafening (I learned afterwards that it could be heard miles away), yet I have only a confused remembrance of it.

How long we were in crossing No Man's Land I don't know. It could not have been more than five minutes, yet it seemed much longer. We were now well up to the Boche. We had to clamber over all manner of obstacles—fallen trees, beams, great mounds of brick and rubble—in fact, over the ruins of Ginchy. It seems like a nightmare to me now. I remember seeing comrades falling round me. My sense of hearing returned to me, for I became conscious of a new sound—namely, the pop, pop, pop, pop of machine-guns, and the con-

tinuous crackling of rifle fire. By this time all units were mixed up, but they were all Irishmen. They were cheering and cheering like mad. There was a machine-gun playing on us near by, and we all made for it.

At this moment we caught our first sight of the Huns. They were in a trench of sorts, which ran in and out among the ruins. Some of them had their hands up. Others were kneeling and holding their arms out to us. Still others were running up and down the trench distractedly as if they didn't know which way to go, but as we got closer they went down on their knees, too. To the everlasting good name of the Irish soldiery, not one of these Huns, some of whom had been engaged in slaughtering our men up to the very last moment, was killed. I did not see a single instance of a prisoner being shot or bayoneted. When you remember that our men were worked up to a frenzy of excitement, this crowning act of mercy to their foes is surely to their eternal credit. They could feel pity even in their rage.

[*French official photograph.*

TRANSPORTING A HEAVY FRENCH GUN.

By this time we had penetrated the German front line, and were on the first flat ground where the village once stood surrounded by a wood of fairly high trees. There was no holding the men back. They rushed through Ginchy, driving the Huns before them. The Hun dead were lying everywhere, some of them having been frightfully mangled by our shell fire. We dug in by linking up the shell craters, and though the men were tired (some wanted to smoke and others to make tea) they worked with a will, and before long we had got a pretty decent trench outlined.

I heard that when Captain ——'s company rushed a trench to our right, round the corner of the wood, a German officer surrendered in great style. He stood to attention, gave a clinking salute, and said in perfect English, "Sir, myself, this other officer and 10 men are your prisoners." Captain —— said, "Right you are, old chap!" and they shook hands, the prisoners being led away immediately. So you see there are certain amenities of battlefields. I believe our prisoners were all Bavarians, who are better mannered from all accounts than the Prussians. They could thank their stars they had Irish chivalry to deal with.

The trench (between ours and the wood) was stacked with German dead. It was full of *débris*, bombs, shovels, and what-not, and torn books, magazines, and newspapers. I came across a copy of Schiller's "Wallenstein."

Our men are very good to the German wounded. An Irishman's heart melts very soon. In fact, kindness and compassion for the wounded, our own and the enemy's, is about the only decent thing I have seen in war. It is not at all uncommon to see a British and German soldier side by side in the same shell-hole, nursing each other as best they can and placidly smoking cigarettes. A poor wounded Hun who hobbled into our trench in the morning, his face badly mutilated by a bullet—he whimpered and moaned as piteously as a child—was bound up by one of our officers, who took off his coat and set to work in earnest. Another Boche, whose legs were hit, was carried in by our men and put into a shell-hole for safety, where he lay awaiting the stretcher-bearers when we left. It is with a sense of pride that I can write this of our soldiers.

The first advance of the Irish carried them to the main road running through the centre of the village. The soldiers on the left reached it in eight minutes, those on the right were held up by machine-gun fire. A trench mortar was hurriedly brought forward, and the Germans forced to evacuate the emplacement. Another trench mortar silenced the mitrailleuses in the ruins of the farm above mentioned. At 5.30 p.m. a second rush carried the Irish out into the open. They pushed up the Ginchy-Morval road about 800 yards to the farther edge of the plateau. Thence they looked down on Morval. To the right of Ginchy the English troops had been no less successful. They had seized over 1,000 yards of trenches from a point just south of the Guillemont-Morval tramway to the south-west corner of Bouleaux Wood. Over 500 prisoners were taken on that and the succeeding days, and

A SHELL-HOLE AS COVER FOR A FIELD-GUN.

COLLECTING THE WOUNDED NEAR GINCHY AFTER THE BATTLE.

the total of prisoners captured since July 1 was raised to over 17,000. The French, who on Saturday carried a small wood and part of a trench east of Belloy, made fresh progress east of Deniécourt, and repulsed an attack north of Berny. Since September 3 in the region south of the Somme they had secured 7,600 German privates and some 100 officers.

As a result of the efforts of Sir Henry Rawlinson's Army, and particularly of the Irish troops from Connaught, Leinster and Munster, of the Rifle Regiments and the regiments from Warwickshire, Kent, Devonshire, Gloucestershire, Surrey, Cornwall, and from Wales and Scotland, the British line, from September 3 to September 9 had been pushed forward on a front of 6,000 yards to a depth varying from 300 to 3,000 yards. The enemy had lost all his observation posts on the main ridge with the exception of those in High Wood and north and north-east of Ginchy. He was being forced more and more to rely on reports from aeroplanes and captive balloons for the direction of his still very powerful artillery. We, on the other hand, had now a clear view of

Courcelette, Martinpuich, Flers, Lesboeufs, Morval and Combles, the knots as it were in the next chain of defences between the British and the Bapaume-Péronne highway. By our victorious offensive through Ginchy and the Leuze Wood we dominated Combles and, consequently, were in a position materially to assist the left of General Fayolle in its projected advance on both sides of the Bapaume-Péronne road towards Sailly-Sallisel. From the eastern edge of the wood of Leuze to that important highway was but a distance of two miles and a half, and batteries established in the wood would be able to enfilade the German guns in the Bois St. Pierre Vaast seeking to impede the movement of Fayolle on Sailly-Sallisel, while from Ginchy a direct thrust at the last named village-fortress might be made through Morval by Sir Henry Rawlinson. Gradually the enemy was being pushed into the low-lying ground in the apex of the triangle Albert-Bapaume-Péronne, the western side of which was formed by the Amiens-Cambrai, the eastern by the Ham-Arras chaussée. The base of the triangle, almost to the gates of Péronne, was already in the possession of the Allies, and they were on the ridge above Martinpuich half-way up the western side.

Perceiving the imminent danger he was running of having his main line of communication with Péronne cut by Sir Henry Rawlin-

[Official photograph.

PREPARATIONS FOR REMOVING A CAPTURED HOWITZER.

son's troops debouching through Ginchy, the enemy, about noon on Sunday, September 10, attacked north of the village and was bloodily repulsed. A second attempt later in the day was equally unsuccessful. Small detachments of German infantry made ineffectual efforts to recover the trenches lost near Mouquet Farm in the vicinity of Pozières. Over 350 more prisoners and 3 machine-guns captured during the last 24 hours were brought in by our men.

While General Baron von Marschall and General von Kirchbach were vainly striving to relax the grip of the British on the ridges between Thiépval and Combles, south of the Somme, General von Quast during the night of September 9–10 launched several attacks in the sector Barleux-Belloy. The *flammenwerfer* were once more employed, and the enemy managed to enter one of the French trenches. He was speedily ejected by a vigorous counter-attack, and four of his machine-guns were captured. To the south-west of Berny, to the east of Deniécourt, and to the south of Vermandovillers, German bombers advanced against the French lines, which had been previously subjected to severe shelling. Fierce hand-to-hand struggles ensued. Finally the Germans were thrown back all along the front, leaving behind a large number of dead. On Sunday, the 10th, two more attacks were made south-west of Berny.

Both failed completely. During the night of the 10th–11th the enemy, undeterred by his heavy losses, delivered a series of charges south of the Somme. From Berny to the region Chaulnes-Chilly, no less than five attacks, in which the bombers were accompanied by bearers of *flammenwerfer*, were made. The French artillery and mitrailleuses scattered and thinned the advancing masses, the survivors of whom sullenly retreated to their own trenches. Meanwhile the French airmen had not been inactive. On the preceding Saturday, Adjutant Dorme had brought down his ninth aeroplane, which fell at Beaulencourt, south of Bapaume. Four other German machines were damaged—one in the region of La Maisonnette, the others to the north and east of Péronne. On Saturday night a squadron dropped 480 bombs on the stations and enemy depôts in the region of Chauny, south-east of Ham, an important point on the railway in the Oise Valley, and another squadron of 18 machines bombed military establishments at Ham on the Somme and between Ham and Péronne.

On Monday, September 11, the ascent of 16 German balloons north of Ginchy gave visible evidence that the Germans were no longer able to direct their guns from posts on the ground at this point. The day passed almost uneventfully save for the furious artillery duels. Our heavy guns caused two large conflagrations in

A WAGON IN DIFFICULTIES.

an ammunition depôt at Grandcourt on the Ancre, north-east of Thiépval. During the night our trenches between Mouquet Farm and Delville Wood were heavily shelled. The battle-field round Guillemont and Ginchy was a gruesome sight. German corpses lay thickly

MR. LLOYD GEORGE AT THE FRONT,   *[Official photograph.*
With (from left to right) M. Thomas, Sir Douglas Haig and General Joffre.

about the roads and craters. In one place straight rows of dead men clad in " field-grey " showed where a massed counter-attack had been caught by our machine-guns. The twisted iron frame of a goods wagon, the foundations of the railway station, and the concrete base of an observation post were now the sole indications that Guillemont had ever existed. South of the Somme the French with grenades beat off a German attack east of Belloy, and our Allies captured an enemy trench south of the cemetery of Berny.

The British having had time to consolidate their positions from Ginchy to Leuze Wood, from which positions they menaced Morval and Combles, General Fayolle decided to advance his left wing between Combles and the Somme.

On Tuesday, September 12, while Mr. Lloyd

FRESH PRISONERS ARRIVING AT A "CAGE."   [Official photograph.

George was visiting the rear of the British salient, and desultory fighting was proceeding in High Wood and east of Ginchy, the turning movement which was designed to sever Combles from Sailly-Sallisel and to place the French astride of the Péronne-Bapaume road began. It was preceded by a terrific two days' bombardment of the enemy's lines, west and east of the road. These consisted of a belt of entrenchments descending from Morval to the banks of the Somme. Behind them on the road the villages of Rancourt, due east of Combles, and Bouchavesnes, due east of Maurepas, had been organized for defence with characteristic German thoroughness. Rancourt was just in front of the large wood of St. Pierre Vaast. On the country road from Combles to Rancourt, the farm of Le Priez had been converted into a small subterranean fortress. Between Clery-sur-Somme and Péronne was the Canal du Nord, which, after crossing the Bapaume-Péronne road north of Mont St. Quentin, entered the river at Halle. Parallel with, close to, and east of the canal flowed the Tortille, a little tributary of the Somme.

On the morning of the 12th the French were on the western slopes of the little plateau, the summit of which was 76 metres high, and at whose eastern foot ran the Canal du Nord. Thence their line ascended just west of the long patch of woodland known as the Bois de Marrières, and curved north-westwards to the Bois d'Anderlu and the southern outskirts of Combles. The front from which the advance started, when at 12.30 p.m. the guns lifted, was nearly four miles long. So admirably had the French artillery done its work that within half an hour the whole of the enemy's battered, crater-pitted trenches were in the possession of our Allies. On the left the infantry debouching from the wood of Anderlu passed round the Priez Farm and reached a little chapel 600 yards or so in front of Rancourt. Simultaneously the troops on Hill 111 mounted the western slopes of the plateau between them and the Bapaume-Péronne road and seized the summit of Hill 145. The Germans rallied behind a ruined windmill west of the road. Meanwhile the troops who had traversed the wood of Marrières, which they did not do till 4.30 p.m., the garrison there putting up a plucky fight, came up on the right, and the French guns placed a barrage east of the high road and prevented reinforcements coming up to the aid of the broken enemy. To check the oncoming French, masses of Germans charged out of

Combles and Frégicourt. Another barrage of shells stopped this flank attack. After several hours of stubborn fighting the Bapaume-Péronne road was gained. The French seized houses at the southern end of Rancourt, and deployed along the road as far as Brioche, south-west of Bouchavesnes. The hamlet of Brioche was carried, and, pivoting on it, the remainder of the French forces advanced eastwards, the troops from the Clery region capturing the plateau of Hill 76, and saw below them the Canal du Nord and beyond it the Péronne-Bapaume highway. Not content with these successes and with the capture of 1,500 prisoners including numbers of officers, towards 8 p.m. the French crossed the highway and assaulted Bouchavesnes. After two hours of severe hand-to-hand fighting the ruins of the village were seized. The troops concerned in this brilliant little episode were the 6th Brigade of Chasseurs (comprising the 6th and 27th Chasseurs and the 28th Alpine Chasseurs), a battalion of the 44th and one of the 133rd Infantry. During the night some units of a division which had been rushed up from the Verdun district were hurled at the Hill 76 plateau. Mont St. Quentin, menaced by the French in Bouchavesnes, would be in great danger if the plateau was not recovered. Time after time the German columns crossed the canal and swarmed up the eastern slopes only to be driven back in hopeless confusion.

At daybreak on Wednesday, September 13, the French resumed the offensive up the road from Bouchavesnes to the village of Haut-Allaines, north-east of Mont St. Quentin. They stormed the German positions on the western slopes of the plateau of Hill 130 and the farm of the Bois l'Abbé, which was half a mile east of the Bapaume-Péronne road. At the same time, in the direction of Combles, they cleared the Germans from the six successive trenches round the Le Priez Farm, which itself was carried on the 14th. In the two days' fighting over 2,500 prisoners had been taken, and in Bouchavesnes alone 10 pieces, several of them heavy guns, and 40 machine-guns.

Enraged at their defeat the German leaders counter-attacked throughout the 13th. Two regiments were sent against the Farm of Bois l'Abbé. The defenders at first gave way, but the chasseurs with irresistible *élan* swept the enemy from the wrecked building. Hill 76 was

also the scene of stubborn encounters. For hours the fighting went on, but at last the plateau remained in French hands. South of the Somme on the same day, in the hope of retrieving his signal defeat north of the river, the enemy advanced again and again at various points. He was everywhere repulsed, a company west of Chaulnes being wiped out by the French fire.

It will be seen that the battles of September 9, 12, and 13 had materially improved the Allied chances of breaking right

GENERAL BARON VON MARSCHALL,
One of the German Commanders on the Somme.

through the German lines north of the Somme. Combles was now under the fire of the British from the west and north-west, and under that of the French from the south and south-east. A section of the Bapaume-Péronne road was firmly held by our Allies, and Mont St. Quentin could be attacked from the north and north-east as well as from the west. Mont St. Quentin, 350 feet high, was, indeed, protected by the Tortille on the north and the Somme on the south-west, but it would be difficult henceforth for the Germans to send supplies of ammunition and guns to its defenders, for most of the roads

The progress towards Thiépval had already been considerable, but between us and that village there lay an intricate organization of trenches, produced by the strenuous exertions of the past two years. The key of this position, an elaborate stronghold embodying the highest examples of the engineer's art, was the central kernel known to the Germans as the *Wunderwerk* behind the Hohenzollern Trench and 600 yards in front of Thiépval. It was placed on the spur which runs south-eastwards from Thiépval towards Authuille, and dominated to a considerable extent the surrounding

THE COMMANDANT PERSONALLY INSPECTS THE DEFENCES.

leading to the hill were under the direct fire of French batteries. Nor had the Germans anywhere between the Ancre and Chilly gained counter-balancing successes. During the night of the 12th-13th they had been repulsed near Mouquet Farm, and on the 13th the British had pushed ahead north of Ginchy. On the 14th there was a lull—the lull which precedes the storm—on the British front, and the French beat off attacks north and south of Bouchavesnes, and south of the Somme advanced by bombing east of Belloy. The situation was decidedly promising for the Allies.

country. The main value of this fortification, beyond its intrinsic strength, was the fact that from it the Germans could sweep the ground to "Sky Line" trench and Mouquet Farm. It was plain, therefore. that before any advance could be made by the British up the valleys on either side of the spur it was necessary to capture it. Moreover, before our centre could move towards Courcelette and Martinpuich the Germans had to be expelled from these advanced posts, whence our troops moving to the assault of the Courcelette sector could be struck in flank.

The *Wunderwerk* itself had formed the target

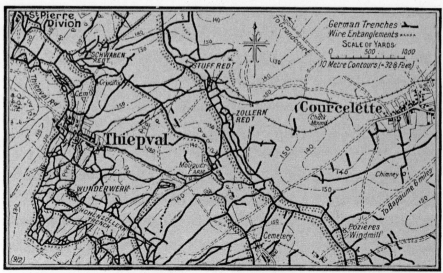

PLAN OF THE "WUNDERWERK" AND ADJOINING GERMAN TRENCHES.

of our artillery for the previous fortnight with the usual result. So far as concerned the works above ground, it had been beaten and blown out of existence and many of the dug-outs had been destroyed or seriously damaged. Yet some still remained which afforded shelter to many of the garrison, and in the trenches before and around it which had escaped to some extent the devastating fire of our guns, the enemy was hanging on in some strength, and it was recognized that the Germans rightly attached great importance to this part of their line. It was part of Sir Hubert Gough's task to capture it, and it was determined that the operation was to be carried out on the evening of September 14.

Before our infantry advanced to the assault the usual tornado of projectiles swept over the doomed spot. Suddenly our artillery increased their range and formed a barrage behind the *Wunderwerk* to keep back the enemy's supports. The effect of this, combined with the havoc wrought on the actual position, had a double effect. The remains of the unhappy garrison had seen their comrades falling all around them, and knew that their retreat could only be made through a veil of shell-fire. Many of them fled before the British infantry closed with them ; others remained to put up a really good hand-to-hand fight. It was not of long duration. Our men had come on swiftly and with determination, and soon cleared out their opponents and drove such of them as survived and did not surrender into the barrage which few lived to pass through. The German

casualties were very heavy, ours but a few, while the total advance we made was along a line of 900 yards and a depth of 350. The *Wunderwerk* and the trenches connected with it on the spur were in our hands and an advance on Mouquet Farm and Courcelette could now be proceeded with without fear of flank attack.

No sooner were our troops in the German position than they began to turn it into a stronghold for themselves. The nature of their task may be judged from the statement of a sapper. "The Germans," he said, "do not stay in their trenches any more. These are so badly blown up that we have to dig them anew." The enemy appreciated that they had been deprived of an important point which it was probable that we should endeavour to hold at any cost. Counter-attacks were, therefore, made, and although these did not actually take place till the next evening, as they had no practical relation to the fighting on the 15th they may here be disposed of. Endeavours to recover the lost ground were made twice by the Germans. One took the shape of a direct attempt to turn the British out of the captured position, but this failed completely ; indeed, it could scarcely be regarded as serious. The assailants came on in half-hearted fashion and made no effort to come to close quarters. Indeed, they contented themselves with a stationary and harmless bombing when quite a hundred yards from our newly occupied line. The only result was a numerous series of harmless explosions in front of the British trench which were totally devoid of effect on it

Against our left a more rational assault was delivered. Here the position was more favourable, for the German trench on the north-western side of the Thiépval slope lapped round the line we held and this somewhat outflanked it. Moreover, the distance between the two opposed lines was small, and the attacking troops were able to get well within bombing range from almost the first onset. The conflict lasted for some time and was severe. There does not seem to have been any actual collision between the hostile forces ; the fighting was conducted chiefly if not entirely with bombs, we alone using up 1,500. But eventu-

GENERAL VON KIRCHBACH,
One of the German Commanders on the Somme.

ally the enemy was driven back, and he then allowed us to consolidate the conquered position without further hindrance.

On Friday, September 15, both Allies had arranged for a further conjoint attack. Sir Douglas Haig had ordered Sir Hubert Gough's army, which formed the left wing of the British in the ensuing battle, and was now on high ground in the Thiépval salient with its left centre secured by the capture of the *Wunderwerk*, to act as a pivot to the 4th Army on its right commanded by Sir Henry Rawlinson. The latter was to direct his efforts to the rearmost of the enemy's original systems of defence between Le Sars on the Albert-Bapaume road and Morval. If he were successful, the left of

the attack would be extended to embrace the villages of Martinpuich and Courcelette. As soon as the advance had reached the Morval line, the left of the British would be brought across the Thiépval ridge in line with the Fourth Army.

To the right of the British, General Fayolle was to continue the line of advance from the slopes south and east of Combles to the Somme, directing his main efforts against the villages of Rancourt and Frégicourt, so as to complete the isolation of Combles and open a road for the attack on Sailly-Sallisel. By this time the whole of the forward crest of the main ridge from Mouquet Farm to the Delville Wood, a distance of 9,000 yards, was held by the British, giving them a clear view over the slopes beyond. East of Delville Wood to Leuze Wood, which is a thousand yards from Combles, we held a line of 3,000 yards, while farther east on the other side of the Combles Valley the French had, as previously narrated, successfully gained ground. The centre of our line was well placed, but on the British flanks there were still difficult positions to be won. Ginchy, which had been taken, is situated on the plateau running towards Lesboeufs and to the east of Ginchy the ground drops somewhat steeply towards Combles. North of Combles, but a little below the edge of the plateau, stood the village of Morval, commanding a wide field of fire in every direction. It was an obstacle to the French advance through Frégicourt on Sailly-Sallisel. From Leuze Wood the British right would have a distance of 2,000 yards to cross, passing over the valley which intervenes between the wood and Morval. Combles itself was strongly fortified and held by a large garrison and, although dominated from the Leuze Wood, and by the French left on the heights across the valley, still remained so serious an obstacle that it was best to avoid taking it by direct assault and to render it untenable by both armies pressing forward along the ridges on either side of it.

The direct capture of Morval from the south presented considerable difficulty, that of Sailly-Sallisel, which was about 3,000 yards to the north of the French left, was an even harder task, for the advance had to be made along a line flanked on one side by the strongly fortified wood of St. Pierre Vaast and over the Combles Valley, which was dominated by the German work on the high ground to the west.

It will be seen how necessary it was to have-

GENERAL FAYOLLE,
Commanded a French Army on the Somme.

close cooperation between the Allied armies to make the sufficient progress on the British right without which the advance of Sir Douglas Haig's centre was impossible. At the time when this operation commenced the Fifth Army followed a line back some distance from Mouquet Farm down the spur which went between Pozières, and then, crossing the intervening valley, mounted the Thiépval ridge to the *Wunderwerk*, which we had captured on the evening of September 14. It will be seen what an important point of support this formed for any further advance against Thiépval. In this direction General Gough had since July 3 been making methodical progress in which great skill and patience had been displayed, and had considerably improved his position. For the moment it was not an essential part of the plan of operations to capture Thiépval itself by a sudden rush, which would only have

GENERAL MICHELER,
Commanded a new French Army south of the
Somme.

Hardécourt across the Somme by Dompierre,
and Fay, to the east of Lihons and west of
Chilly. Since July 1 General Fayolle had
made a considerable inroad into the German
fortified belt north and south of the Somme.
The French, as related, had taken Maurepas
and reached the southern outskirts of Combles
and were also at Priez Farm, across the country
road which ran from Combles to Rancourt,
which was on the summit of the plateau overlooking the narrow valley at the northern end
of which was Combles. South of Rancourt
our Allies had severed the main road running
between Péronne and Bapaume by occupying
Bouchavesnes. Along the right bank of the
Somme the French had pushed their way
through Curlu and Clery-sur-Somme until
they were within a few thousand yards of
Mont St. Quentin, which is close to Péronne on
the south side of the Tortille.

Sir Henry Rawlinson, after clearing the
Bouleaux Wood—the northern end of the
wood of Leuze—was to push on towards
Morval, while the French from Priez Farm
would advance on Frégicourt, the fortified
hamlet between Combles and Rancourt. South
of Frégicourt was a collection of trenches
which had to be carried, and to the west of
this point a trench ran north-westwards and
joined the southern defences of Morval. From
this trench another behind Frégicourt went
westwards to Combles station. Combles was
a strongly fortified point possessing vast
underground caverns extending under the
village over an area of nearly 400 yards.

Rancourt, a straggling village traversed by
the Bapaume-Péronne highway, was defended
on the south by a network of trenches, on the
west by the works at Frégicourt and on the

been successful at the price of heavy casualties.
An advance in the direction of Courcelette
would indirectly threaten the Germans on the
high ground in the neighbourhood of Thiépval
and render the capture of this village easier.

What direction was the French Army to
take to connect with the British forward
movement and facilitate the advance towards
Bapaume ? Plainly it was desirable, after
Rancourt and Frégicourt had been won, to
capture the wood of St. Pierre Vaast and to
gain the height on which Sailly-Sallisel was
situated.

At the beginning of the Battle of the Somme
the French line extended from a point near

**TRENCH CUT THROUGH A
RUINED VILLAGE.**

east by the wood of St. Pierre Vaast, through which was cut a road from Rancourt to Manancourt, and Etricourt. The wood of St. Pierre Vaast and the Vaux Wood to the east of it had been treated by the German engineers in the same way as the woods of Mametz, Trônes and Delville. Entrenched on several lines, entangled with barbed wire, freely provided with communications, they formed together a most formidable defence, with the village of Manancourt in support. At the northern edge of the wood, close to Sallisel and Sailly-Sallisel, the ground was almost on a level with the highest point north of Ginchy. Beyond Sailly-Sallisel the ridge rapidly descended towards Bapaume. Between Rancourt and Sailly-Sallisel a German trench crossed the high-road

Taking the foregoing into consideration and looking at the map, it will be seen that if the French secured Frégicourt they had turned both Combles and the St. Vaast Wood and thus facilitated the acquisition of the defensive group formed by the two woods and the village of Manancourt. Once this was gained, with the ridge line in the Allies' possession, they would have before them the more gentle slopes descending to the north.

South of the Somme, while the British and General Fayolle were making their advance north of the river, General Micheler was to advance between Barleux and a point south

of Vermandovillers, a front of between 7 and 8 miles. Here the French had to deal with a strong line of German defences based upon the fortified villages of Barleux, Berny, Deniécourt, Soyécourt, and Vermandovillers. Of these Soyécourt had already been captured, but the remainder still formed an unbroken chain of strong posts. Deniécourt was of special value to the Germans. It consisted of the village of that name, together with the country house and park belonging to the Comte de Kergorlay. The house itself had long been reduced to ruins, but these had been utilized to form a most formidable keep with the park defences to the German position in this part of their line. Barleux stood at the bottom of a narrow valley dominated by high ground, of which the French held the northern and western sides. The French trenches then ran across flat ground for a mile and a half and crossed the Barleux road at Berny-en-Santerre. The retrenchment formed by this latter village in the German position had, so far as its outer edge was concerned, been occupied by French troops since the early days of September, but they had not been able to penetrate beyond a little park at the east end of the village.

Berny-en-Santerre was a point of considerable tactical interest to the Germans. Placed at the entrance of a long, narrow valley, which ran for a distance of 3 miles to the Somme

THE FIGHT IN THE CEMETERY AT CURLU.

north of Briost, it completely commanded it. The valley cut across the German lines, which were here almost parallel with the Somme. If the French could occupy Berny-en-Santerre and the valley they would cut the German position in two A mile farther to the west was Deniécourt, already described, and three-quarters of a mile beyond it Soyécourt. The village of Vermandovillers stood in the re-entering angle of the French front.

The front of battle from Thiépval to Chilly, measuring 20 miles as the crow flies and about 25 along the actual trench front, may be looked upon as divided into three sections. One of these was south of the Somme from Barleux to Chilly, and it was here that General Micheler commanded what may be regarded as the right flank of the operations. The troops of General Fayolle extended the French line from Barleux across the Somme at Omiécourt and thence to the wood of Douage, where it joined on to the British forces.

The history of the operations hitherto given shows that these three groups—the British, Fayolle and Micheler—had not attacked simultaneously, but that each in accordance with the plan laid down by the supreme commanders had operated to some extent independently—one at a time, each having its own special objectives. On the 15th, however,

this was changed. for the whole force of the Allies moved forward at the same time from the line Thiépval to Vermandovillers in a combined endeavour to thrust the enemy back over the whole front of attack.

The fighting described in this chapter represented considerable gain of ground, with the noteworthy feature that there was a distinct falling off in the resisting power of the Germans. This was shown not only by the increasing number of unwounded prisoners, but also by the fact that our successes were obtained with diminished losses, proving clearly that the enemy's power of continued contest was not what it had been.

A force which feels it is being beaten is apt to have recourse to means very often futile, but which it fondly hopes may have some useful effect. Such was the case with the Germans. To hide bombs just before abandoning trenches which go off when trodden on may cause a few casualties, but can produce no useful military results. Still less justifiable is the employment of the old-fashioned man-trap, probably known to some of our readers as an object of curiosity in a museum. This enlarged rat-trap will break the leg of a soldier who manages to get caught in it, but such dastardly devices as these bring in time their own revenge. They infuriate the men who see these atrocities, and they punish them.

[*Official photograph.*

ONCE A DWELLING, NOW A STABLE.

CHAPTER CLXXV.

THE BATTLE OF THE SOMME (V.).

ON the morning of September 15, 1916, the British troops attacked the Germans along the line extending from Bouleaux Wood, between Guillemont and Combles, to the north of the Albert-Bapaume road—*i.e.*, a distance of some six miles.

The ground over which the fighting took place was generally undulating on the south side of the watershed extending from Bouleaux Wood through Delville Wood and High Wood to Thiepval. To the east of Bouleaux Wood the ground sloped down with some sharpness to the valley in which was Combles. This valley divides into two horns, one going north-west and upwards to the west of Morval, the other north-east rising up to Sailly-Saillisel. Morval was on a prolongation of the Delville Wood-Ginchy ridge and somewhat below it. North of the main backbone the ground sloped down more gently. The villages which dotted the battlefield were strongly defended and had been largely sheltered from view by trees till the British bombardment swept these away and pounded the villages themselves into mere masses of ruins. Still the trenches round them afforded some cover, and although any protection near the surface had been largely destroyed, sufficient was left, combined with the deeper dug-outs, to shelter the garrisons until they had to resist the near approach of the British troops.

Everywhere the attack was successful; the first and second German lines were captured

and, along a good part of their position, even the third line was pierced. The depth of the British in-burst, varying in places, measured on an average from one to two miles, and included Courcelette, Martinpuich, High Wood, Flers, and a large portion of Bouleaux Wood. Thus the British now stood on the high ground extending through Bouleaux Wood and Martinpuich, nearly to Thiepval. Many, too were the trophies gained. Prisoners to the number of over 2,300 were gathered in, including 65 officers, of whom no less than six were battalion commanders, a sure proof that the enemy had been taken, or had surrendered, in large units.

The bombardment of the German position had been going on since early morning on September 12, and had become highly intense before the infantry were launched to the assault at 6.20 a.m. It was a remarkable achievement even for the British artillery, which had done so much good and efficient work since it had been adequately equipped. The duties of every heavy battery had been most carefully and exactly worked out, its targets were defined and it knew when to switch off one and switch on to another. It understood when a barrage was to be carried out and what points behind the enemy's line were to be expressly dealt with.

The field batteries acted with a brave audacity worthy of the highest praise, taking up position after position nearer to the enemy as the latter was pressed back. The forward observing officers pushed up to the high ground as soon

Fig. 1. FRENCH ARMOURED CAR WITH MACHINE GUN.

as the infantry captured it, and so were able to telephone back the directions in which fire was wanted, and to pass back corrections in range and direction when needed.* The fire of our guns of every kind was arranged with a mathematical precision marvellous in itself, yet necessary, to get the full effect from

* The Forward Observing Officer is an officer who from an advanced position notes the fall of the shells from his battery and telephones back to it, so that the Battery Commander may know how to correct the aim of his guns.

modern weapons. The enemy's artillery was still strong and well worked, but it was not so powerful as ours, which was soon able to dominate it.

Before discussing the fighting in detail it is necessary to describe the famous "Tanks," which on September 15 made their first appearance on the field of battle.

An armoured train had been proved useful at Alexandria, in 1882, and others had been

Fig. 2. BELGIAN ARMOURED CAR WITH MACHINE GUN.

employed in the South African War, producing,
however, no particular effect. They were only
improvised arrangements of no great tactical
value, being entirely limited to the railways.
A car which could move over ordinary ground
had to await the arrival of the internal com
bustion engine before it could be made in any
way successful.* Nor had the first protected
automobiles been capable of producing much
influence on battle tactics, though they were
of some utility as supports to reconnoitring
cavalry, or advanced guard infantry, or for
reconnaissances on their own account. The
reason for this was that they were just ordinary
motor-cars, more or less protected by steel

gives the Rolls-Royce armoured car used in
Egypt with such good results in the expedition
against the Senussi.*

It will easily be seen how liable all these types
were to injury of their wheels, the shielding
of which was very imperfect. Moreover, the
engines and air coolers were not well protected.

The designers of the Tanks worked on different
lines entirely. In them the whole of the motor
machinery was securely housed inside the car
itself. The latter did not run on wheels, but
on the two side caterpillar constructions
which, revolving, drew the car forward. A
glance at Fig 6 will show how much safer
and better this method was. Moreover, the

Fig. 3. BELGIAN ARMOURED CAR WITH QUICK-FIRER.

shields fixed to them. Types of these are shown
in figs. 1, 2 and 3. Fig. 1 shows the French
type of armoured car with machine gun.
These did good work for the French Army.
Fig. 2 is a type made use of by the Belgian
Army with a machine gun. Fig. 3 is another
Belgian type with a quick-firer. Fig. 4 is an
armoured car, the quick-firer of which could
be used as an anti-aircraft weapon. Fig. 5

wedge-like shape of the front part of the car
made it possible to drive through or over
obstacles which an ordinary car could not
traverse, as its hood would be doubled up;
while the longer caterpillar sides formed as it
were a movable girder, which enabled the Tank
to pass over ditches and trenches. For if the
point but reached the other side the caterpillars
could claw it forward. The Tank also had a far
superior armament to that of any ordinary
armoured car, which can take but one or two
machine guns or small quick-firers at the most.

* In 1860 a steam-driven armoured car was brought to
the attention of Napoleon III. It was armed with two
guns and furnished with revolving scythes which were
intended to mow down any of the enemy's infantry which
might attempt to close with it. Nothing came of the
suggestion.

* See Vol. IX., Chapter CXLV.

Several weapons of either or both of these classes could be carried in the Tank, while there was no comparison between the security it afforded its crew and that given to the ordinary armoured cars. No armoured motor-car could charge a brick wall without damage, and even passing over a wire entanglement would be dangerous. But experience soon showed that the Tank could deal with quite considerable obstructions. Its special form enabled it to overcome opposition and pass through or over many obstacles which would be quite unnegotiable by the ordinary motor-car, ar-

these monstrous engines, and it is urgent to take whatever measures are possible to counteract them."

The correspondent of the *Düsseldorfer General-anzeiger* said that, as the Germans saw the monsters coming on through the mist at the moment when some cessation of the bombardment allowed them to emerge from their shelters, " their blood froze in their veins " :

Stupefied by the earthquake which had raged around them they all rubbed their eyes, which were riveted as if deprived of sense on the two fabulous creatures. The imagination, flogged by the storm of fire, was full of excitement, and no wonder it had the mastery over these

Fig. 4. ARMOURED MOTOR-CAR WITH ANTI-AIRCRAFT QUICK-FIRER.

moured or unarmoured. To render it as indistinguishable as possible, it was painted in a curious medley of browns, greens and yellows, which harmonized with the broken ground over which it had to pass. We shall see in the description of the fight on September 15 and following days that these novel engines of war played an important part.

They certainly proved an objectionable surprise to the Germans. The chief of the Staff of the Third Group of German Armies said : " The enemy in the latest fighting has employed new engines of war as cruel as they are effective. No doubt he will adopt on an extensive scale

men, tried by suffering, who were well aware that the enemy would push with all the means of destruction through a wall hard as steel, though made of frail human bodies. They have learnt not to fear men, but there was something approaching which the human brain, with tremendous mechanical powers, had fitted out for a devil's trick, a mystery which oppressed and shackled the powers, because one could not comprehend it with the understanding—a fatality against which one seemed helpless. One stared and stared as if paralysed.

The monster approached slowly, hobbling. moving from side to side, rocking and pitching, but it came nearer. Nothing obstructed it ; a supernatural force seemed to drive it onwards. Someone in the trenches cried " the devil comes," and that word ran down the line like lightning. Suddenly tongues of fire licked out of the armoured hide of the iron caterpillar, shells whistled over our heads, and a terrible concert of machine-gun orchestra filled the air. The mysterious creature

Fig. 5. ROLLS-ROYCE ARMOURED CAR
As used in Egypt.

had surrendered its secret, and sense returned with it, and toughness and defiance, as the English waves of infantry surged up behind the devil's chariot.

Describing the participation of two of these "land Dreadnoughts" at Flers on September 16 the correspondent said :

Our machine-gun fire and hand grenades rattled ineffectively on their iron hide. As our rear connexions

Fig. 6. A BRITISH "TANK" IN ACTION CROSSING A SHELL-CRATER.

STAR · SHELLS IN THE EARLY MORNING OF SEPTEMBER 15.

were cut, the artillery could not be summoned to help against the mass fire of these iron towers, as they easily destroyed what remained of the garrisons of the advanced shell holes. They then advanced over the first German line away into Flers village, remaining there some time. When the English infantry had arrived and occupied the village they proceeded further on the Ligny-Thilloy road. Meanwhile, as their appearance became known in other rear positions, well-placed shots made an end of their triumphal march behind the village.

But although one Tank seems to have been disabled, the Germans did not succeed in capturing any of them. The Tanks, for their part, brought in many German prisoners, usually following submissively behind, or, as in the case of a few officers, inside.

It is plain that the moral effect of the new weapons was great, and it will be seen from the narrative which follows that tactical gains were very considerable. Officially called His Majesty's Land-Ships, each of them had a name given it by its crew; two which were attached to the New Zealanders on September 15 were known as "Cordon Rouge" and "Crême-de-menthe."

September 15 was fine, but the morning mist still clung to the ground and somewhat obscured the movements of the infantry. The huge projectiles from the big guns and heavy howitzers

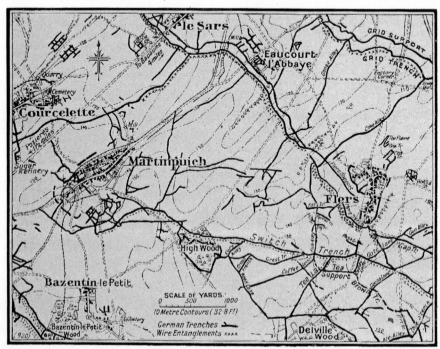

THE CAPTURE OF COURCELETTE AND FLERS.

boomed over the heads of our men in the front line and burst with terrific explosions on their target, destroying the front line of German trenches. At first the enemy did not appreciate that an assault was imminent, probably because the British artillery had expended so much ammunition on the German position as to keep the majority of its garrison lying close for shelter, and thus the sudden intense fire was regarded as a mere incident in the artillery duel and not as a prologue to the coming infantry assault. The Germans, too, in the days immediately preceding the attack, had been distributing a considerable amount of shell fire

and made a rush at the trenches where part of the Canadians were assembled; coming suddenly out of the mist which concealed their approach, they flung their bombs into the trench and, following on, succeeded in entering it. The success was but a short one. It was the hour fixed for the British advance and forward accordingly went our men, sweeping the Germans back before them. This was the only incident before our attack began, and it had no effect whatever on the arrangements.

The left of our attack executed by one Army Corps was engaged with the German positions from Thiepval down towards the Stufen (called

[*Canadian War Records.*

CANADIANS FIRING A HEAVY HOWITZER.

against their opponents' position, and are said to have had over 1,000 guns in action against us. But we had more, and our artillery had distinctly gained the upper hand before our infantry went over the front trench parapet at 6.20 a.m.

There is some reason to believe that the Germans were planning an attack at the same time as we were, for the number of men in their position was larger than usual, although this may also have been due to the reliefs arriving and being there with the outgoing garrison before the latter had left. Still it is certain that shortly before our advance began a German force covered by bombers crossed No Man's Land

by us the Stuff) Redoubt; beyond it the Canadians directed their efforts against Courcelette. Beyond these again the remainder of General Gough's command was aimed at High Wood and Martinpuich.

On the right of the Fifth Army was the Fourth Army under Sir Henry Rawlinson. The village of Flers was the objective of the left of this force. Against it were engaged the left of Rawlinson's men, one Corps going for Flers, and the New Zealanders pushing forward to the west of the village.

The length of the right portion of this attack was about 2,500 yards, and extended from the east side of Delville Wood to some distance

THE SEAFORTHS HOLDING A FRONT-LINE TRENCH OPPOSITE MARTINPUICH.

east of Flers. Beyond this was the remainder of the Fourth Army connecting with the French.

The German position to be attacked formed a treble line of works well strung together by connecting trenches amply provided with bomb-proof shelters and covered by a very strong wire entanglement. A fourth formidable line had also been recently constructed in front of Le Transloy, facing almost west and covering the road from that important village to Bapaume. In advance of the first line were several advanced works with the usual machine-gun emplacements, which allowed a powerful flanking fire to be brought on any troops who endeavoured to pass between them. It was necessary to silence these before an attack could make progress.

One of them was the so-called " Mystery Corner " at the eastern end of Delville Wood, which at this time was still in German hands, though most of the rest of the wood had been for some time in our possession. It was a formidable redoubt, well provided with machine-guns which would enfilade any British attack moving northward across its line of fire. Moreover, it protected two lines of communication trenches which went back from this point towards the great length of trench known as the Switch Trench, which ran from the

neighbourhood of High Wood to the south of and past Flers, towards the east. It was plainly necessary, therefore, to storm this redoubt and turn the enemy out of the connecting trenches before the main advance could be pushed forward towards Flers.

Somewhat before the time fixed for the assault, when the half light of commencing dawn had scarcely appeared, two detachments, about a section each, crept swiftly and quietly forward. One tackled the redoubt, the other the communicating trenches. The assailants of the former were over its parapets and in the midst of the garrison before the latter could get their machine-guns into action. A short, sharp combat sufficed to settle the question of possession—the redoubt was ours, and with it some 50 prisoners and its armament of machine guns.

The other detachment was accompanied by two Tanks, and supported by them went for the two communication trenches. But little opposition was met with, for here our artillery had been able to enfilade the hostile defences, and they found them almost filled up with dead and dying, the result of the recent bombardment. Now the way was clear for the main advance.

The first thing to be done was to capture the

Switch trench. But in advance of it there were two other trenches, roughly parallel to it, known as the Brown Trench and Tea Support Trench, while more to the east, and behind the Switch, was the Gap Trench, which connected up with the trench running from the front of Lesboeufs, past Gueudecourt to the Grid Trench $1\frac{1}{2}$ miles to the rear.* In addition to these more elaborate works there were many shell-craters organized for defence, many little projections from the innumerable connexion trenches in which machine-guns and riflemen were nested. The position was, indeed, a powerful one, and had it not been thoroughly searched out by our artillery fire would have been impregnable to an infantry attack. Fortunately our guns had dealt with it thoroughly, and those who were about to assault it were first-rate fighting men.

The men told off went over the parapet in a succession of waves, and in advancing went by the two detachments which had taken the redoubt and communication trenches, and were now resting after their labours. These,

* The reader will do well to refer to the coloured maps of the battle area which form the frontispieces of Vols. IX. and X.

although their task was done, and all their officers wounded, declined to be left behind, and acted as a connecting link between two units of the attack, which became a little separated as the advance went on. The troops concerned in the direct attack on Flers and to the right of it were chiefly Londoners who had not had much previous experience, but they bore themselves that day as well as any war-seasoned troops. They showed their readiness in the intricate fight both in trench storming and the more individual work of hunting the Germans out of the village. The Switch Trench was quickly entered by the first two waves of men, who then proceeded to round up the few—very few—living Germans, the majority having been killed by the British artillery fire.

Leaving the front line of men to hold the newly won ground, the officer in command sent the supports forward against Flers. Forcing their way over shell craters under machine-gun and shrapnel fire, they reached the outer line of the village defences. Here they were held up, for the German trench was covered by a strong wire entanglement. It was a job for a Tank, and one arrived to do the business. Coming

AWAITING THE ORDER TO ADVANCE.

up in its own fashion with a deadly persistence, it passed over shell craters, reached the wire, and then proceeded to iron out flat a sufficient length of the obstacle to give the infantry room to advance, meanwhile bringing a deadly flanking fire to bear on the defenders of the German trench. Once the way was clear, our foot soldiers moved forward once more, and Flers was taken with a rush. There was really very little resistance, and the position does not appear to have been held with any determination. Perhaps the garrison had fled before the terrifying monster which proceeded up the main street amid the cheers of our men, as calmly as an omnibus up Oxford Street. Two counter-attacks were made about three and four in the afternoon; both were stopped without difficulty by machine-gun fire.

On the right of this portion of Sir Henry Rawlinson's army, the fight at this time was of a tentative nature.

The New Zealanders took a considerable part in the battle of the 15th. The position against which they advanced lay between Flers and High Wood, on the high ground at the top of the plateau. Their flanks were protected by the British troops attacking

Flers and on their left. The assault was furnished by the men of Auckland, Canterbury, Otago, and Wellington, and their main objective was the German trench 500 yards ahead of the British line. Our men advanced in a series of waves with distances between them, and they suffered on the upward move from both shrapnel and machine-gun fire. But nothing could stop them, and they burst into the German trench. A prolonged and desperate close-quarter fight ensued, in which scarcely any other weapon was used than the bayonet. It was a terrible combat of comparative silence, in which little was to be heard except the clash of steel and the half-smothered cries of the wounded. But eventually the garrison were completely conquered; few, indeed, escaped with their lives. A slight pause was made there, and then the advance began again, a distance of 800 yards to the second German position, consisting of two lines of trenches covered by deep wire entanglements.

This time the New Zealand Rifles led the assault, moving in open order, yet keeping touch and their alignment. The enemy's defences had been considerably damaged by

[*Official photograph.*]

WOUNDED GUARDSMEN NOWISE DOWNHEARTED.

[*Official photograph.*

THE CANADIANS ADVANCING TO THE CHARGE.

our artillery fire, but several machine-gun emplacements were still in working order, and much of the wire obstacle was still effective. The New Zealanders suffered heavily, but stuck to their task, in which they were soon aided by a powerful auxiliary. Two Tanks, which had been somewhat delayed in their progress over the shell-pitted ground, now came up and proceeded with characteristic deliberation to flatten out the wire for the infantry to pass, then getting astride the German trench and beating out the machine-guns and their detachments by their fire. In vain the Germans bombed them and covered them with rifle fire; they carried out their task. A German battery 1,500 yards off brought its fire to bear on them, but obtained no direct hits, and was itself soon reduced to silence by British guns. Then the infantry came on and drove back the rest of the German garrison. The New Zealanders went on still farther, accompanied by one of the Tanks. They succeeded, indeed, in progressing beyond the troops at Flers and on their left flank, in both of which directions the fighting had been stiffer, and their fire swept down the shallow gulley which points north-east 1,500 yards west of Flérs.

The projecting salient they made threatened the lines of the enemy from either flank. The Germans naturally made a strong counter-attack, and the New Zealanders were drawn back to a straighter line which ran westward from the north end of Flers village, and there they held their ground.

A more desperate counter-attack was delivered by the enemy in the afternoon in conjunction with a similar effort against Flers

already mentioned. It was equally unsuccessful; but in this case it was not fire only which stopped the Germans. The downward slope of the ground appears to have afforded some shelter to the latter in their advance, and they came on in a more or less dense line, to use cold steel. The New Zealanders were ready to meet them with their own weapon, and gallantly led, dashed into them at the double with their bayonets, while the Germans stood to receive them. Such was the impetus of our troops that they drove back their opponents after a short struggle. Their slow retreat grew faster, and then became a run, until, finally, they took to their heels and fled helter-skelter, pursued by the New Zealanders. There were no more counter-attacks by the enemy in this part of the field.

While the fighting had been going on round Flers, the Guards had been engaged in another part of the front. All five regiments took part.

The place of assembly, before the advance, had been on the hither slope of the Thiepval-Ginchy Ridge, and the nature of the ground on the farther side and its occupation were not very well known. It had been thought that there was some little distance before the line of trench to be taken would be reached. But no sooner had the men gone some 200 yards and breasted the crest than they found themselves before two lines of trenches covered by an unbroken wire entanglement defended by machine-guns and bombers to back up the infantry. The three battalions of Coldstreams led the advance, supported by the Grenadiers, with the Irish Guards in reserve behind them

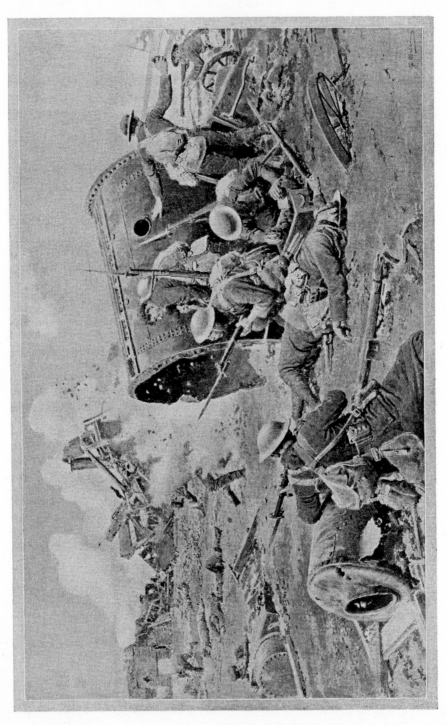

THE CAPTURE OF THE SUGAR REFINERY AT COURCELETTE BY THE CANADIANS.

The troops on the right of the Guards had been held up by obstacles, and thus the Coldstreams going on beyond them exposed their right flank and suffered accordingly. But they drove steadily onwards, over wire, over parapet, till Briton encountered German in the trench. Nor were our opponents loth to meet the attack. Both sides fought desperately with bomb and bayonet. The Coldstreams were reinforced by the Grenadiers, and the Irish Guards came up too, while later on the Welsh joined in the fray. After an hour or more of handy-strokes we gained the victory, and once more the Guards went on. They saw the German infantry beating a hasty retreat before them, they saw the German gunners endeavouring to remove their guns. They had advanced more than 2,000 yards from the point of departure, they had broken a gap in the German lines, but they had come to the limit of the possible and wisely determined to halt where they were and dig in. They had taken 200 prisoners, and disposed of many hundreds of the enemy.

The night by no means brought peace. The Germans launched counter-attack after counter-attack on them, but in vain, and so the Guards won through the darkness and held the position they had conquered.

Martinpuich and High Wood formed the connexion points of the battle between Flers and Courcelette.

High Wood had only been partly in our possession, the northern portion being still in the hands of the Germans when the battle of September 15 began. What they held they held strongly with a mass of machine guns. Here the Tanks gave great assistance, and, indeed, it was they that really turned the enemy out. Going on over trees, over wire, over trenches, they flattened out the enemy, and by 10 o'clock the whole wood was in our hands. Meanwhile the infantry had moved to the assault of Martinpuich. The front defences of the village were taken with a rush, but a counter-attack drove our men back. They went forward, once more supported by Tanks, and this time with entire success. The Bavarians fled before them, and the Tanks plied them with fire, enfiladed their trenches, sat on their dug-outs and thoroughly dominated them in every way. Many were the prisoners who fell to them—over a hundred surrendered to one alone, and two of the crew sufficed to keep them till the infantry came up. Another

captured a regimental commander who came out of a dug-out to see what was going on.

The share taken by the Canadians in the advance of September 15 and 16 was considerable. When they went over the parapet and advanced over the ground towards the German position they saw Martinpuich on their right and Courcelette to their left front, with an intervening network of trenches. Mouquet Farm, or rather the trenches round it, formed

SETTING FUSES.

their first objective, and part of these were captured after a short but severe struggle. Farther forward pressed the Maple Leaves, towards the brick ruins and white chalk heaps of what had once been the renowned sugar refinery, the subterranean defences of which still served to shelter the enemy, who also held the trenches right and left of it. These together formed the main objective of our troops. But before they could be reached other works had to be taken. Nor were they captured without a considerable fight. As usual, the German trenches were so laid out that portions of them, manned with machine guns, flanked their lines. These for a time held up the movement. But soon a new auxiliary arrived to aid the Canadians—His Majesty's Landship " Crême de Menthe." Moving deliberately but continuously forward, lurching a bit as it bumped over the shell craters and other obstacles, but always getting nearer and nearer to the German line, the steel-clad automobile battery passed through the cheering foot-soldiers and went on amid a hail of rifle and machine gun bullets to which it paid no attention. Then, taking position across the German front trench, its fire swept to right and left down it, and thus eased the way for Canadian infantry to continue their advance. The enemy's machine-guns were silenced and a considerable number of prisoners taken, and the main line of the German entrenchments here was captured, and even parts of the trenches on the outskirts of Courcelette. Soldiers from all parts of Canada took part in the triumph—Mounted Rifles from the eastern provinces with men from Toronto, London, and Kingston; while from the western side came the men from Vancouver and Regina, with the volunteers of Winnipeg, from the centre of the Dominion. It was a glorious combination. Having reached the point above indicated, the storming force proceeded to dig itself in, while the reserve battalions were brought up to complete the occupation of the ground gained.

The attack had indeed been so successful that Sir Julian Byng, the Canadian Corps

Commander, determined to push on still farther and take Courcelette, although the evening was advancing. The reserve battalion had now come up, and was told off to lead the new assault. A French Canadian battalion swung round to the left and struck the village on the eastern side, while other Canadians pressed straight forward against it. It was through a hot fire of artillery and small arms that our troops advanced, but they would not be denied, and, in the darkening shades of evening, the outer ring of the Courcelette fortification was broken through and the greater part of the garrison, now thoroughly demoralized, were made prisoners. Defences were improvized, and these served to beat off several counter-attacks made during the night against the newly won village. The prisoners taken numbered over 1,000, together with two pieces of artillery and a number of machine-guns and trench mortars.

On the extreme left, in front of Thiepva and down towards the Bapaume road, it was not the policy of Sir Douglas Haig to push matters to extremities at this period. But here, too, fighting went on; attacks

[*Canadian official photograph.*

CANADIANS HANDING DRINK TO GERMAN PRISONERS TAKEN BY THEM AT COURCELETTE.

[*Canadian official photograph.*

A KITE BALLOON PREPARING TO ASCEND.

were driven off, and some little progress was made.

The victory gained was a great one, and the Germans had been taught a lesson. Sitting down beyond the risk of danger the higher commanders might order their men to hold on till death or make counter-attack after counter-attack. But there is a limit to the capacity for resisting loss beyond which troops will not go. This had been reached by the Germans on the ground where the fighting of the 15th took place, and hence the great results gained this day by the British Army. In the language of General Haig, the fighting of the 15th and 16th was of great importance, and probably the most effective blow which had yet been dealt to the enemy by British troops. The damage to his *moral* was probably of greater consequence than the seizure of dominating positions and the capture of between 4,000 and 5,000 prisoners. Guards, Northumbrians and London Territorials, Scottish and English New Army divisions, with troops from Canada and New Zealand, shared the glory of the battle between them. Nor were our aviators without their share. They destroyed 15 aeroplanes of the enemy and drove others off, then they

came down lower and used their machine-guns on the enemy's guns and on the infantry in his trenches. At the same time they kept constant count of the enemy's movements, observed his batteries, and informed our own where to fire. The perfection to which the work of the Royal Flying Corps had been brought is impossible to put into words.

September 16 was chiefly a day of consolidation of our new position and of driving back counter-attacks of the enemy which were entirely unsuccessful. Late in the evening our troops obtained a considerable success, taking the " Danube " Trench near Thiepval on a front of about a mile, and with it many prisoners and a considerable quantity of rifles and equipment abandoned by the enemy. The network of defences round Mouquet Farm, which had been in dispute for some weeks past was almost completely conquered, and we extended our gains near Courcelette on a line of 1,000 yards. A number of minor advantages were secured on other parts of the British Front.

On the 17th, to the south of the Ancre, the Germans made several heavy counter-attacks, which were all repulsed. One which came from the direction of Lesbœufs and from the country

[*Official photograph.*

PRISONERS COMING IN.

north of Flers was caught by our artillery barrage and suffered heavy loss. Between Flers and Martinpuich a German brigade commenced an attack in the direction of High Wood. Our troops, only two battalions, did not wait for them to join issue, but leaving the shallow trenches which they had recently made, went on at a double to meet them. The result was never for a moment in doubt. Although the Germans were in threefold strength they were driven back with great slaughter.

[*From the official Ancre film.*

PRISONERS CLAIMING THEIR LETTERS AND OTHER PROPERTY.

To the north of Mouquet Farm more ground was gained. Our artillery, too, maintained its fire generally against the German line, and among other successes blew up an ammunition dump at Grandcourt. During the night further progress was made east of Courcelette and our line was appreciably advanced, and we gained more ground south of Thiepval, thus threatening to surround this position.

The Germans, on the other hand, under cover of a heavy bombardment, managed to enter one of our trenches west of Mouquet

Farm, but were at once counter-attacked and driven back with heavy loss. During the night they kept up an intermittent artillery fire against various points of our line.

It was at this juncture that the French and British Commanders-in-Chief exchanged the letters published below :

TO GENERAL SIR DOUGLAS HAIG.

General Headquarters of French Armies.
September 17.

My Dear General,—I desire to convey to you my most sincere congratulations on the brilliant successes gained by the British troops under your command during the hard-fought battles of the 15th and 16th of September. Following on the continuous progress made by your Armies since the beginning of the Somme offensive, these fresh successes are a sure guarantee of final victory over our common enemy, whose physical and moral forces are already severely shaken.

Permit me, my dear General, to take this opportunity of saying that the combined offensive which we have carried on now for more than two months has, if it were possible, drawn still closer the ties which unite our two Armies ; our adversary will find therein proof of our firm determination to combine our efforts until the end to ensure the complete triumph of our cause.

I bow before those of your soldiers by whose bravery these successes have been achieved but who have fallen before the completion of our task : and I ask you to convey, in my name and in the name of the whole French Army, to those who stand ready for the fights to come, a greeting of comradeship and confidence.

J. JOFFRE.

TO GENERAL JOFFRE.

General Headquarters, British Armies in France.
September 19.

My Dear General,—I thank you most sincerely for the kind message of congratulation and goodwill that you have addressed to me and to the troops under my command on their recent successes. This fresh expression of the good wishes of yourself and of your gallant Army, without whose close cooperation and support those successes could scarcely have been achieved, will be very warmly appreciated by all ranks of the British Armies.

I thank you, too, for your noble tribute to those who have fallen. Our brave dead, whose blood has been shed together on the soil of your great country, will prove a bond to unite our two peoples long after the combined action of our Armies has carried the common cause for which they have fought to its ultimate triumph.

The unremitting efforts of our forces north and south of the Somme, added to the glorious deeds of your Armies unaided at Verdun, have already begun to break down the enemy's power of resistance ; while the energy of our troops and their confidence in each other increases from day to day. Every fresh success that attends our arms brings us nearer to the final victory to which, like you, I look forward with absolute confidence.—Yours very truly,

D. HAIG, General,
Commanding-in-Chief, British Armies in France.

On September 18 another important advance was made. East of Ginchy and north-west of Combles we captured the important work known as the Quadrilateral, which gave us an important gain of ground and straightened our line. We also captured five heavy howitzers, two field guns, and lighter pieces.

While the British on the 15th were capturing Courcelette, Martinpuich and Flers, the French,

trench north-east of Berny was carried the same day.

On the 17th, in the afternoon, a great battle was delivered south of the Somme between Barleux and Vermandovillers. Numerous trenches were carried south of Barleux. The enemy was cleared out of the last houses held by him in Berny, and his lines from Berny to Deniécourt were pierced. Deniécourt was completely surrounded, and the German entrenchments thence to Vermandovillers were stormed. Simultaneously the enemy was ejected from such portion of Vermandovillers as he had still managed to retain. Violent counter-attacks towards nightfall were repulsed with terrible punishment to the foe. When

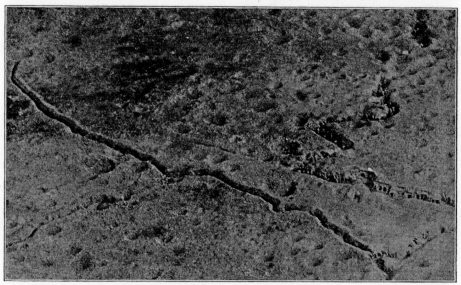

[French official photograph.

THE TRENCHES AT VERMANDOVILLERS: ARRIVAL OF FRENCH REINFORCEMENTS.
Photographed from an aeroplane.

who at nightfall on the 14th had carried enemy trenches just south of Rancourt and some hours later had repulsed attacks east of Clery, moved forward north of Priez Farm, threatening Combles from that region. South of the Somme also, at 4 p.m. in the sector Deniécourt-Berny they delivered two charges. To the east of Deniécourt a trench and small wood were wrested from the enemy ; and north-east of Berny three German trenches were seized. Two hundred prisoners and 10 mitrailleuses remained in the hands of our Allies. The next day the troops of General Fayolle from Bouchavesnes struck northwards in the direction of the wood of St. Pierre Vaast, and reached a narrow depression south of the wood. Another

sun set the French had been everywhere successful and had captured 700 unwounded prisoners, among them 15 officers. The battle went on through the night, counter-attack succeeding counter-attack. Vainly the troops of the 10th Ersatz Division strove to retake the ground lost near Berny. On the 18th the French finally secured Deniécourt, and pushed on towards Ablaincourt. At nightfall they were before the hamlet of Bovent. They had also captured three little woods south-east of Deniécourt and a trench west of Horgny, a village east of Berny.

During the night of September 18-19 the British beat off several determined counter-attacks south of the Ancre, destroyed two gun emplacements, and exploded an ammunition store. South of Arras we cleared the enemy from 200 yards of trenches, and the French made further progress south of the Somme to the east of Berny, taking some prisoners. The next day, September 20, north-east of Béthune, in the neighbourhood of Richebourg l'Avoué, three raids resulted in the capture of prisoners and a machine-

GENERAL DUPORT,
Chief of the French General Staff.

gun. A hostile balloon was brought down south-west of Arras. In the Somme area a German attack on the British trenches east of Martinpuich was easily repulsed. The next evening, south of the Ancre, in a torrential downpour, the New Zealanders were violently and continuously attacked, but at no point did the Germans penetrate their lines, and at daybreak the ground in front of their trenches was seen to be littered with the dead and dying. Many prisoners were captured in this and other regions.

On September 20 the main event was the determined effort of the Germans to drive back the French north of the Somme. The 18th Corps had been brought up from the Aisne and the 214th Division which was on its way to the Eastern Theatre of War, had been hastily recalled. It had arrived on the 14th. With these fresh troops, the Crown Prince of Bavaria, at 9 a.m., attacked General Fayolle's position between the Priez and l'Abbé farms, and east of Clery to the Somme. The 214th Division operated in the Bouchavesnes region. Preceded by violent bombardments, mass after mass of the enemy were precipitated against Bouchavesnes and the French trenches north and south of it. Four waves of grey-green infantry were cut down by the French guns before Priez Farm. The survivors fled, leaving the ground covered with corpses. But at 3 p.m. the Germans after a succession of bloody checks burst into the north-east end of Bouchavesnes. It was only a momentary triumph, for the French rallied and drove them out at the point of the bayonet. Few of them escaped and several officers and men were captured. The 75- and 120-mm. guns and the mitrailleuses had here, and at Priez Farm, caused frightful losses. At ridge 76, which is crossed by the road from Clery to Haut Allaines, regiments of the 18th Corps were kept at bay by the barrages of shell and shrapnel fire, but, nearer the Somme, parties of Germans succeeded in entering some trenches. They were swiftly ejected by counter-attacks. At nightfall the desperate contest died down. Prisoners stated that one company alone in the 11th Bavarian Division lost 110 men out of 210, that two battalions of the 123rd Prussian Regiment had been almost wiped out and that the 12th Reserve Division had suffered terribly. " I cannot understand," said a French artillery officer present, " how, after so many disastrous experiences, the German Higher Commanders can order attacks to be carried out in massed formation. The road from Combles to Rancourt is covered with dead Germans, sacrificed to no purpose." General Fayolle was able to report the victory to the new Chief of the French General Staff, at the Ministry of War, General Duport, who took the place the next day of General Graziani, whose health had broken down. Since the first months of the war the latter had filled this onerous post attached to the French War Office. It must not be confused with that occupied by General de Castelnau, who still continued to direct the movements of the armies at the front. Duport, a colonel in August 1914, was an infantry officer. He had been educated at the Military College of St. Cyr, and had fought on the Algerian frontier between 1885 and 1888. Promoted General of Brigade in

June, 1915, he had been since August 31, 1916, Commander of the 14th Corps d'Armée. Like so many other officers almost unknown at the beginning of the war, he had forced his way up by the exercise of conspicuous abilities.

So bloody had been the repulse of the German 18th Corps and 214th Division, that the next day, Thursday, September 21, Prince Rupprecht made no further attempt to pierce the lines of General Fayolle north of the Somme.

On the British front in the neighbourhood of Flers, bombing parties vainly endeavoured to wrest from us the positions taken in the battle of the 15th–16th. The night before, in vile weather, there had been encounters on the edge of Courcelette and north of Martinpuich. A hostile kite-balloon fell to the ground in flames, but, as against this, we had to record the loss of an aeroplane.

During the night of the 21st–22nd, while our troops were raiding enemy trenches south of Arras and north of that point, seizing a crater in the Neuville St. Vaast region caused by the explosion of one of our mines, an advance was also made by the British between Martinpuich and Flers. Up to the 21st our line sagged eastward from Courcelette round the northern end of Martinpuich and hugged the eastern face of the village. Thence it zigzagged towards Flers. It was now decided that the mill of Martinpuich,

500 yards north of the village, must mark the alignment of our front from Courcelette cemetery to Flers, and that a redoubt between the mill and the Albert-Bapaume road must be carried, and the German salients in our position flattened out. After desperate fighting two lines of hostile trenches were carried, and 24 hours later the redoubt was stormed. On the 23rd a strongly fortified system of trenches east of Courcelette was captured and we advanced on a front of about half a mile. The day before (September 22) at nightfall a violent German attack west of Mouquet Farm had been driven back by our fire with heavy losses. In the course of the 22nd our guns had destroyed 10 hostile gun-pits and damaged 10 others, while five ammunition dumps were blown up. A squadron of 50 aeroplanes the same day bombed an important railway junction. Two trains loaded with ammunition were smashed and many violent explosions caused. Railway works and sidings elsewhere and aerodromes and other points of military importance also received attention. As a consequence of aerial duels, three enemy machines were destroyed, five damaged severely and others driven to earth. Our loss was five machines.

Meantime, on September 22, the French had pushed a little nearer to the doomed village-fortress of Combles. On the northern slopes of

FRENCH RED-CROSS MEN WAITING IN A TRENCH OUTSIDE COMBLES

the hillock beyond the wood of Anderlu, towards the road from Maurepas to Frégicourt, the enemy had converted into a small fortress an isolated house in front of Combles and close to the road. The machine-guns in it held up the French advance. After an attack very ably executed the house was surrounded and carried by assault. Ninety-seven men and three officers were captured. Simultaneously between Frégicourt and Priez Farm the French stormed German trenches on the east slope of the Combles ravine. The enemy's endeavours to hinder the French movements in this direction by renewed counter-attacks between Priez Farm and Rancourt were repulsed by curtains of shell fire.

By this date the total of the prisoners captured by the Allies in the Battle of the Somme had swelled to over 55,800, of which 34,050 had been taken by the French.

Preparations were now being made by the Allies to fight another battle similar to that of September 15–16. It was preceded by aerial enterprises on a large scale and by bombardments of almost incredible intensity. The French wrecked 25 enemy machines on September 23, we seven. The same day five bombing raids against railway stations on the German lines of communication were successfully executed by the British. In the course of an air fight one of our airmen collided with his opponent. The German plane fell to the ground, while ours, after a vertical descent of several thousand feet, was righted and returned safely, the pilot flying over 30 miles with an almost uncontrollable machine. Our losses on the 23rd were five machines.

Among other noteworthy incidents at this date, the celebrated French airman Guynemer brought down his seventeenth and eighteenth hostile machines, and on the 24th Captain de Beauchamps in the "Ariel" and Lieutenant Daucourt executed one of the most daring flights on record. For the first time Essen, the great military manufactory of Germany, was bombed in broad daylight. The workshops of Krupp were defended by no fewer than 250 anti-aircraft guns, and numerous German aeroplanes were naturally on the watch to intercept raiders. Nevertheless, the intrepid Frenchmen succeeded in dropping twelve bombs on Essen and in returning safely to their base. Captain de Beauchamps, who was not 29 years old, had for many months been commanding the squadron "des As" stationed on the eastern front of the French lines. He had had under him Guynemer and other distinguished pilots,

[*Official photograph.*

BRITISH FIELD BATTERY CROSSING A FORD.

including Daucourt. Of his then recent exploits the destruction of a Fokker on April 7 and of a Drache on May 22, 1916, had caused him once more to be cited in an Order of the Day.

The night before the visit of De Beauchamps and Daucourt to Essen a fleet of Zeppelins, probably 12, had crossed to England. Two were destroyed in Essex, while they did no material injury to us.*

As for the Allied bombardments north and south of the Somme which had commenced on the 23rd, a French artillery officer remarked : " A terrible drama is being enacted on the Somme. I have been through the whole of the Verdun battle and I have been two months here, but I have not seen anything like the havoc wrought by the Allied artillery yesterday. It surpasses anything I have witnessed."

It speaks for the stubborn courage of the Germans that on Sunday, September 24, while their trenches were being inundated with high-explosive shells, they took the offensive at several points. A British post east of Courcelette was assaulted ; three attacks were delivered west of Lesbœufs against our men and the French garrison of the Abbé Farm, and troops in trenches south of it had to withstand a violent assault. These efforts on the part of the enemy were all unavailing.

Monday, September 25, was the anniversary of the Battle of Loos, which now seemed as remote an event as the Battles of Le Cateau, the Marne, and Ypres. It was a beautiful, clear autumnal day. Not a cloud was in the sky ; a golden haze rose from the fields and crept over the ruined villages and the litter of what once were woods. Anticipating from the frightful violence of the bombardment that the Allies were about to renew their general offensive between Thiepval and the Somme, the Germans dispatched in the early morning two flocks of aeroplanes to reconnoitre. They were peppered with shrapnel, met in mid-air by our aeroplanes, and driven back followed by our pursuing airmen, who, with the observers in the " Ruperts " (kite balloons), directed the fire of our artillery. The balloons, iridescent in the sun-light, seemed like aerial monsters decked with glittering trappings for some State occasion.

The plan of General Fayolle and Sir Douglas Haig was to break farther into the lines of the enemy between the Albert-Bapaume road and the Somme. Should success attend their efforts, Sir Hubert Gough was the next day to storm

* See Vol. X., p. 192.

Thiepval and the ridge behind it. The whole night-long guns of all calibres had been firing incessantly.

At 12.30 p.m. the final bombardment before the infantry attack opened. The din was indescribable. Perhaps four times as many guns

LIEUT. GUYNEMER.

as had been in action along the whole front of the great Battle of Liao-Yang in the Russo-Japanese War were concentrating their fire on a belt of ground only about 14 miles in length. Most of those guns were immensely more powerful than any employed by Oyama or Kuropatkin, and the front of battle was very much shorter. At the end of 10 minutes the deafening noise slightly diminished. The infantry combat had begun.

At the Battle of Loos-Vimy the efforts of the Allies had not been properly co-ordinated, the French attacking several hours after the British. No such mistake was made on this occasion. The tension was applied simultaneously to every link in the German chain of fortified positions. Several systems of trenches between the Bapaume-Péronne chaussée and the Canal du Nord were carried by the French, who arrived in places at the banks of the canal. East of the road the French captured Hill 130, south-east of Bouchavesnes, and Hill 120 to the north-east of that village. Gradually the

FRENCH SOLDIERS ENTRENCHED IN A SHELL-HOLE OUTSIDE COMBLES.

Germans were being thrust back into the valley of the Tortille. Still more important, Rancourt, due east of Combles, was taken. Situated on the southern side of a bare narrow plateau, one of the highest points in the neighbourhood, it dominated the great wood of St. Pierre Vaast, the edge of which ran about 500 yards to its east. Part of Rancourt was traversed by the Bapaume-Péronne highway; the remainder of the village was clustered about a road through Frégicourt to Combles. From the centre of Rancourt a narrow ravine descended to the wood, in the hollows of which the Germans had installed batteries bombarding the French lines from the Priez Farm to Bouchavesnes. This ravine bristled with machine-guns. With the capture of Rancourt, which formed, as it were, the main link between the wood and Combles, the fall of Combles could not long be delayed. The only communication now connecting it with the rest of the German lines was the road which ran upwards through Frégicourt across the Bapaume-Péronne highway to Sailly-Saillisel. As will shortly be related, the last of the other roads by which the garrison of Combles could be supplied with food and munitions had been cut by the British when they stormed Morval.

Frégicourt, a hamlet of 10 houses with a chapel in it, still remained to be taken. On the 24th our Allies pushed up to the southern side of it, and evicted the Germans from their powerful organizations between Frégicourt and Hill 148, which is on the northern edge of Rancourt. Thus the connexion of Combles with Sailly-Saillisel was snapped and, as the British were by now in Morval, there was no longer any road by which the garrison of Combles could be reinforced. The enemy's sole access to the village was by a narrow ravine twisting north-eastwards to Sailly-Saillisel and the Bapaume-Péronne highway. This ravine was under the fire of the Allied artillery, machine-guns and rifles.

During the night the French continued their advance on Combles, from which the Germans were dragging some of their guns up the ravine, down whose centre ran a little stream. While four French aeroplanes armed with guns fired 82 shells on the convoys and enemy's organizations in front of Sailly-Saillisel and in the wood of St. Pierre Vaast, the infantry of our Allies stormed Frégicourt. Patrols descended the slopes towards the Combles ravine and reached and seized the cemetery of this town, situated at the point where the route from Sailly-Saillisel reaches the western mouth of the ravine. Other Allied detachments moved up to the southern edge of Combles. One of them captured a trench at the south-west end and in it a company of Germans. The unwounded prisoners taken already amounted to 800. Violent counter-attacks delivered at nightfall against the French right between the Bapaume-Péronne highway and the Somme, with a view to forcing the French to suspend their movement on Combles, had been bloodily repulsed.

It is now time to describe the operations on the 25th of Sir Henry Rawlinson's army, which prolonged the Allied line from the wood of Leuze above Combles on the west to Martin-puich. Among Sir Henry Rawlinson's objectives were the villages of Morval—which, as we have seen, was on one of the roads used by the Germans to supply Combles—of Les-bœufs to the north-north-west of Morval on the Ginchy-Le Transloy road, and of Gueude-court farther down the slope on the way to Bapaume. A belt of country about 1,000 yards deep curving round the north of Flers, which is south-west of Gueudecourt, to a point mid-way between Flers and Martinpuich, was also to be cleared of the enemy. The battle-front was six miles long.

Morval, it will be recollected, stands on the height north of Combles, which lies below it at the bottom of the valley. With its subterranean quarries, trenches and wire entanglements, it

was a formidable obstacle. The Germans still held part of the wood of Bouleaux, north of the wood of Leuze. Their machine guns lined two trenches, "Lemco" and "Bovril," south-west of Morval, and two sunken roads leading from the village to Lesbœufs. After the tremendous bombardment already described the British infantry, at 12.30 p.m. on the 25th, advanced to the attack. The enemy expected that the wood of Bouleaux would be assaulted, but our efforts at this point were confined to seizing two trenches west of it. Nearly at right angles to these was an embankment pitted with deep dug-outs, held by a large force equipped with machine-guns and *minenwerfer*. Here the

[*Official photograph.*

GERMAN GUN EMPLACEMENT AT COMBLES.

SHATTERED GERMAN WIRE ENTANGLEMENTS AT COMBLES.

THE MAIN STREET OF COMBLES.

fighting went on half way through the afternoon. Finally the dug-outs were cleared, and 80 prisoners and five *minenwerfer* captured, together with a great store of shells. After dark patrols entered Bouleaux Wood, which was being evacuated by the Germans owing to the result of the struggle in Morval.

Meanwhile, north-east of the wood our troops simultaneously advanced on both sides of the Ginchy-Morval road. The northern sector of Morval gave little trouble. At the approach of our bombers the garrison surrendered. In the southern sector there was more resistance. The Germans manfully defended the "Lemco" and "Bovril" trenches and a trench cut from the eastern end of the village in a quarter circle to the road to Frégicourt. As the British were north and the French in the Frégicourt region south of them the position of these brave men was untenable and they began to dribble off in the direction of Sailly-Saillisel.

The British troops to the left of the detachments assaulting Morval were equally successful. Exposed to severe machine-gun fire they seized the road from Morval to Lesbœufs and stormed into the latter village.* Some of the men swept up the road to Le Transloy, others encircled the village, from the ruined chateau in which machine-guns for a time continued their fire. Between Lesbœufs and Gueudecourt eight

German battalions attempted to stem the British advance but were quite unable to do so. "My men," said a Baden officer, "would not stand. I could not make them fight ; they had had enough."

The attack on Gueudecourt did not yield such good results. At the point where the Ginchy-Gueudecourt and Flers-Lesbœufs tracks cross one another a German redoubt barred the way. In the neighbouring shell-craters groups of Germans with machine-guns assisted its garrison.

Before the village on the west and southern sides there were two trenches strongly fortified and protected with barbed wire. They were known as Grid Trench and Grid Support. The Ginchy-Gueudecourt road crossed them just below the village in a deep ravine, which at this point forked, one branch passing up the western, the other up the eastern, side of Gueudecourt. Across both branches of the ravine went the road from Le Transloy to Eaucourt l'Abbaye. In Gueudecourt itself were machine-gun posts and numbers of defended shell-holes and hidden strongholds.

Advancing from the line held by them east of Flers our men closed on Gueudecourt. The German artillery in the background deluged them with shells, and the redoubt at the crossroads swept the advancing infantry with machine-gun fire. From a redoubt at the junction of Grid Trench with another trench a hail of bullets proceeded. This redoubt was eventually carried by a bombing party, but at

* A captured German Army Order, dated September 21, emphasized the importance at that time of the position at Lesbœufs as "the last protection of the artillery, which must in no circumstances be lost."

nightfall we had not succeeded in storming Gueudecourt. West of this place Sir Henry Rawlinson's troops secured the fortified belt already referred to between Flers and Martin-puich. Apart from the failure to capture Gueudecourt, victory had everywhere attended the efforts of the Allies. Slowly but surely they were passing from the basin of the Somme into that of the Scheldt.

During the night of the 25th–26th the struggle went on. The sky was lit up from below by white flares, throwing a vivid light over parts of the battlefield and showing the rims of the shell-craters snowy white. Combles, a dark spot in the middle of the semi-circle of fiery explosions caused by the Allied artillery, seemed deserted.

While the French stormed Frégicourt and descended into the cemetery and the eastern houses of the ruined town and reached those to the south, our troops picked their way down from the wood of Leuze and through the abandoned wood of Bouleaux. At 3.15 a.m. on the 26th a strong patrol with machine-guns

"CEUX SONT LES ANGLAIS !"
The meeting of British and French in the village of Combles, September 26, 1916.

reached the railway which ran from the Somme up the valley and ended in Combles. Through the gloom they saw figures approaching them. One of these drew near and reconnoitred.

"Ceux sont les Anglais !" he cried. The Allies had joined hands in Combles.

This town, which before the war had contained 3,000 inhabitants, had been, as it were, an arsenal for the Germans at the Battle of the Somme. Most of the stores had been previously removed, but more than 1,800 rifles, four *flammenwerfer*, and thousands of rounds of artillery ammunition and of grenades were taken by the British alone. Fighting continued in the ruins and the caves under the village, but the whole town was soon entirely cleared of living Germans. The dead lying in heaps bore witness to the terrible effects of the fire of the Allied guns.

Besides taking their share in the capture of Combles, the French in the afternoon of the 26th seized a small wood north of Frégicourt half-way to Morval, and also the greater part of the enemy's fortifications from this wood

RUINS OF COMBLES CHURCH.

COMBLES, AS THE ALLIED ARMIES FOUND IT.

to the western border of the wood of St. Pierre Vaast.

With the seizure of Morval and Lesbœufs, almost the whole of the high ground between the Albert-Bapaume and Péronne-Bapaume roads came finally into the possession of the Allies. The Germans in the apex of the triangle Albert-Bapaume-Péronne were everywhere under the observation of the British posted on the captured heights. But on the Péronne-Bapaume road the enemy was still entrenched on Hill 148, just north of Rancourt, and on Hill 153, east of Morval. These hills were parts of a winding ridge, cruciform in shape, on which Sailly-Saillisel and Saillisel, practically one village, were built. The road to Bapaume crossed the ridge and went through Sailly. It then descended to Le Transloy, rose again at Beaulencourt, and thence descended to Bapaume. The villages of Morval and Lesbœufs were on the eastern slopes of Hill 154, north of Ginchy, and were separated from Sailly-Saillisel by the ravine up which most of the garrison and guns in Combles had been withdrawn.

In the early hours of Tuesday, September 26, the advance on Gueudecourt was resumed. A Tank had been brought up in support of the infantry. It was especially useful at the point where Grid Trench and Grid Support crossed the Ginchy road in the ravine, and in reducing a strong post at the south-east end of the village. When this fell Gueudecourt was

CHEERING A "TANK."

speedily entered, and 650 prisoners were taken. While our men were rounding them up the Tank proceeded into the open country, and, something going wrong with its machinery, it was surrounded by the Germans, who peppered it with bombs, shot at every chink in it, even climbed on its roof, and hammered at it with the butts of their rifles, the crew meantime being engaged inside in repairing the Tank and shooting down its assailants, who made no impression on it. Possibly the Tank might have been captured had not its plight been perceived by our infantry who, issuing from Gueudecourt, rescued it. Some 250 to 300 dead Germans lay around the Tank, evidences of its effective fire.

Cavalry patrols pushed beyond the village. Our line from Morval to Gueudecourt now ran parallel with the Bapaume-Péronne road.

In the afternoon the Germans debouching from Le Transloy flung themselves on our trenches between Gueudecourt and Lesbœufs. Checked by shell and rifle fire they were charged with the bayonet and flung back in utter confusion. Another counter-attack was directed on the eastern corner of Courcelette from the warren of German trenches between the sunken Courcelette-Le Sars road and the Albert-Bapaume highway. It was temporarily successful, the enemy penetrating the outskirts of the village. The British troops rallied,

and bayoneted and bombed the intruders, and, following in pursuit, began to clear out the Germans from their dug-outs.

Between the British and the Péronne-Bapaume road still lay the large village of Le Transloy, from which the counter-attack already narrated had issued. To reach Le Transloy and the highway our troops would have to move down bare slopes and then into and up the western face of the ravine under the fire of the enemy on the Sailly-Saillisel ridge. Nevertheless, with the Allies also in Combles and the French in Rancourt, the German hold on the road north of Rancourt, on the wood of St. Pierre Vaast and on Sailly-Saillisel was becoming every hour more precarious.

To take Bapaume, the capture of which would have a psychological, as well as a strategical, effect on the war, it was not, however, necessary to move from the heights down the highway. At Gueudecourt we were but three miles from the edge of this important town. In the night of the 26th–27th, Sir Henry Rawlinson pushed his troops from Flers on Eaucourt l'Abbaye, on the road from Gueudecourt to Le Sars, through which village runs the Albert-Bapaume highway, and during the 27th we carried trenches north of Flers on a front of 2,000 yards, and gained a foothold to the east of Eaucourt l'Abbaye. Our lines

TRENCH MORTARS FOUND IN COMBLES VILLAGE.

in the apex of the triangle Albert-Bapaume-Péronne now resembled a wedge pointed towards Bapaume.

By nightfall on September 25, the results of the offensive conducted by Generals Fayolle and Rawlinson had been so great and the resulting position of our forces so favourable, that Sir Douglas Haig decided that the moment had now arrived for Sir Hubert Gough to push on northward in the direction of the Ancre, and drive the enemy out of Thiepval and off the main ridge behind that village. As the ridge commanded the valley of the Ancre it had been fortified with peculiar care by the Germans, some of whom were still on the edge of Mouquet Farm. In Thiepval, the 180th Regiment, composed of Wurtembergers, had been placed as early as September 1914, when the race for the sea was beginning. An apple orchard before the village formed an advanced work. At the southern end of the ruins was a great pile of red bricks and raw earth—all that remained of a château occupied by a German tenant before the war. It is significant that, according to report, its large cellars had been made before the opening of hostilities. These cellars were the central point of a vast labyrinth of tunnels. All served for shelters and storehouses. A sunken road, with passages

to dug-outs along its course, ran northward from the middle of Thiepval towards the cemetery, which as usual was a fortress in itself. On the bare ridge behind and to the north of it, at a thousand yards distance, was the Schwaben Redoubt, an irregular oval measuring nearly 700 yards long by 300 wide, built in the fork of the roads leading from Thiepval to St. Pierre Divion and Grandcourt, both villages on the Ancre. A thousand yards east of it, and connected with the Schwaben Redoubt by the Hessian Trench, was the Stuff—or Stufen—Redoubt, garrisoned by the 153rd German regiment. These fortifications were furnished with innumerable underground shelters. From the western end of the Schwaben Redoubt a maze of trenches descended steeply to the ruins of St. Pierre Divion. Well-timbered alleys connected the Schwaben and Stuff Redoubts with the village of Grandcourt in the valley below, and a couple of hundred yards north of the Stuff Redoubt was another redoubt called "The Mound." The whole face of the ridge down to the Ancre had been hollowed out by the Germans during their two years' occupation. The size of the caves constructed by them may be gathered from the fact that one used as a dressing station and hospital contained 125 beds.

From the vicinity of the Stuff Redoubt a trench called "The Regina" ran eastwards, parallel with the Albert-Bapaume chaussée to the road which proceeds northwards out of Le Sars to Pys and Miraumont, the village next to Grandcourt going up the Ancre. Between Thiepval and Courcelette, lower down the up-slope of the ridge and to the north of Mouquet Farm, which, as previously mentioned, was not completely cleared of the enemy, was the Zollern Redoubt.

It may be imagined how formidable were the barriers from the Zollern Redoubt and Thiepval upwards still barring our way to the valley of the Ancre, from St. Pierre Divion eastwards. The whole of the works were heavily wired, and the lines of approach to this position were swept by the fire of German batteries from the high ground north of the Ancre.

When, on July 1, the Ulster troops had, in spite of their great gallantry, vainly assaulted its western face, the enemy was brimming over with confidence in his own courage and skill and in the supremacy of German military engineering. He had not yet seen villages as elaborately fortified as Thiepval wrested one by one from his grasp. By September 26, judging from letters found on soldiers of the German 180th and 153rd Regiments, the nerves of many of the men hidden in the dug-outs on the Thiepval ridge were shaken. "We must reckon," wrote a soldier of the 180th Regiment on the morning of Sir Hubert Gough's offensive, "with

FIRING THE BOMB.

the possibility of an attack at any moment, and we are in a tight corner. The British now have aerial torpedoes, which have a frightful effect."*

* Large trench bombs, or possibly Stokes bombs.

Another soldier of the 180th Regiment put his ideas on paper (apparently a little later on the same day) :—

We relieved a machine-gun crew who had the only entrance to their dug-out knocked in by a shell after a

HEAVY FRENCH TRENCH BOMB.

gas bomb had fallen in it. You cannot imagine what misery this is. Our company commander was gassed, and is now in hospital. The bombardment has begun again at a rate to make a man dizzy. I think we shall soon have either to get out or be taken by the British.

Men of the 153rd Regiment, which was holding the Stuff and Zollern Redoubts and the outskirts of Mouquet Farm, were equally despondent. Four days before—on September 22—one of them wrote :—

In case of attack we are not in a position to defend ourselves, much less to attack—the rifles have been dragged through the mud and are useless. All we have are bayonets and hand grenades, but I think if the

"Tommies" came over no one would put up a fight;
the men would gladly go over to them.

And on September 25, when Sir Henry Rawlinson and General Fayolle were making their great push and Sir Hubert Gough was preparing his, the following was penned by another man of the same regiment :—

We are about an hour from the trenches, 36 of us in a dug-out. It is not surprising to hear that men are missing, for they are torn to pieces ; many are buried and never get out again. It would be better if German women and girls could be here, for the war would soon be over then.

It was from the South, from the Wunderwerk to Mouquet Farm, that Sir Hubert Gough, on the morning of the 26th, delivered his attack. The capture of Courcelette, east of the Zollern redoubt, had appreciably lightened his task. After a very severe bombardment our troops, following behind the ever-advancing barrage and accompanied by Tanks, came over the parapets of their trenches at 12.30 p.m. The right wing, passing by the few Germans still hidden beneath the outbuildings of Mouquet Farm, whose influence by this time was of but little moment, made for the Zollern Redoubt in three successive waves. As they charged forward they were unexpectedly attacked in the

rear by enemy machine-guns which had been suddenly hoisted to the surface at some outbuilding of the farm. A working party of pioneers who happened to be near dropped their tools, and headed by a young officer and followed by other units, rushed for the gun emplacement and forced a way into the dugouts. For six hours a desperate struggle went on in the tunnels and chambers below the farm, which stopped all attention of the garrison to outside matters. Finally our men emerged with 56 German privates and an officer taken prisoners. Meanwhile the Zollern Redoubt had been stormed and prepared for defence by our men.

In Thiepval itself the struggle was of the fiercest. From the apple orchard machine-guns played on the advancing infantry, while streams of bullets proceeded from the château, the sunken road and the cemetery. Passing round the eastern side of the village our bombers got between it and the cemetery and then turned back and entered Thiepval from the northern end. Slowly the surface of the ruins was conquered, but no impression could be made on the château. Suddenly, amid wild cheering from our men, a Tank hove in sight, its guns

WITHIN A HUNDRED YARDS OF THIEPVAL.

BRITISH ADVANCE TO ATTACK.

firing their hardest. A hail of shot pattered ineffectually on its sides ; bombs burst on them but did not penetrate. Nothing could stop its onward movement. It charged the mound of red-brick and earth ; and the garrison of the isolated château despairingly surrendered. Another Tank which had rendered good service reached an obstacle over which it could not climb. It halted and became for the nonce a stationary fort.

The Wurtembergers driven from the surface took refuge in their tunnels and caverns, and for hours the fight went on with bomb, knife and bayonet. Loud cries mingled with the sound of the exploding bombs gave testimony to the deadly nature of the struggle. Night fell but brought no cessation of the contest. By the light of electric torches our men hunted the enemy from one lair into another, and it was not till 8.30 a.m. on Wednesday the 28th that Thiepval was finally in our hands. The Germans had believed that it was impregnable. It had been defended, not by raw levies, but by some of those troops who in August, 1914, had swept victoriously through Belgium and who had had many months in which to prepare their strongholds without much interruption by fighting.

The cemetery of Thiepval, the Schwaben Redoubt, and the Stuff Redoubt, with the trenches binding them together, had still to be carried before the summit of the Thiepval salient would be securely held. From this chain of fortified works the enemy descended again and again into the ruins of the village, each time being beaten back with heavy loss. On the 27th we resumed the offensive. The south and west sides of the Stuff Redoubt were carried, together with the trench connecting it with the Schwaben Redoubt. During the afternoon the latter was assaulted and, in spite of desperate resistance, the southern face of it was captured and our patrols pushed to the northern face and towards St. Pierre Divion. The next day (September 28) our guns concentrated on the cemetery of Thiepval, the Schwaben Redoubt, and the neighbouring work known as the Crucifix. A *Times* correspondent who was present gave a graphic description of the barrage of gun-fire and the subsequent assault :—

Beyond the little company of ragged trees and mottled patch of ground which are all that there is of Thiepval we saw the region of the Cemetery—marked by another small company of tattered tree-stumps—and all the rise beyond where the Crucifix was and the Redoubt lay, disappear in an instant behind the dreadful veil. The barrage lifted for a moment, and we knew that the infantry were going into that hell of smoke and fire and death. We saw the cloud spread northward as our guns increased their range to positions beyond, and, as the wind drifted the smoke away, the region on which our storm had first broken came out peacefully into the sunlight again. Our men had gone beyond it.

Presently on that same region the enemy's shells began falling—sure sign that it was our ground now and not his —and still the tide of battle moved on. Ever northward the curtain of our bursting shells passed steadily, until it engulfed only the farther side of the Redoubt and down to the German first line on the Ancre ; and there it hung. Between it and us the enemy's shells dropped in increasing numbers, on Thiepval, on the ground which our men

[Official photograph.

THE CAVALRY LINES ON THE SOMME, SEPTEMBER, 1916.

had just swept over, and at large over the middle distance and the foreground of the picture. But always the centre of the fight hung at the farther side, where the last slope from the high ground of the ridge goes down to the valley.

Well into the afternoon we watched, and then went to meet the wounded, to seek prisoners, to find anyone who could tell us of what was happening behind the pall. But I still know nothing definite beyond what we saw ourselves. We broke through the position at the Cemetery and stormed into the Redoubt. Fighting there appears to be still going on. All the ground from here down to the valley is a maze of trenches, the German front line which he has held for two years and all the support lines and communication trenches and strong points with which in that time he has supplied himself. Among these trenches and along the front line the struggle still rages, and British soldiers are finishing the task, half done yesterday, which Germany for two years has

Bapaume, and, in places, but two miles from the Bapaume-Péronne highway, a section of which from Rancourt southwards to beyond Bouchavesnes had been secured by our Allies.

On the evening of September 27, it having been discovered that in the neighbourhood of Courcelette we had broken through the last line of the German entrenched positions, some Canadian cavalry were promptly dispatched to Pys, a hamlet between the Ancre and Le Sars, the last village fortress blocking the approach to Bapaume by the Albert-Bapaume road. Two lieutenants and 24 troopers proceeded straight up the road itself. The next morn-

[Canadian official photograph.

CANADIANS ADVANCING WITH PICKS AND SHOVELS READY TO DIG
THEMSELVES IN.

believed that no troops could ever do. Whether they have yet succeeded or not, and whether this last corner of the ridge is ours, we shall know to-night.

When the sun set the ruins of the cemetery were in the possession of the British, and we had also penetrated into the Schwaben Redoubt.

By the 28th the prisoners captured by the British in the fortnight's fighting amounted to 10,000. Sir Hubert Gough and Sir Henry Rawlinson had reached most of their objectives. Almost the whole of the summit of the ridge from above Thiepval to Morval and beyond were in the possession of the British. We looked down on the valley of the Ancre from the south side, we were within three miles of

ing two patrols located Germans in Destremont Farm, which was a mile beyond our trenches and 300 yards south-west of Le Sars, on the Albert-Bapaume road. There was a skirmish, in which one Canadian was killed and a second wounded. Another patrol discovered enemy units between Le Sars and Pys, and still another threaded its way across the Regina trench, which ran north-west of Courcelette and parallel to the Bapaume road nearly as far as Le Sars, but was driven back by snipers. As a consequence of the reports furnished by the Canadian cavalry, a Toronto battalion on Thursday, September 28, advanced a thousand yards to the north-east of Courcelette, while a New Brunswick battalion established itself close to the south of the Regina trench. A Montreal battalion also took part in these operations, the machine-guns of a Brigade protecting its flank. German details counter-attacking were wiped out by the fire of the latter. The Borden Battery assisted. Three of its guns were hit, and some casualties incurred.

While the Canadians at the point of junction between the armies of Sir Hubert Gough and Sir Henry Rawlinson were wedging themselves in north of the Albert-Bapaume road, the Germans to the west of Courcelette clung desperately to the northern edge of the Thiepval salient. On the 28th, when the fine weather broke up and rain began to fall we had, as already described, captured the Thiepval cemetery, and broken into the southern face of the Schwaben Redoubt. During the night of the 28th-29th the Germans shelled heavily the lost positions, and our bombers were at work on the remainder of the redoubt and in the Hessian trench, which connected it with the captured Stuff Redoubt.

The next day, Friday, September 29, rain fell in torrents, but the fighting still went on at these points. A counter-attack drove us

from a section of the Hessian trench, but later in the day this was recovered. A single company in the morning had stormed Destremont Farm, which formed an advanced post to Le Sars. Four miles away to the east Sir Henry Rawlinson's troops had occupied 500 yards of enemy trenches in the direction of the Bapaume-Péronne road, while between Morval and Frégicourt our Allies were approaching that chaussée. Morval had been handed over to the French in order to facilitate their advance on Sailly-Saillisel.

The activity exhibited by the Allied artillery was maintained on Saturday, September 30. The German guns replied to the best of their ability during the night of September 29-30, heavily shelling our battle-front south of the Ancre. It was the prelude to violent counter-attacks in the vicinity of the Stuff Redoubt and the Hessian trench. The last of them was delivered at 5 a.m. on September 30. At noon we again advanced and gained the whole of the trench with the exception of a small section which was attached to the sunken road to Grandcourt on the Ancre. This road had been entrenched and enemy reinforcements were constantly ascending it from Grandcourt

LOADING UP LIMBERS WITH AMMUNITION.

HOWITZER IN ACTION ON THE ANCRE.

[*Official photograph.*]

to aid the Germans in the Schwaben Redoubt, Hessian trench and Regina trench previously referred to. On the French front progress had been made north of Rancourt by grenade fighting.

Up to this date the gains of the British since September 14 had been as follows : *

The number of prisoners captured had swollen to 26,735. We had secured 27 enemy guns, 40 trench mortars and over 200 mitrailleuses. Of the 38 German Divisions—which at full strength would have numbered about 450,000 infantry—no less than 29 had had to be withdrawn in an exhausted or broken state. The half-moon of upland ground south of the Ancre with every height of importance had been carried ; we had now direct observation to the east and north-east ; and the enemy had been driven back upon his fourth line behind the low ridge just west of the Bapaume-Péronne road between Bapaume and Le Transloy.

The importance of the three months' offensive was, however, not to be judged solely by the distance advanced, but had to be gauged by the effect upon the German numbers, material and moral. Hindenburg had been obliged since September 15 to reinforce the Crown Prince of Bavaria with twelve new divisions or roughly

* See further Official Summary of October 3, published in *The Times* of October 5.

100,000 infantry, of which seven divisions had been launched against the troops of our New Army. The enemy had used up his reserves in repeated costly and unsuccessful counter-attacks without causing the Allies to relax their steady and methodical pressure. Shelled, bombed and bayoneted from villages, woods and trenches which their engineers had fondly believed they had rendered impregnable, the Germans were at last beginning to doubt the gain of any decided victory. Some extracts from letters or diaries found on prisoners at this time will show their feelings. One unfortunate wrote :—

We are actually fighting on the Somme against the English. You can no longer call it war, it is mere murder. . . . The slaughter at Ypres and the battle in the gravel pit at Hulluch were the purest child's play compared with this massacre, and that is much too mild a description.

We are here now on the Somme in such an artillery fire as I have not experienced—indeed, no one has in the whole war. Cover there is none ; we lie in a shell-hole and defend ourselves to the last man. He who comes out of this fire can thank God. It's frightful ; such a murder here.

I have not been through anything like it in the whole war. It may well be called sheer hell. It is unendurable.

Another in hospital said : " We are already sick of the damned war. . . . My feeling about it is such that if I am to go back I shall serve for three weeks and then get ill again, for there is no object in fighting any more." Here is a picture of the conditions under which some of

SOME OF THE PRISONERS.

the garrisons of the subterranean fortresses were living :—

> The gallery in which we now are is tolerably well constructed. . . . In it are also a machine gun and its crew of four men, two sentries, one wounded, two men with carrier pigeons, two men who have lost their way— altogether 29 men. The gallery is full from top to bottom. There are two men sitting on every other step of the stairs. The air is fearfully bad and hot, as there is no proper ventilation. . . . We have to live here for four days. Several of us were ill, and fresh air was not to be had. We dare not stick our heads outside the entrance, for enemy airmen are continually on the watch, and the artillery sweeps the entrances with shrapnel.*

Most of the prisoners complained of the superiority of the Allied airmen.

> There are no trenches in the front-line position. The men lie to a large extent in shell-holes. The enemy aviators descend to a height of about 80 metres and fire on them with machine-guns and signal with horns. The enemy's aviators are far superior, especially in numbers. Our airmen are powerless and are put to flight as soon as the enemy machines approach our trench lines.

Occasionally a German relieved his mind with hysterical and comic abuse :—

> We will not spare our insolent, villainous enemy, but destroy everything that comes into our hands, for the cowardly blackguards see that they cannot do anything with us in the trenches, and so now their aircraft have to fly to our towns and there destroy our poor innocent women and girls—a very shameful proceeding on the

* Manchester Guardian.

part of the cowardly blackguards, and one which will stand to their credit later on. But, thank God, we can say that we have not led our Fatherland against poor women and children, but with an iron fist have raised our weapons in the fight against the venomous hosts of our enemy and have nobly and justly defended our Fatherland, and so that we hope a victorious and lasting peace may ensue.

No doubt the slaughter of unoffending British citizens on land by Zeppelins or on sea by submarines was, in this egregious person's eyes, commendable. But he howls like a whipped dog when his own people suffer.

As a matter of fact, however, our airmen never intentionally bombed civilians. They had other work to do. "For every enemy machine," wrote the British Headquarter Staff on October 3, "that succeeds in crossing our front it is safe to say that 200 British machines cross the enemy's."

The French military authorities, also summed up the situation at the end of September, 1916. They pointed out that at the time of the commencement of the Somme offensive the Germans had possessed two main lines of fortifications. The first, from 500 to 1,000 yards in depth, was based on the powerfully organized positions of Thiepval, Ovillers-la-Boiselle, Fricourt, Mametz, Curlu, Frise on the

Somme, Dompierre, Fay and Soyécourt, and consisted of a series of parallel trenches—usually three n number—between which were innumerable shelters for men, machine-guns and ammunition. Behind it came a second line of positions from Grandcourt on the Ancre, through Pozières, the two Bazentins, Longueval, Guillemont, Maurepas, and across the Somme to Herbécourt, and from Herbé-court southwards through Assevillers and Belloy en Santerre to Ablaincoùrt. Between the first and second lines were in places systems of intermediate trenches, and along the whole front of the second barrier ran wide barbed-wire entanglements. Farther back were a series of other organizations constructed during the battle.

Such had been the tremendous obstacles

GERMANS, CAPTURED BY THE FRENCH, PASSING THROUGH A TRENCH
UNDER THE EYES OF THE BRITISH.

Official photograph.

DRAWING WATER FOR COOKING.

encountered by the British and French on the 25 miles front. Nearly all the first and the greater part of the second of the lines had been carried between July 1 and July 6. Between July 6 and September 3 the remainder of the second line had been occupied. From September 3 onwards the Allies had continued their offensive, constantly proving their superiority over the enemy. Between July 1 and September 17, the French alone, continued the report,

Official photograph.

DINNER-TIME ON THE ANCRE.

had taken 30,000 unwounded and 4,500 wounded prisoners, and had captured 144 guns of which more than half were heavy pieces, a number of trench mortars, about 500 machine-guns, vast quantities of shells and a captive balloon. The Allies had conquered a zone of territory considerably greater than that won by the Germans after six months' fighting at the Battle of Verdun. Up to September 17, no less than 67 fresh divisions and 17 fresh battalions had been opposed to them. The greater part of these divisions and battalions

September 17, or with the operations of General Micheler's Army between Ablaincourt and Chilly. Since September 17 the French, north of the Somme, had, as related, captured Rancourt, and they were now on the outskirts of Sailly-Saillisel, while General Micheler's thrust eastwards had rendered it more and more difficult for the enemy to maintain himself in the area west of the Somme from Ablaincourt through Barleux to Péronne. In the Biaches region, General Fayolle's troops were already in the south-western environs of

SORTING THE MAIL FROM HOME.　　　*[Official photograph.*

had been drawn from sectors where no battle was in progress. " The Battle of the Somme," said the French report, " has destroyed the German will to conquer before Verdun. As the Somme battle has developed the German attacks on Verdun have become weaker and weaker, and the German troops that were concentrated before the great French eastern fortress have ebbed away regularly toward the Somme. Better still, with the development of the Somme battle the enemy before Verdun soon changed from the offensive to the defensive."

The French report, it will be perceived, did not deal with the momentous fighting since

Péronne, and from the east of Clery and from Bouchave-nes they were within striking distance of Mont St. Quentin; the northern key to the city. The points of the blades of, as it were, a pair of scissors, which crossed at Frise, on the Somme, were closing, and Péronne, like Bapaume, might be expected in the near future to be cut off and compelled to surrender.

Whether, however, Péronne and Bapaume were secured mattered comparatively little. In this warfare of attrition the great question exercising the minds of the Staffs on both sides was how to reduce the opponent's effectives. Until the enormous forces yet at the disposal of Hindenburg had been materially reduced

[Official photograph.

INDIAN CAVALRY DISPATCH RIDER COMING BACK FROM FLERS.
Road-makers are at work among the wreckage of a wood.

by casualties it was idle for the Allies to expect decisive victories. The *Frankfurter Zeitung* of September 27 boldly asserted that in strategy the Entente had won nothing. This was a criticism derived from the study of old wars, when battles were decided by piercing positions or outflanking them. But, by September, 1916, the test to be applied when considering the result of a battle was almost an arithmetical one. Had the balance of effectives, weapons, and munitions shifted as a result of the struggle? Applying this test to the Battle of the Somme from July 1 to September 30 the answer was unequivocal. The writer in the *Frankfurter Zeitung* might allege that Hindenburg's calm course had not "swerved a hair's breadth from its intended path"; but if that were true, why had the Battle of Verdun subsided and the Germans, after their prodigious losses, abandoned their offensive?

The movements of the German forces in the Western theatre of war during the Battle of the Somme also told a significant tale. At this epoch the enemy appears to have had in the field 193 divisions, of which 117 consisted of three, 57 of four regiments, the remaining 19 being of various sizes. One hundred and twenty-four divisions had been stationed on the Western front. Now, at the beginning of the Battle of the Somme, from July 1 to July 9, the 25 miles long line of entrenchments had been held by 18 divisions. From the 10th to the end of July, 15 of them were withdrawn and replaced by 12 fresh ones. In the last week of August no fewer than 26 divisions were shuffled from one position to another on the front of battle, and in the third week of September six divisions were brought up to the Somme from other positions between Ostend and Mülhausen, and seven divisions retired and six divisions which were resting displaced. Simultaneously two divisions were withdrawn from the Verdun region. One was sent into Champagne, and the other into Belgium.

It is obvious that if Hindenburg had not been obliged by dire necessity he would never have imposed the immense labour involved in moving these masses of troops to and fro, especially when his object was not to fight an offensive but a defensive battle. It must, moreover, be remembered that the extraordinarily complicated character of the lines north and south of the Somme rendered it most inadvisable suddenly to send new troops to garrison them. In the struggles of earlier periods officers and men could quickly understand the features of a position which they were called upon at a moment's notice to occupy, but here the mazes of tunnels and trenches, and the thousands of dug-outs, required to be studied for days before their tactical value could be fully appreciated. To rush men ignorant of the locality into the labyrinthine entrenchments was to court disaster.

The truth was that the initiative in the Western theatre had at last passed from the Germans to the Allies.

CHAPTER CLXXVIII.

THE BATTLE OF THE SOMME (VI.).

FROM the line held by the British on September 30, 1916, the ground sloped gently downwards to a shallow valley which ran north-westward from near Sailly-Saillisel—the immediate objective of the French from Morval and Rancourt—past Le Transloy and Ligny-Thilloy, then westward south of Irles, where it narrowed into comparatively abrupt slopes ; at Miraumont it joined the valley of the Ancre. From the Thiepval-Morval ridge a series of long well-marked spurs ran down into the first-named shallow depression. The most important of these was the hammer-headed one immediately west of Flers. At the end of it, just east of the Albert-Bapaume road and north-east of Le Sars was the ancient tumulus, some 50 feet high, known as the Butte de Warlencourt. Another spur ran from Morval north-north-westwards towards Ligny and Thilloy, villages north-east of the Butte de Warlencourt forming the southern slope of the depression just described, and on it lay the German fourth position. To get within assaulting distance of this it was necessary to carry Le Sars and the two spurs, which were held in strength, every advantage having been taken of sunken roads, buildings, and the undulating nature of the country. Le Sars itself was strongly fortified ; to its east was an agglomeration of trenches round Eaucourt l'Abbaye : and to its north-west the ground to Pys and Miraumont contained numerous artificial

obstacles. At Petit Miraumont, on the south bank of the Ancre, began the Regina trench, which ran from the neighbourhood of the Stuff Redoubt nearly to Le Sars. Destremont Farm was already in our hands. But before Bapaume could be reached this further formidable barrier had to be overcome.

During the night of September 30-October 1 the French were bombing south-east of Morval and along the banks of the Somme towards Péronne. At the other end of the battlefield, north of the river, the enemy was dislodged by Sir Hubert Gough's troops from ground near the Stuff Redoubt and we increased our gains at Schwaben Redoubt, only a minute fragment of which remained untaken.

Between Neuve Chapelle and Ypres no less than sixteen raids were successfully carried out, and a number of prisoners taken, and some progress was made in the area to be attacked the next day.

It was on Sunday, October 1, in rainy weather, while the French were moving out of Morval and Rancourt and capturing trenches in the direction of Sailly-Saillisel, and our guns were bombarding Le Transloy, that the Canadians from the Courcelette region attacked the Regina trench and Sir Henry Rawlinson's troops advanced on a front of some 3,000 yards from the Albert-Bapaume road, north-east of Destremont Farm, to a point east of Eaucourt l'Abbaye. The 1st and 2nd Marine Regiments of the 2nd German Division had been brought

THE BUTTE DE WARLENCOURT.
In the foreground a light railway for transporting ammunition and supplies

down from the Belgian coast, so hard put to it were the German leaders owing to the terrible losses which their troops had sustained in the Battle of the Somme. They replaced the 26th Regiment of the 7th (Magdeburg) Division in the Regina trench. From the Lille district the 17th Regiment of the 6th (Bavarian) Division had also been summoned to help defend the Bapaume region. After the customary intensive bombardment the attacks were delivered at 3.30 p.m. The sailors fought stubbornly, but the Canadians pushed up a German trench running north-westward nearly to its junction with the Regina trench, which itself was entered in several places. Fighting there went on well into the night, attack and counter-attack succeeding one another. The Canadians succeeded in establishing themselves at a point 1,200 yards north of Courcelette in the direction of the Hessian trench but were ejected from a section of the Regina trench. This operation was in the nature of a demonstration to protect the troops moving on Le Sars and Faucourt l'Abbaye from being attacked in flank ; the serious business of the day consisted in the drive to be undertaken towards Bapaume.

The foremost line of trenches between Sir Henry Rawlinson's men and Le Sars and the ruined abbey was of old construction. It had been made before July 1, at a date when the whole system of defence of the region had been planned. A second trench, 50 yards or so behind

the first, was of more recent construction. Both trenches were well-wired and furnished with dug-outs. A mill east of Le Sars and west of the abbey had been fortified. The chapel and the deep crypts and cellars of the monastery were alive with machine-gunners, and garrisoned by the 17th (Bavarian) Regiment. At 3.30 p.m. our men went over the parapets. In five minutes they had seized the first trench before Le Sars. The barrage lifted and, following in its wake, the British charged for the second entrenchment. Weakly defended, it was speedily taken, and patrols pushed forward into and beyond Le Sars. For a moment it looked as if the village would be carried with little loss, but as the evening drew on German reinforcements poured into it down the Bapaume-Albert road and the operation of reducing Le Sars had to be postponed.

Simultaneously with the movement on Le Sars, infantry had advanced from the north-east and south-east on Eaucourt l'Abbaye. The Abbey was protected on the north-east by two lines of trenches, of which the outer one was known as Goose Alley. Neither offered any serious resistance, and by nightfall our men had established themselves on a line which ran from the northern end of the buildings due east and west, connecting with our positions to the north-west of Factory Corner, parallel with the German trench from the Butte de Warlencourt to the outskirts of

Gueudecourt. They even captured and held positions farther to the north on the country road to Le Barque and west of it. On this, the right of the attack, the gain was from 1,200 to 1,500 yards.

The assault on the trenches south of the Abbey was less successful. It was held up by barbed wire and machine-guns. Two Tanks, however, arrived on the scene. One of them stuck in the mud and became a stationary fortress. The crew left her later, and the Commander was wounded. Two of the crew remained with him in a crater and stayed there for a couple of days. The other Tank tore through the entanglements and went along the borders of the trenches, crushing or shooting down all who came in its way. Our troops, with the aid of the Tanks, were soon ensconced in the southern outskirts of the Abbey, where they remained, though drenched to the skin. They were now violently attacked from the direction of Warlencourt. Throughout the night the struggle went on, and by the morning of October 2 the Abbey was finally cleared out.

While these events were proceeding, cavalry patrols pressed on towards Pys and Warlencourt. They reported on their return that they had reached " fresh fields, green trees, and untouched villages " behind the enemy's lines. They had ridden over some empty trenches and had found open country between the Courcelette-Warlencourt road and Pys. " It is a very cheering thing," said an officer, " to find that you have got past the great network of trenches. Even the horses want to go on when they feel that once more they have firm ground underfoot."

On Monday, October 2, the enemy counterattacked with great violence and succeeded in recovering Eaucourt l'Abbaye. We, in our turn, improved our positions north and east of Courcelette and south-west of Gueudecourt. The French, in the night of October 1–2, had carried a trench east of Bouchavesnes and taken some prisoners. During October 2, they made further progress in this direction, and south of the Somme repulsed a German attack between Vermandovillers and Chaulnes. In the night of October 2–3, their barrages and machine-gun fire drove back German columns attempting to debouch from the Wood of St. Pierre Vaast.

On the Sunday and Monday President Poincaré and the French Minister of War,

A WASH IN A SOMME SWAMP.

[Official photograph

141—2

General Roques, visited the Allied battle-front. On this occasion the President decorated Sir Hubert Gough with the insignia of Grand Officer of the Legion of Honour.

Rain had now been falling for two days, and the operations were almost brought to a standstill. Fighting for Eaucourt l'Abbaye, however, continued, and by the evening of October 3 it finally passed into our hands. The same day the French drew nearer to Sailly-Saillisel, capturing an important trench north of Rancourt, and took 120 prisoners, including three officers.

On Wednesday, October 4, in heavy rain, the Germans attempted a bombing attack between Eaucourt l'Abbaye and Gueudecourt. It was driven off, the enemy abandoning his wounded. The French completed the capture of the powerful lines of German trenches between Morval and the Wood of St. Pierre Vaast. They captured 200 prisoners, including 10 officers. At 8 a.m. three companies had bombed the enemy out of the Brunswick Trench, and one company had rushed over the double line of trenches west of the Morval-Frégicourt track. Nine 88 mm. guns had thus

been secured. The way to the northern end of the St. Pierre Vaast woods, which covered nearly two miles of country, and acted as a centre from which German attacks radiated, was now open, and the western face of the woods could be assaulted from Rancourt. South of the Somme the Germans violently bombarded the French works in the region of Belloy-en-Santerre, and there was cannonading near Assevillers. The next day the enemy's artillery was particularly active south of the Somme, chiefly in the Barleux-Belloy-Deniécourt sector and about Quesnoy, which lay north-west of Roye. The French, in the course of the day, repulsed a counter-attack on the trenches captured north of Frégicourt, and we repulsed two enemy attacks in the Thiepval area. North of the Schwaben Redoubt our guns caught bodies of Germans on the move and inflicted heavy losses on them. The rain had now ceased, but the ground was so soft and muddy that operations on a large scale were impossible.

Friday, October 6, the day before another forward move on the part of the Allies, passed in comparative quietude, but we captured the

[*Official photograph.*

ARTILLERY OFFICER DIRECTING GUN-FIRE BY MEANS OF DATA RECEIVED BY WIRELESS TELEGRAPH.

A GERMAN HOWITZER LEFT BEHIND. [*Official photograph.*]

mill between Le Sars and Eaucourt l'Abbaye. During the previous night we had advanced north-east of the Abbey. East of Loos, where three raids were carried out, and east of Armentières, the British discharged gas. This diabolical invention of the enemy had reacted on him. It enabled the Allies with little effort to keep the Germans on the alert at almost any point of their long line of battle and so to disturb their calculations. Not having the command of the air, they could never be certain that a gas discharge would not be followed by an attack of infantry which had been secretly concentrated behind the cylinders.

The French on the 6th advanced slightly east of Bouchavesnes. Otherwise there was little to report from the Somme front. It was the lull before another determined advance by the Allies.

During this period our aeroplanes patrolled far behind the German lines, fought aerial duels, swooped down on trains and attacked German depots and troops The following incidents extracted from reports of the Royal Flying Corps are illuminating :

October 1.—On the evening of September 30 one of our patrols encountered many hostile machines. A formation of seven Rolands near Bapaume was dispersed, two of them being driven down out of control.

On October 1 Captain " A " drove down two patrolling machines out of control near Gommecourt. He afterwards waited and attacked three hostile machines

which came up from a neighbouring aerodrome. He forced one to land and dispersed the remainder.

Lieutenant " B " and Lieutenant " C," when taking photographs, were attacked by seven Rolands. The attack was driven off with the assistance of two of our patrolling machines, who joined the fight. One of the Rolands fell in a nose dive and was seen to plunge to earth.

October 10.—Lieutenant " D " and Lieutenant " E " had six encounters between 7 a.m. and 8.45 a.m. while on artillery patrol. In an encounter with three L.V.G.'s one German machine dived emitting clouds of smoke, having been engaged at 20 yards range. The remaining machines declined close combat.

Second Lieutenant " F," in the course of an encounter with several hostile machines, had all the controls of his machine, with the exception of the rudder, shot away. His machine turned a somersault and was wrecked ; the pilot was unhurt.

A highly successful bombing raid was carried out against railway trains and stations at Quéant, Cambrai, and Bapaume at about 11 p.m. on the night of the 10th inst. A train entering Cambrai was attacked and wrecked, a bomb being observed to hit the first carriage behind the engine. The second bomb hit the station buildings, whereupon all the lights were extinguished.

Second Lieutenant " G " fired a drum of ammunition from 1,400 feet at a closed touring car. The car immediately stopped and three people got out of it and ran away.

On Saturday, October 7, it was decided that Sir Henry Rawlinson's Army should move still farther forward between Destremont Farm and Lesboeufs, and that General Fayolle's left wing should advance from Morval through Rancourt to Bouchavesnes on Sailly-Saillisel. Le Sars, the last considerable village on the Albert-Bapaume Road, was to be stormed, the British salient between Destremont Farm and Lesboeufs rendered less pronounced, while the ridges on the road from Lesboeufs to Le Transloy, and the approaches to Sailly-Saillisel astride the Péronne-Bapaume road, were to be gained. Le Sars was held by the 4th Ersatz and the

[*Canadian official photograph.*

A BURSTING SHRAPNEL SHELL.

ground behind Eaucourt l'Abbaye by the 6th (Bavarian) Divisions. So uncertain did the German commanders consider the outcome of another struggle with the victorious British that these two Divisions were deployed on a front of less than 3,000 yards. The succession of blows delivered by the Allies since July 1 had forced the enemy to resort to massed defence as well as massed attack.

The offensive had been fixed for a little before 2 p.m. Though the rain had ceased and the weather was comparatively fine, the ground in places resembled a morass and the craters were mostly filled to the brim with water. During the night the Germans had delivered an unsuccessful bombing attack north-east of Eaucourt l'Abbaye. The British advance was preceded by the customary violent bombardment which churned up the ruins of Le Sars and knocked the Butte de Warlencourt behind it into a shapeless mass. When the guns lifted the Canadians from the Courcelette-Destremont Farm line again attacked the points in the Regina trench not yet held by us and the quadrilateral formed by the junction of the Below and Gallwitz double line of trenches between Pys and Le Sars. The village of Le Sars itself was assaulted on two sides, from Destremont Farm and from Eaucourt l'Abbaye, which with its mill house had formerly been a strong German position. Le Sars consisted of a street of wrecked houses, crossed midway by the sunken road connecting it with Eaucourt l'Abbaye. A redoubt, the Tangle—walled and cemented—blocked the approach to Le Sars on the east ; 1,200 yards north-west of the village were a strongly fortified quarry and chalk-pit.

The ground between Le Sars and the Abbey dipped into a hollow or gully running northward almost up to the Butte de Warlencourt. This gully was swept by machine-guns from the neighbourhood of the tumulus. In craters before and on the flanks of the village were German snipers, who held their ground despite the fact that some of them were up to their armpits in water. The whole area swarmed with hostile machine-gunners, riflemen and bombers. But to the troops who had stormed the Thiepval-Morval ridge the obstacles in the low-lying ground before Bapaume appeared almost insignificant. At two in the afternoon the British infantry went over the parapets and, undeterred by bullets, bombs, shells, and the huge projectiles lobbed at them by *minenwerfer*, advanced up the Albert-Bapaume road and to the left and right of it on the village and the strong points in its vicinity. At the first rush our men reached the sunken road, and waited till our guns had operated on the houses beyond it. The barrage again lifted and then, with grim determination, the British, supported by those attacking from Eaucourt l'Abbaye and its mill, burst through the village and dug themselves in 500 yards or so nearer Bapaume across the highway. "The British," said a captured sergeant of the German 361st Regiment, "fought like tigers."

Meanwhile a desperate struggle had gone on

between Le Sars and Eaucourt l'Abbaye. The machine-gunners in the Tangle mowed down our infantry, the survivors of which were forced to fling themselves face downwards on the muddy soil. Once more the Tanks justified their inventors. One of these huge machines made its appearance and splashed its way up to the redoubt. In vain the Germans flung bombs at it. From each flank its guns fired into the Tangle, which was speedily carried. Only in the hollow leading to the Butte de Warlencourt were the Bavarians able to resist the British onset. When night fell the enemy there were maintaining a precarious hold on this narrow salient. The quarry and chalk-pit north-west of Le Sars were gained the next morning and counter-attacks of the Germans during the night of the 7th and at 5 a.m. on the 8th on the Schwaben Redoubt above Thiepval were heavily repulsed. The troops employed by the enemy were drawn from the 110th and 111th Regiments.

Thus the operations on the 7th between the Schwaben Redoubt and Le Sars had been brilliantly successful. East of the Butte de

Warlencourt we had pushed forward on Le Barque and Ligny-Thilloy; to the right of Gueudecourt we had penetrated the enemy's trenches to a depth of 2,000 yards; and north-east of Lesboeufs we had gained a footing on the crest of the long spur which screened the defences of Le Transloy. Nearly 1,000 prisoners had been captured in the fighting and the enemy's losses in killed and wounded had been very heavy. Unfortunately rain fell on the evening of the 7th and prevented us from pursuing our onward progress.

Simultaneously with the advance of Sir Henry Rawlinson's infantry the French, after a devastating bombardment, moved on Sailly-Saillisel from the west and south. They had in front of them the Karlsbad, Teplitz and Berlin trenches and the well-organized fringe of the eastern end of the St. Pierre Vaast Woods. Beyond these trenches the enemy had constructed a very strong fortress on the western edge of Sailly-Saillisel Château, and close to the Péronne-Bapaume road was a redoubt known as "The Bluff" which had to be taken. At 2 p.m. the French left their

[Official photograph.

PRISONERS FROM THE LESBOEUFS DISTRICT.
A Tank is seen in the distance.

trenches. A company recruited from the Parisian districts of the Temple and Belleville, and known as the "Belleville Boys," had been deputed to storm "The Bluff." They crossed 300 yards of destroyed trenches and shelters and came under machine-gun fire. The moment for assaulting "The Bluff" had come. A non-commissioned officer described what followed :

The Lieutenant called me, saying : "Now is the time for us to use our wits. Take your section to turn the Bluff. Crawl within 20 yards of the first trench, and as soon as you are ready to attack I will fall upon the Boches with the remainder of the company." So I, with 40 men, made for the spot selected, going forward by six-foot bounds, and, thanks to the craters, only losing two comrades. Then I gave the agreed signal and we leapt into the trench. A fierce fusillade on my right told me that the Lieutenant also was busy. I wish you could have seen my little "Belleville Boys" bayoneting the Boches. Then they rushed on to help their comrades, who were engaged in a hot struggle with a Silesian battalion. They were fighting like lions blowing a path through the enemy's ranks with grenades. At 10 minutes past 3 Sailly Bluff was ours and the blue and white colours of the "Belleville Boys" were fluttering joyfully on the summit

Elsewhere the Germans, taken by surprise, offered little resistance, and soon after 3 p.m. the French had reached all their objectives. They were within a couple of hundred yards of the twin villages.

Fearing that Sailly-Saillisel would be at once attacked, the German commanders packed into automobiles of every description troops hastily withdrawn from other parts of their line and sent them post haste to the north of the village. Their presence was at once reported by observers in aeroplanes, and the French heavy guns discharged on them a hurricane of shells with great effect. By nightfall the troops of General Fayolle had carried their line forward over 1,300 yards north-east of Morval ; they crowned the western slopes of the Sailly-Saillisel ridge, and, as mentioned, were on the Péronne-Bapaume road within 200 yards of the southern entrance of Sailly. East of the road they were ensconced in the western and south-western fringes of the St. Pierre Vaast Wood. Over 400 prisoners, including 10 officers, with 15 machine-guns, had been captured.

The next day (Sunday, October 9) the German reinforcements sent to support the garrison of Sailly-Saillisel were flung against the French positions in front of Morval. Wave after wave advanced to the attack, only to be shattered by the *rafales* from the " 75 " guns. Not a single living German reached the French

[*Official photograph.*

WOUNDED GERMAN PRISONERS AT A BRITISH DRESSING STATION.

[*French official photograph.*

A GERMAN SNIPER'S POST OCCUPIED BY A FRENCH MARKSMAN.

trenches. Meanwhile the aerial squadrons of our Allies were particularly active. They bombed the Bois des Vaux, due east of the Bois St. Pierre Vaast and the village of Moislains to the south of it.

On the British front, besides the fighting round the Schwaben Redoubt already referred to, there was an engagement north of the Courcelette-Warlencourt road where we gained ground, and we also advanced south-west of Gueudecourt. North of the Ancre-Somme battlefield Irish, Midland, and Yorkshire troops had during the night executed successful raids in the Loos, Givenchy and Fauquissart (north of Neuve Chapelle) areas. Against these achievements the Germans could only set the recovery on the evening of the 8th of a small portion of their lost trenches north of Lesbœufs.

On Monday, October 9, in somewhat drier weather, while raids were being carried out in the regions of Loos and Neuville St. Vaast, we successfully discharged gas at different points north of the Ancre, and our patrols were able to enter the enemy trenches and secure prisoners. During the night our troops had progressed east of Le Sars in the direction of the Butte de Warlencourt, and in the course of the afternoon of the 9th we attacked 1,000 yards east of the Schwaben and north of the Stuff Redoubt. Round "The Mound," a redoubt on the edge of the ridge descending towards the Ancre Valley, there were some fierce encounters, ending in our taking 200 prisoners, including six officers. In the Le Transloy region our artillery dispersed a party of the enemy which had ventured into the open. The French the same day repulsed an enemy attack starting from a salient of the St. Pierre Vaast Wood to the east of Rancourt, and shortly afterwards a reconnaissance debouching from a small wood to the north-east of Bouchavesnes was dispersed by machine-gun fire.

At this point it will be well to consider the tactical situation between the Ancre and the Somme created by the series of victories gained by the Allies since July 1. It was well explained in Sir Douglas Haig's dispatch of December 23 as follows :

With the exception of his positions in the neighbourhood of Sailly-Saillisel, and his scanty foothold on the northern crest of the high ground above Thiepval, the enemy had now been driven from the whole of the ridge lying between the Tortille and the Ancre.

Possession of the north-western portion of the ridge north of the latter village carried with it observation over the valley of the Ancre between Miraumont and Hamel and the spurs and valleys held by the enemy on the right bank of the river. The Germans, therefore, made desperate efforts to cling to their last remaining

[*French official photograph.*

FRENCH CATERPILLAR TRACTORS.

trenches in this area, and in the course of the three weeks following our advance made repeated counter-attacks at heavy cost in the vain hope of recovering the ground they had lost. During this period our gains in the neighbourhood of Stuff and Schwaben Redoubts were gradually increased and secured in readiness for future operations ; and I was quite confident of the ability of our troops, not only to repulse the enemy's attacks, but to clear him entirely from his last positions on the ridge whenever it should suit my plans to do so. I was, therefore, well content with the situation on this flank.

Along the centre of our line from Gueudecourt to the west of Le Sars similar considerations applied. As we were already well down the forward slopes of the ridge on this front, it was for the time being inadvisable to make any serious advance. Pending developments elsewhere all that was necessary or indeed desirable was to carry on local operations to improve our positions and to keep the enemy fully employed.

On our eastern flank, on the other hand, it was important to gain ground. Here the enemy still possessed a strong system of trenches covering the villages of Le Transloy and Beaulencourt and the town of Bapaume ; but, although he was digging with feverish haste, he had not yet been able to create any very formidable defences behind this line. In this direction, in fact, we had at last reached a stage at which a successful attack might reasonably be expected to yield much greater results than anything we had yet attained. The resistance of the troops opposed to us had seriously weakened in the course of our recent operations, and there was no reason to suppose that the effort required would not be within our powers.

This last completed system of defence, before Le Transloy, was flanked to the south by the enemy's positions at Sailly-Saillisel, and screened to the west by the spur lying between Le Transloy and Lesboeufs. A necessary preliminary, therefore, to an assault upon it was to secure the spur and the Sailly-Saillisel heights. Possession of the high ground at this latter village would at once give a far better command over the ground to the north and north-west, secure the flank of our operations towards Le Transloy, and deprive the enemy of observation over the Allied communications in the Combles Valley. In view of the enemy's efforts to construct new systems of defence behind the Le Transloy line, it was desirable to lose no time in dealing with the situation.

Unfortunately, at this juncture, very unfavourable weather set in and continued with scarcely a break during the remainder of October and the early part of November. Poor visibility seriously interfered with the work of our artillery, and constant rain turned the mass of hastily dug trenches for which we were fighting into channels of deep mud.

The country roads, broken by countless shell craters, that cross the deep stretch of ground we had lately won, rapidly became almost impassable, making the supply of food, stores, and ammunition a serious problem These conditions multiplied the difficulties of attack to such an extent that it was found impossible to exploit the situation with the rapidity necessary to enable us to reap the full benefits of the advantages we had gained.

None the less, my right flank continued to assist the operations of our Allies against Saillisel, and attacks were made to this end, whenever a slight improvement in the weather made the co-operation of artillery and infantry at all possible. The delay in our advance, however, though unavoidable, had given the enemy time to reorganise and rally his troops. His resistance again became stubborn, and he seized every favourable opportunity for counter-attacks. Trenches changed hands with great frequency, the conditions of ground making it difficult to renew exhausted supplies of bombs and ammunition, or to consolidate the ground won, and so rendering it an easier matter to take a battered trench than to hold it.

Such, in short, were the considerations which determined the future Allied movements between the Ancre and the Somme. It remains to be seen how Sir Douglas Haig's plans were eventually carried out.

By Tuesday, October 10, the advance beyond the Stuff Redoubt had enabled us to push our line forward east of that point and to carry it eastward and a little to the north to about half-way between Le Sars and Warlencourt. In the vicinity of Grandcourt, west of Le Sars, German infantry in the open were dispersed by our artillery on the 10th. Otherwise the day was uneventful for the British. It was very different with the French. South of the Somme between Berny-en-Santerre and Chaulnes on a front of over three miles they advanced to the attack. Their line ran from Berny southwards to Hill 91 and thence in a westerly direction towards Deniécourt. A few hundred yards east of Deniécourt it swerved to the south-west in front of Soyécourt and Vermando-villers and then proceeded to a point a few hundred yards west of Chaulnes. The German position in the area formed a salient and the object of General Micheler was to expel the Germans from it. They were strongly en-trenched in the hamlet of Bovent, the villages of Ablaincourt and Pressoire and in the woods round Chaulnes. General von Kothen, defend-ing the salient, had been strongly reinforced and believed that his Silesian " shock " troops were capable of resisting any attack. The 44th Reserve Division and a Division of Wurtem-bergers had been sent to his assistance, and the 23rd Saxon Division was held in readiness against unexpected eventualities.

During Monday the French artillery bom-barded the selected sector with their usual thoroughness. Among other targets which had been in the last week struck by the French guns was an observation-post in an orchard at Bovent, six feet high and constructed of great blocks of reinforced concrete. It resembled the conning-tower of a battleship, and at its top there were two narrow slits, through which observers could watch the French lines or machine-guns could fire. Eight rooms, 30 feet deep, with numerous concealed exits sur-rounded the tower. So long as the summer lasted this observation post was hidden by the foliage of the trees and undergrowth. But in October it had become visible and a French artillery lieutenant had noticed that the orchard contained some structure unusual in orchards. He promptly directed the " 75 " guns to clear away the surrounding trees and bushes and the naked grey concrete of the tower was revealed. The attention of the big guns was then drawn to this formidable obstacle. Projectile after projectile burst on it. Still the tower, although becoming more and more ragged, resisted. A salvo of gas shells was next discharged. The gas being heavier than air descended into the subterranean shelters. Finally a huge shell burst a few yards to the left of the tower, opened a hole in the ground about 15 feet deep, hurled great masses of concrete into the air, which fell and blocked the exits. When Bovent on Tuesday was captured a French soldier squeezed his way down into the cavern below the tower and found 30 Germans, including two colonels, lying dead

A GERMAN PRISONER LENDS A HELPING HAND TO A BRITISH
DISPATCH RIDER.

[Canadian official photograph.

LOADING AMMUNITION ON A MOTOR LIGHT RAILWAY BEHIND THE FIRING LINE.

with their gas-masks on and apparently un-wounded. Two of them had been playing chess when the gas caught them, and the table was laid for dinner.

The effect of the French bombardment was to shake the nerves of the Germans, who on Monday evening, in anticipation of an offensive, replied with copious *barrages* and tear shells. It was not, however, till Tuesday that the attack was really delivered. One column, starting from the woods outside Deniécourt, carried the hamlet of Bovent after a short and fierce struggle. A second column from Ver-mandovillers assaulted Ablaincourt. Five times they carried the village and five times it was recovered by the enemy, to whose aid the 23rd Saxon Division had been rushed up in motor lorries. At the end of the day the northern and western outskirts of Ablaincourt were in the possession of the French. Farther to the south our Allies progressed to within 200 yards of Pressoire. A third column from Lihons deployed and attacked the Chaulnes Woods, bristling with entanglements and machine-guns and garrisoned by a brigade of Wurtembergers, who were finally chased away. The prisoners taken in the fighting amounted to over 1,700.

During the day bivouacs and cantonments in the vicinity of Péronne, the Tergnier aviation sheds, the railway stations of St. Quentin and Guiscard and the Wood of Porquericourt, had been bombed by French aeronauts and there had been 14 aerial duels between French and German airmen south of the Somme, and 44 north of it. Four German machines were brought down and six others injured. A train running between Offoy and Ham was attacked with machine-gun fire. The British aeroplanes destroyed two gun emplacements and damaged others. They penetrated well behind the German lines and bombed with good effect railway stations, trains and billets. Two of our machines engaged seven hostile aeroplanes, destroyed one, damaged two, and dispersed the rest. Four British machines were lost.

The next day (Wednesday, October 11) the enemy attempted to retake the Chaulnes Wood and was repulsed after violent hand-to-hand fighting. The struggle still went on in Ablain-court and began round the sugar refinery of Genermont, east of Bovent. North of the Somme, in the evening and throughout the night, bombing encounters took place along the Morval-Bouchavesnes front, especially on the edge of the St. Pierre Vaast Wood. The German 68th Infantry Regiment and 76th Reserve Infantry Regiment put up a fierce resistance. North of Courcelette the British artillery stopped an attack and elsewhere dealt effectively with hostile infantry mustering in the background.

In dull weather on Thursday afternoon, October 12, Sir Henry Rawlinson and General

[French official photograph.

ARMY TELEPHONE STATION ON THE SOMME.

Fayolle launched an offensive between Le Sars and Bouchavesnes against the troops of General Sixt von Armin, General von Boehn and General von Garnier. No progress was made in the vicinity of the Butte de Warlencourt, but south of Ligny-Thilloy, east of Gueudecourt and Lesboeufs, our line was advanced. Between Lesboeufs and Le Transloy the gain was about 1,000 yards and we approached to within 500 yards of the cemetery of the last-named village. The enemy appeared to have been about to advance when our offensive began, for there had been a considerable accumulation of troops in their trenches, as was shown in some of them north-east of Gueudecourt, which were found to be packed with the dead and dying. Two hundred prisoners besides numerous machine-guns were secured. During the night a German attack north of the Stuff Redoubt was repulsed. Meanwhile the French scored some small successes west of Sailly-Saillisel, and Sir Hubert Gough pushed forward

GENERAL VON BOEHN.
A German Commander on the Somme.

round the Schwaben Redoubt, capturing 300 prisoners, belonging to the German 110th Regiment.

Apart from a skirmish north of the Stuff Redoubt little that was noteworthy occurred on the British front during Friday, October 13, but there was considerable activity in the Morval, Bouchavesnes, Ablaincourt and Chaulnes sectors. A German attack with *flammen-werfer* resulted in the capture of some parts of trenches at the outskirts of the St. Pierre Vaast Wood.

On Saturday, October 14, Sir Hubert Gough's troops advanced their line well to the north and west of the Schwaben Redoubt and cleared two German communication trenches north of the Stuff Redoubt for a distance of nearly 200 yards, capturing two officers and 303 privates. The French bombarded the Sailly-Saillisel position and south of the Somme again joined battle with the enemy.

On October 14 our Ally, who had progressed on the Malassise Ridge between Bouchavesnes and Moislains, beat back after desperate

fighting masses of Germans counter-attacking in Ablaincourt. At the close of the day the French line ran through the ruins of the village. Between Ablaincourt and Barleux, which lies in a hollow, our Allies had dug deep into the German lines. The sugar refinery on the Ablaincourt-Genermont road had been pulverized by 15-inch and 16-inch howitzers and it was carried with little loss, and from Bovent the French entered Genermont, which fell after an hour's fighting, 250 Germans of the 150th Prussian Regiment being captured. When the sun set the French were only a few hundred yards from the villages of Fresnes and Mazancourt. Farther to the north, starting from the Berny-Barleux road, the Colonial Division, commanded by the heroic General Marchand, who with Kitchener had prevented France and Great Britain from playing into the German hands over the Fashoda affair, brought the French line nearer to the heights of Villers-Carbonnel, the batteries on which covered the Barleux-Chaulnes road. A Silesian detachment in a ruined work barred the way. It was submerged by the waves of the Colonial infantry.

GENERAL VON GARNIER.
A German Commander on the Somme.

In places five lines of trenches had to be carried. They were crammed with German corpses, among which surviving bombers, riflemen and machine-gunners, rendered desperate by the fact that they were fighting with their backs to the marshy Somme, fought with great courage. After a terrible struggle, reminiscent of the scenes in Charleroi when the Colonial troops had at the opening of the war crossed bayonets with the Prussian Guardsmen, the position was taken and the French front extended in depth from six to eight hundred yards. It now overlapped Barleux, and turned the heights of Villers-Carbonnel.

Unwounded German prisoners to the number of 1,100, including 19 officers, had been taken in the Belloy-Ablaincourt sector. The counter-attacks of the enemy in the evening were all beaten off. The French aeroplanes splendidly cooperated in the fighting. The clouds were but 600 feet from the ground, and they had flown close to the enemy's barrages. One machine returned riddled with over 200 bullets. North of the Somme two pilots had attacked the enemy in his trenches with machine-guns.

The next day (Sunday, October 15), while the Colonials repulsed a German attack at the St. Eloi Wood, south-east of Belloy, and the British in the morning advanced slightly north-east of Gueudecourt, the attack on Sailly-Saillisel was delivered. For forty hours the villages and their outworks had been systematically pounded. The cemented trenches east of the Tripot work had been obliterated; the redoubt on the Morval road had been wrecked and its defenders buried in the ruins. Afterwards the French counted, in a vast underground chamber there, the corpses of 200 asphyxiated Germans. On the evening of Sunday the bombardment ceased and Sailly was assaulted.

This village is traversed by the Péronne-Bapaume highway, on the west side of which lie the château, a chapel, and half of the village. The road from Morval crosses the highway just south of the château. East of Sailly, through Saillisel, runs a road branching off from the highway to the village of Roc-quigny, due east of Le Transloy. One French column, starting from north-east of Rancourt up the highway, attacked the château from the south. A second column entered the park of the château from the north-west and stormed the ruined chapel, which was stubbornly defended by a machine-gun section. A third column, after passing two lines of trenches, descended on the village from the north and isolated it from the garrison of Le Transloy. Long and terrible was the fighting for the

chapel and château. The Germans disputed every inch of the ground, but were finally driven helter-skelter through the underground passages connecting these buildings with the houses along the Péronne-Bapaume highway.

GENERAL MARCHAND.
In command of the Colonial Division of the French Army of the West.

After the chapel and château had fallen the contest continued in the western half of the village, which ran for 800 yards north and south. In the meantime the British had during the night repulsed with heavy loss a strong *flammenwerfer* attack at the Schwaben Redoubt delivered after heavy artillery preparation, and a small hostile bombing attack north of Courcelette.

[French official photograph.

BRITISH GUNNERS, WEARING GAS MASKS, LOADING A FIELD GUN.

On Monday, October 16, the French consolidated the position gained by them in Sailly, repulsed a violent counter-attack east of Berny-en-Santerre, carried a small wood and captured two guns of 210 mm. and one of 77 mm. between Genermont and Ablaincourt.

During the next day (October 17) the French, whose aeroplanes fought 65 duels, in the course of which five German machines were put out of action, heavily repulsed counter-attacks east of Berny and Belloy and bombarded the portion of Sailly-Saillisel still in the possession of the Germans. In the morning the enemy forced his way into the ruins between the chapel and the central crossroads. He was promptly expelled, and towards sunset three more counter-attacks from the north and east were repulsed. In thick and murky weather on October 18 the clearing out of the Germans from the rest of Sailly was undertaken. An enormous concentration of guns had been ordered by General Fayolle. "It seemed incredible," said *The Times* correspondent, "that there could be so many guns and so much ammunition in the world, and still more impossible to believe that any sort of

defence could possibly stand up against the hurricane of shell for more than a few minutes." The German artillery was completely outclassed. Faintly, through the mist, about 11.45 a.m., red balls of fiery light announced to the German gunners that the French infantry was leaving its trenches and dug-outs. The garrison, composed of mixed elements of the 1st Bavarians, the 16th Division, and the 2nd Bavarians, received but little assistance in the nature of barrages. By noon the action was over, and the enemy, leaving behind him masses of dead and wounded, had been ejected from the whole of Sailly, and from the ridges north-west and north-east of the village. Again and again, accompanied by waves of asphyxiating gas and the fire-spouting *flammenwerfer*, the frantic Germans were hurled at their relentless foe. No fewer than 20 attacks in mass formation were delivered and repulsed. Across a fiercely disputed outbuilding German corpses formed a rampart three feet high.

The completion of the conquest of Sailly was not the only memorable event of October 18. South of the Somme the French, under Generals Lacapelle and Cugnac, rushed the whole of the

German front-line trenches between La Maisonnette and Biaches, defended by troops of the
11th Reserve Division. Five officers, 245
privates, and several machine-guns were
captured, and the German batteries across
the Somme, near Doingt and Bussu, were
silenced. A German advance at 5 a.m. against
a French trench east of Berny-en-Santerre
had also failed to achieve its object. Some
enemy parties entered the French lines and
were promptly bayoneted. The waves of men
following on behind them were caught in
barrages, and fell back in disorder, leaving
numbers of their comrades dead on the
ground.

The same day at 3 a.m. Sir Henry Rawlinson
had pushed forward on the Butte de Warlencourt, to the north-east of Gueudecourt and
beyond Lesboeufs. Aided by a Tank the
British secured a further section of the Grid
and Grid Support trenches. Some 150 prisoners
were captured. A counter-attack in the Butte
de Warlencourt region was repulsed.

On Thursday, October 19, the French
attacked and captured the village of Saillisel,
which straggled 1,400 yards on either side of
the Sailly-Moislains road. The eastern half of the
village was secured after half an hour's fighting,
and a struggle then began for a ridge 400 feet
high flanking the village between the Péronne-
Bapaume road and the road to Rocquigny.
By the end of the day the French line before the

St. Pierre Vaast Wood formed a semi-circle
from Sailly to between Rancourt and Bouchavesnes East of the wood the Germans still
held the Vaux Wood, behind which ran the
Tortille. But the enemy's batteries on the
ridges north-west and north-east of Sailly-
Saillisel which had raked our troops advancing
from Lesboeufs on Le Transloy had been dislodged, and his batteries on the high ground
towards Le Mesnil were under the direct fire of
the French guns. But for the abominable
weather it is probable that Bapaume would
have been speedily captured by the Allies in
1916. Unfortunately, in the words of Sir
Douglas Haig, " the moment for decisive action
was rapidly passing away, while the weather
showed no signs of improvement. By this
time," he added, " the ground had already
become so bad that nothing less than a prolonged
period of drying weather, which at that season
of the year was most unlikely to occur, would
suit our purpose."

For the moment, indeed, it seemed that
fortune would favour the Allies. A spell of
fine, hard weather set in on Friday, October 20.

**SAILLY: RUINS OF A HOUSE FORTIFIED BY THE GERMANS.
INSET: REMAINS OF THE CHÂTEAU.**

Advantage of the changed conditions was promptly taken by our airmen.

The number of combats in the air on October 20 exceeded 80. Seven enemy machines were seen to crash down or to fall out of control, and there can be no doubt that some which were driven down by our airmen were wrecked in landing. Three of our airmen were killed, three reported missing, and five wounded.

The *communiqués* record at least two instances of conspicuous pluck and endurance. Second Lieutenant " S," though mortally wounded by

machines having withdrawn, Captain " D," the leader of our formation, tried to complete his reconnaissance, accompanied by only two escorting machines. He was again attacked, and another of our machines retired, with engine and propeller damaged. Captain " D " then fought his way homeward, surrounded by hostile machines, and landed safely.

Nor were the French aviators inactive. Seven German machines were brought down, Lieutenant Herteaux increasing his " bag " to ten. During the night 41 bombs of 120 mm.

SHELLS FOR THE 15-IN. HOWITZERS.

[*Official photograph.*]

gun fire, brought his machine and observer safely back to his own aerodrome. He died of his wounds next day. Lieutenant " S," though wounded in the head at the beginning of a combat in which he and Second Lieutenant " G " were opposed to six German machines, continued to fight for a considerable time and drove down one of the enemy machines out of control. Six of our machines, while taking photographs, were heavily attacked by anti-aircraft guns, and, soon after, by twelve hostile fighting machines. One of our machines was brought down by the enemy to his lines, and another brought to land behind our lines, with the pilot severely wounded. The enemy

were dropped on the stations of Noyon and Chauny, and later a train between Appilly and Chauny was bombed. The enemy cantonments and the bivouacs in the region of Nesle and Ham, and the aviation grounds at Matigny and Slez were also hit.

Saturday, October 21, was another day of battle. On the 20th the Germans had delivered an ineffectual attack against the Schwaben Redoubt. Another in the early morning of the 21st was repulsed, five officers and 79 privates being captured. Shortly after noon, preceded by a tremendous bombardment, Sir Hubert Gough's Army advanced on a line of some 5,000 yards between Schwaben Redoubt and

Le Sars. Our line towards the Ancre was pushed forward from 300 to 500 yards; advanced posts to the north and north-east of the redoubt were secured and most of the Stuff and Regina trenches captured. Over 1,000 prisoners were taken, a figure only slightly exceeded by our casualties.

In the meantime the Germans renewed their desperate efforts to recover Sailly-Saillisel.

verse. Near Belloy that day General Marchand, who had been badly wounded at the Battle of the Champagne Pouilleuse, was slightly injured. He refused to relinquish his command.

Finally, on the 21st, the French mastered the Bois Etoile north of Chaulnes from its western edge to the central cross-roads. They captured 250 prisoners and beat off an attack of part of the Chaulnes garrison which had issued from

[*Official photograph.*]

LOADING A HEAVY BRITISH HOWITZER.

Three regiments of the 2nd Bavarian Division were flung at the ruins after artillery preparations of an extremely violent character. Barrages and machine-gun fire broke the waves of the assaulting infantry. Thrice they came forward and thrice were they driven back. South of the Somme at 2 p.m. the Germans with *flammenwerfer* attacked the positions recently lost by them between Biaches and La Maisonnette. The struggle was peculiarly bitter in the Blaise Wood, in some trenches north of which the enemy obtained a footing. At all other points they met with a bloody re-

the village to support the Saxons garrisoning the wood.

On Sunday, October 22, the French extended their gains west of Sailly-Saillisel, south of the Somme. The Germans attacked the French positions in the wood north of Chaulnes. The attack was repulsed with heavy losses. At 1 p.m. the Germans again advanced on the French trenches on the southern end of the wood, but only to be driven back, leaving behind them a litter of dead and wounded, and losing numerous prisoners; in the previous attack alone 150 had been captured.

The next day (October 23) the Germans, who
before dawn had attempted to raid our trenches
in the Gommecourt region, massed south of
Grandcourt, on the Ancre, as if they intended
to commence a counter-attack on the Regina
trench. This movement was at once notified
to our artillery, and the British gunners hurled
high explosives and shrapnel at the enemy, who
speedily dispersed. About the same time Sir
Henry Rawlinson's troops, in conjunction with
the French, pushed forward east of Gueudecourt
and Lesboeufs. The rain had increased during
the night, and numerous German trenches—

Dewdrop, Rainbow, Hazy, Misty, Sleet, Frosty,
Zenith, Orion, Spectrum—and the craters were
full of water.

The object of this minor operation was to
straighten the British front before Le Transloy.
The Germans had dug two lines of trenches in
front of the village embracing the cemetery on
the Lesboeufs road. Behind them were many
machine-gun emplacements, giving a wide field
of fire against the British and against any
French troops moving on Le Transloy down
the Péronne-Bapaume road, who had to pass
over an average distance of 1,200 yards of No-

BRITISH TROOPS REPELLING A STRONG COUNTER-ATTACK.

OFFICERS OBSERVING FROM A CAPTURED TRENCH.

Man's Land. The fighting which ensued was of a confused character. One strip of trench changed hands no less than five times, and a group of gun pits, in which the guns had been replaced by machine-guns, was obstinately attacked and obstinately defended.

Details of the 64th Brandenburg Regiment, the regiment which took Douaumont in February, 1916, and of the 24th Bavarian Regiment, which had carried Fort Vaux, with Hamburgers and Hanoverians, strove desperately to keep the British from approaching nearer to Le Transloy, the most formidable of the village fortresses still blocking the road to Bapaume. Nevertheless, at nightfall, we had captured over 1,000 yards of trenches, while the French had made appreciable progress north-east of Morval in the direction of Le Transloy.

Nothing occurred worth recording on October 24 and 25. The rain continued to pour down, converting low-lying portions of the battlefield into a quagmire. But on Thursday the 26th there was a sudden liveliness. The British raided enemy trenches north-east and south of Arras, and in the morning, after a preliminary bombardment, the Germans attacked the Stuff Trench. They were driven off with considerable loss, leaving 41 prisoners in our

hands. An attempt of the enemy to recover the Abbé Wood, south of Bouchavesnes, was unavailing.

Heavy rain once more fell on Friday, October 27, and the operations on both sides were, apart from the never-ceasing artillery duels, suspended.

On Saturday, October 28, our artillery shelled the Germans out of some strong points north-east of Lesboeufs. As the enemy emerged from his hiding places he came under a murderous fire from our infantry. Several important trenches passed into our hands, and about 100 prisoners were captured.

On Sunday, October 29, we made a further forward movement in the same region, and the French by advancing 300 yards north-west of Sailly, parallel with the Bapaume Road, brought their front into line of our new positions. But in the afternoon they suffered a somewhat serious reverse to the south of the Somme. Their progress between Biaches and La Maisonnette had seriously alarmed the German commanders, for our Allies were almost in the outskirts of Péronne, and threatened Barleux from the north. Accordingly, at 3 p.m., the 360th Regiment, composed of Berlin and Brandenburg men, whose advance had been preceded

[Official photograph.

PACKMULES CARRYING AMMUNITION TO THE TRENCHES.

by an unusually severe bombardment, was launched at the farm of La Maisonnette. Other troops attacked on both sides of the farm, and the assaulting masses were accompanied by a liberal supply of *flammenwerfer*. For a time the French, supported by their artillery, held their own, but during the night the enemy was once more in the farm. It was claimed by him that he captured 412 men and 15 officers. All efforts, however, to drive the French from Hill 97 failed. The next day the French as an offset to this reverse carried a system of trenches north-west of Sailly-Saillisel.

On Wednesday, November 1, the Germans, after a vigorous bombardment and discharges of poisonous gas, attacked Sailly-Saillisel. Seven battalions drawn from different divisions were launched against the village on the north and east. No fewer than six attempts were made by the enemy's columns to force their way in; but apart from a small success the German efforts were abortive. In the after-

[Official photograph.

WATERING HORSES BEHIND THE BATTLE-FRONT

noon the Allies took the offensive in this region. North-east of Lesboeufs the French captured two trenches and made 125 prisoners, while the British gained some ground between Lesboeufs and Le Transloy. Another attack, made by the French to the south-east of Saillisel, secured them a strongly organized system of trenches on the western outskirts of the wood of St. Pierre Vaast.

On November 2, in despite of heavy rain, more ground was gained by the French between Lesboeufs and Sailly-Saillisel; the total

Vaast Wood. The attack was shattered by curtain and machine-gun fire.

On Sunday, November 5, according to the German Higher Command, the British and French "began a gigantic blow against the Army front of General von Below." According to the same veracious account, "the troops of the various German tribes, under Generals von Marschall, von Deimling, and von Garnier, tenaciously resisting, inflicted on the enemy a severe defeat." The real facts were as follows :

[French official photograph.

GERMAN GUNS AND FLAME-THROWERS CAPTURED BY THE FRENCH.

prisoners captured on the 1st and 2nd amounted to 736, including 20 officers, and a dozen machine-guns were also taken. The net result of the fighting was that the British were within 200 yards of Le Transloy, which was also threatened by the French from the south.

On Friday, November 3, the enemy counter-attacked the British east of Gueudecourt and were beaten back, suffering heavy losses and losing four machine-guns. The Germans left behind them over 100 dead and 30 prisoners.

On November 4 the Germans vainly endeavoured to expel the French from the trenches on the western edge of St. Pierre

In the morning of the 5th the troops of Sir Henry Rawlinson moved towards the Butte de Warlencourt and seized the heights east of Le Sars and north-east of Gueudecourt on a front of 1,000 yards, approaching some 400 yards nearer to the Butte. For a short time the Butte passed into our power; but during the night the Germans drove us back. In the Lesboeufs region we captured what was known as the Hazy Trench, and reached a point almost at the further edge of the minor ridge running northwards before Le Transloy. In the meantime the French, from the south of Le Transloy to the south of St. Pierre Vaast Wood, took the' offensive. Between Lesboeufs and Sailly-Saillisel they progressed in the direction of Le Transloy. Issuing from Sailly they reconquered the greater part of Saillisel and works to the south of it ; then attacking on three sides at once the St. Pierre Vaast Wood, they captured three trenches defending the northern corner of the wood, and the whole of the hostile position on the south-western

GENERAL MAISTRE.
A French Commander under General Micheler.

outskirts. All through the afternoon German reinforcements from Moislains struggled hard to regain the lost ground ; but by 4 p.m. they were beaten, and another attempt in the evening made by them was also driven back. Over 600 prisoners, including 15 officers, were taken by the French.

On November 7, in an almost incessant deluge of rain, the French scored another brilliant success, this time south of the Somme. Bretons and Parisians of General Micheler's Army, under the command of Generals Anthoine and Maistre, issued at 9.45 a.m. from Genermont sugar refinery, from the Serpentine Trench south-east of Vermandovillers, and from the northern spur of Chaulnes Wood. The two lines of concreted trenches, forming the outwork of the long Germania trench which ran as far south as Hyencourt-le-Grand, were at once captured, all the occupants being either killed or taken prisoners. Similarly, the Germans between the south of Pressoire and Chaulnes Wood received short shrift. Only

in Ablaincourt and Pressoire itself did the Germans put up a good fight. During the preliminary bombardment they had taken refuge in their subterranean chambers, and as soon as the attack began they came to the surface and played their machine-guns on the French attacking waves. In the southern portion of Ablaincourt a severe struggle took place. A stack of houses defended by Bavarians were thrice taken and retaken. In the church a Bavarian company fought almost to the last man. The cemetery, 500 yards east of the village, was also the scene of fierce encounters : it was carried at the point of the bayonet. Between Ablaincourt and Pressoire a single French company routed a whole Prussian battalion. By nightfall the French had secured Pressoire and were on the outskirts of Omiécourt. They had captured hundreds of prisoners and a position from which their guns could command the plateau of Villers Carbonnel, the batteries on which prevented the French from taking Barleux.

The weather had now somewhat moderated ; it remained dry and cold, with frosty nights and misty mornings. Final preparations were pushed on by Sir Douglas Haig for the attack which he proposed to deliver on the Ancre. On November 9, while fighting continued round Saillisel and south of Pressoire, the British remained quiescent—at least so far as their infantry was concerned. The day was, however, rendered memorable by a great aerial battle, in which a squadron of 30 British aeroplanes engaged from 36 to 40 German machines. The action took place between 9 a.m. and 10 a.m. north-east of Bapaume. Near the Villa of Mory close to Vaulx-Vraucourt, the British, who were on a bombing expedition, sighted the enemy's squadron. Some of our machines were at a higher level than the enemy. They plunged down to join their comrades in the engagement which was fought some 5,000 feet above the ground. For twenty minutes among the clouds there was an inextricable tangle of darting, swirling machines. Four of ours were lost, six of the enemy were sent to earth, and the whole enemy formation broke and scattered. Our airmen bombed Vaulx-Vraucourt and returned home unmolested.

On the 10th the French captured more trenches north-east of Lesboeufs, and in Saillisel repulsed a counter-attack.

The next day, in the early hours of the

morning, the Canadians attacked troops of the
Prussian Guard and Saxon Regiments holding
the Farmers Road, an easterly extension of
Regina Trench, on a front of 1,000 yards ;
60 prisoners, including four officers were taken.
An unpleasant interruption to our line had
been removed, and we were close upon the
strong German position running immediately
in front of Pys and Warlencourt. On the same
day the French seized the north-eastern and
south-eastern outskirts of Saillisel, but the
Germans still maintained themselves in the
easternmost houses of the village. South of the
Somme, at 2.30 p.m. the enemy with *flammenwerfer* attacked in the neighbourhood of Deniécourt. He was beaten back with heavy losses.

On November 12 there was a lull on the
British front, but the fighting went on in Saillisel,
which finally passed into the possession of our
Allies, who captured 220 men and seven officers,
with eight machine-guns. South of the Somme
the Germans, attacking south-east of Berny,
succeeded in entering some advanced trenches
but were immediately driven out by a counter-
attack.

Before the winter set in Sir Douglas Haig
determined to strike a last blow at the almost
shattered line of the Germans now running
from the east of Arras to Péronne. The main
ridge between the Schwaben Redoubt and
Sailly-Saillisel being now in the hands of the
Allies, it was possible to attack successfully
from the west and south the enemy's salient
on both sides of the Ancre Since the ineffectual
assault by the British on July 1, Sir Hubert
Gough's troops had step by step crept towards
the hamlet of St. Pierre Divion on the left and
the village of Beaucourt-sur-Ancre on the right
bank of the river. They were well within
assaulting distance of the maze of vast dug-outs,
caverns and trenches which were all that was
left of Beaumont Hamel ; Beaucourt, higher
up the Ancre, was situated in a hollow. North
of Beaumont Hamel the plateau up to the village
of Serre was also strongly organized. Before
the western edge of Beaumont Hamel, down to
and across the low ground before our lines, ran
successive lines of trenches. So thick were the
rusty wire entanglements—in places five tiers
deep, each often 8 feet high and 90 to 120 feet
wide—that from a distance they looked like a
belt of brown ploughed land. Behind the
trenches and entanglements the face of the
slope beyond in the crease of the hills and the

LIEUT.-GENERAL SIR E. A. FANSHAWE,
K.C.B.
In command of the Fifth Army Corps.

banks of the Ancre was pierced everywhere with
the entrances to the caverns and dug-outs.
From the road through Beaumont Hamel to
the Ancre a deep forked ravine descended to
the enemy's front line trench, where the
extremities of the prongs, as it were, of the
ravine ended. It was known to us from its
shape as the " Y " ravine and was 1,000 yards
or so long. At these western points the prongs
were 30 feet and more in depth, with precipitous
sides that in places almost overhung. Below
the bottom of these gullies in the ground, caves,
some of them large enough to hold a battalion
and a half of men, had been constructed, and a
tunnel ran back to the fourth line trenches. In
caves and tunnels the enemy lay absolutely
safe from shell-fire. The ruins of the village of
Beaucourt on the right bank of the Ancre were
not furnished with underground works com-

BRINGING IN RIFLES AND EQUIPMENT FROM NO-MAN'S LAND.

parable with those of Beaumont Hamel and its vicinity, but deep dug-outs there provided accommodation for the masses held in reserve.

Equally formidable were the defences of the hamlet of St. Pierre Divion on the south bank of the river. Starting from four recessed and sheltered entrances on the river level a great gulley ran back some 300 yards into the hill. Then it branched and from the ends of the branches passages and steps led up to the communication and other trenches on the Thiepval ridge west of the Schwaben Redoubt. This network of tunnels and caverns, some of which were used as hospitals, formed perhaps the largest collection of underground case-mates yet discovered. These works formed one immense fortress with a front of nearly five miles lying astride the Ancre from the Schwaben Redoubt to Serre. At the end of October an additional Division—the 223rd, one of Hindenburg's newly constructed divisions —had been added to the garrison. The 2nd Guard Reserve Division was on the north of the Ancre; it was supported by troops of the 12th, 55th, 58th, 62nd, and 144th Divisions. For the attack on the 3,000 yards of entrench-ments and burrows south of the Ancre and of the 5,000 yards north of the river only troops recruited in the British Isles were employed. It was a good trial of strength between them and the inhabitants of Germany.

At 5 a.m. on the morning of November 11, the preliminary bombardment of the Ancre

fortress had begun. It continued with bursts of great intensity until the morning of No-vember 13. The acres of barbed wire en-tanglements by then had melted away, and the surface works had been knocked to pieces. The assault was fixed for 6 a.m. It was preceded by a sudden and very effective barrage fire. A dense fog covered the ground, and the fog coupled with the darkness prevented the Germans from perceiving that our men were concentrating before their positions in un-usually large numbers. Consequently the operation partook largely of the nature of a surprise. South of the Ancre our troops between the western end of the Regina Trench, 700 yards north of the Stuff Redoubt and the Schwaben Redoubt, attacked the formidable enemy trench known as "the Hansa line," which ran unevenly north-westward down to the Ancre just opposite Beaucourt and de-scended on St. Pierre Divion. By 7.20 a.m our objectives east of the hamlet had been reached and the garrison hemmed in between our troops and the river were isolated. At 7 a.m. the number of prisoners captured was greater than that of the attacking force. Soon after St. Pierre Divion and its caverns and tunnels fell. In this area alone nearly 1,400 prisoners were taken by a single Division at the expense of less than 600 casualties. A Tank had rendered considerable assistance preceding the infantry. The new ground won was a wedge-shaped piece 3,000 yards in extreme length tapering to an acute angle where it reached Regina Trench.

North of the river the enemy offered a more stubborn resistance. The British Naval Division had been allotted the task of storming the enemy's position from the Ancre to the " Y " Ravine. The extreme right of the Division went with a rush across the level of the valley bottom. The centre had to attack diagonally along the slope of the hill and the extreme left to mount the highest point of the crest. At the top of the slope, some 500 yards from the Ancre, and invisible owing to being hidden in a recess, was a redoubt comprised of three deep pits with concrete emplacements for machine-guns, which could fire almost flush with the surface of the ground in all directions. This redoubt was situated between the first and second trenches. While the extreme right of the Naval Division swept up the valley, the right centre was hung up round the redoubt. The left of the Division, however, stormed the ridge, joined hands with the extreme right and formed up on the Beaumont Hamel-Beaucourt road. There they remained for the rest of the day and during the night, while the redoubt and other strong points were being reduced.

At 3 a.m. on November 14, a Tank arrived near the redoubt. Unable to reach it, the crew got out and trained their machine guns on it. The survivors of the garrison—360 unwounded men—surrendered, and the advance on Beaucourt of the men of the Naval Division proceeded, the same Tank or another accompanying our infantry. After a quarter of an hour's fighting the village was captured, and at daylight our men were digging themselves in on its further side. The Division in the two days' fighting had taken 1,725 prisoners and advanced 2,000 yards on a front of 1,200.

Meanwhile a Scottish Division had been busy in the " Y " Ravine and at Beaumont Hamel. At all points except at the entrances to the prongs of the ravine, the Scottish infantry broke over the German defences without a check. Some of them descended into Beaumont Hamel, and before midday were over the site of the village and the entrances of the caverns beneath it. The " Y " Ravine was the theatre of a long and bloody contest. It was attacked from the north and south. At a point just beyond the fork of the " Y " the Scots tumbled down the precipitous sides, bombing and bayoneting the Germans in this

BRITISH AND FRENCH SOLDIERS CLEANING UP CAPTURED TRENCHES AT ST. PIERRE DIVION.

open cutting. Simultaneously the western entrances of the ravine were attacked and farther up towards the Beaumont Hamel-Beaucourt road other parties of Scots flung themselves into the chasm. The surviving Germans fled over the crest of the ridge or took refuge in their subterranean lairs, from which they were gradually evicted. The Scots, as a whole, took 1,400 prisoners and 54 machine-guns Farther north the enemy's first-line system for a distance of half a mile beyond Beaumont Hamel was also in our hands. Opposite Serre the attack was not pressed

end in the middle of November, being brought to a termination by the bad weather, and henceforward to the end of the year there was no really important fighting, although of minor skirmishing there was no cessation, and we still continued to make some little but continuous progress. On November 15 the gains of the two previous days on the Ancre were consolidated and further gains made. One division advanced a mile on the north side of the river and took a thousand prisoners at the cost of only 450 casualties. South of the Ancre the ground captured east of the

[*By permission, from the Official Ancre Film.*]

SCOTTISH TROOPS ADVANCING TO THE ATTACK.

owing to the morass-like character of the ground to be traversed. On the morning of November 14 our line was extended from Beaucourt to the north-west along the road across the southern end of the Beaumont Hamel spur. We had now secured the command of the Ancre on both banks of the river at the point where it entered the enemy's lines. On the evening of the 14th, Sir Douglas Haig was able to report that he had captured over 5,000 prisoners in the battle of the Ancre. The serious reverse which we had suffered on July 1 at this part of the field had been wiped out.

On the 14th a successful advance had also been made east of the Butte de Warlencourt, 400 or 500 yards of the " Grid Trench " being taken from details of the Prussian 1st Guard Reserve Division.

Active operations practically came to an

Butte de Warlencourt was secured, and the enemy massing for a counter-attack was dispersed by our artillery fire. The next day there was considerable fire from the German artillery north and south of the Ancre, but without any appreciable result : and the same was the case between Le Sars and Gueudecourt. On the other hand our guns caused several explosions in the German positions. The British front was also extended to the east from Beaucourt along the north bank of the Ancre. The enemy, however, managed to regain a part of the ground near the Butte de Warlencourt, which had been captured from him on the 14th.

Our airmen assumed active operations against the Germans. Two important junctions on their lines of communication, places on their railways, billets and aerodromes, were attacked with bombs and machine-gun fire both by night and day. It must be admitted that the enemy displayed more enterprise than usual, but he lost three machines on the British side of No Man's Land and two on his own, while five more were compelled to descend to earth in a damaged condition. Our own loss was three aeroplanes. By this time (since September 13) we had taken 6,190 prisoners, against which he had no appreciable offset.

On Saturday, November 18, further progress was made on both sides of the Ancre, but mostly on the south, where we gained some 500 yards on a front of about 2½ miles and reached the outskirts of Grandcourt. On the right bank of the river we advanced about three-quarters of a mile to the north-east of Beaucourt, capturing the Bois de Hollande. Altogether 258 prisoners were taken.

During these days the French had also been heavily engaged. On November 7 they had captured the important points of Ablaincourt and Pressoir to the north of Chaulnes. It was not till the 15th, after a two days' bombardment, that the Germans made any attempt to recapture this portion of their lost position.

A very serious fight then ensued, and at one time they managed to gain a footing in the eastern part of Pressoir, but they were repulsed at all other points with great loss. A like fate befel them north of the Somme. Here regiments of the Prussian Guards attacked from Lesboeufs to the south of Bouchavesnes. They managed to capture the northern corner and western fringe of the St. Pierre Vaast Wood, but were beaten back all along the rest of the front attacked. On the other hand, the French progressed on the northern spur of the St. Pierre Vaast Wood. On the 16th the Germans claimed to have entered Saillisel in the morning, but by the evening they lost it again, and were also turned out of Pressoir. It was a severe repulse for three German Divisions in which they suffered very heavy losses. On the 16th French airmen fought 54 engagements with German aeroplanes, and during the night they dropped a ton and a half of bombs on a railway station and aviation park.

General Headquarters reported that on the 22nd the enemy's aeroplanes showed more enterprise, and some of them crossed the British lines. Three fell into our hands, and a

PRISONERS FROM BEAUMONT HAMEL.

RUINS OF BEAUMONT HAMEL CHURCH.

[Official photograph.

fourth was driven down behind the German line—one of ours was missing. On the 23rd twelve of our machines attacked an enemy formation of twenty, and dispersed it. One of them was destroyed and several driven down damaged; all of ours returned safely. But in other fights, where our men destroyed four of the enemy's, we lost three.

The weather was now very bad, and the struggle was confined to the artillery with a few spasmodic efforts in the shape of trench raids and a little work by the airmen.

Thus the struggle went on till the end of the month. Nor did December bring any increase in military enterprise on either side, although on the 12th the German report was that the artillery activity again temporarily increased. It was backed up by an infantry attack on the French line south of Roye. A few small parties managed to enter our Ally's trenches,

[Official photograph.

BEAUMONT HAMEL.

but they were driven out by a bomb attack, and the position was completely re-established.

Our trench raids were continued along the whole line held by the French and ourselves. They produced a certain tale of prisoners, and many of the German dug-outs were injured.

The end of 1916 found the Allies in the Western Theatre of War in a position far different from that which they had held twelve months before. Above all, the pro-

destruction of the military forces of the Central Powers. Thus the war, both on the Eastern and Western Fronts, formed part of the general plan for the defeat of the Germans. Nor could the Austro-Italian Front be left out of the Allied Commanders' calculations. In this theatre by the beginning of June the Austrians had made considerable impression on the Italian line. Plainly, therefore, the situation required fresh, determined, and united efforts on the part of the Allies.

The Russians, for their part, in the campaign

[Official photograph

A QUIET RESTING-PLACE BEHIND THE TRENCHES.

gress made in the last half of the year had been great.

It is true that the Germans in February, 1916, had begun their attack on Verdun, and they had continued their assaults with sometimes varying success, but, on the whole, with substantial progress, and it became evident in the days of late spring that some counter blow must be delivered by the Allies to relieve the pressure on this important point. Moreover, it was necessary not to look upon the different campaigns in Europe as isolated efforts without relation to one another, but rather as forming parts of one scheme for the

which they opened at the beginning of June won most decided successes over the Austrians, and led to the transfer of considerable German forces from the Western to the Eastern Theatre of War. This was advantageous, but more was needed. The British and French leaders therefore determined on a combined offensive at the end of the month to pin the Germans to that part of the front of operations and prevent them from aiding the Austrians with troops whether against the Russians or Italians. The Macedonian operations were at this time only a minor consideration.

The Allied offensive would fulfil two other

objects. It would relieve the pressure on Verdun, and, at the same time, inflict such losses, both in men and material, on the Germans in France as to diminish their strength, while the moral effect of driving them from positions which they had fortified in the past twenty months and believed to be impregnable could not fail to be great. No systematic and combined effort had yet been made against them on a large scale, extending over a considerable stretch of country, but now the time had come when it could be undertaken with considerable prospect of success. When, with inferior numbers, both of men and guns, the Allies had held their own against their opponents, they had still contrived to win isolated successes, and the attacks of the Germans had been without a lasting or striking result. But, by the middle of 1916 both British and French had equipped themselves with an adequate artillery, and the preponderance in guns no longer lay with their opponents. The supplies of ammunition were large and allowed the continuous bombardment of the German lines, while the British Infantry had been enormously increased. France, too, had strengthened her armies, and both Allies

were now capable of carrying out a definite and continuous offensive against the German positions. Their preparations during the last months had put, indeed, a very different complexion on the situation. No longer were they in any inferiority with regard to weapons : on the contrary, both in numbers and efficiency they were better off than were Germans. This has been clearly shown in the previous chapters dealing with the operations on the Western Front. It seems probable that the Germans had some idea of a limited offensive in the early summer, for on May 21 an attack had been made by the Germans on our positions on the Vimy Ridge and south and south-east of Souchez, and they had gained some ground. But as their success was of no strategic or tactical value, Sir Douglas Haig came to the conclusion that it was better to take up a fresh position a little to the rear of the original line rather than use up troops in a counter-attack who could be better employed in the larger operation he had in view.

On June 2 the enemy made a determined attack on a front of over a mile and a half from Mount Sorrell to Hooge, and succeeded in penetrating our line to a depth which, at its

[*Official photograph.*

A MEAL AMONGST THE WRECKAGE.

[*Official photograph.*

MOVING A FIELD-GUN TO A NEW POSITION.

greatest, measured some 700 yards. As the Germans in the southern part of the captured position commanded the British trenches more to the rear, it was therefore necessary to expel them from it. This was done on June 13 by a well-planned and well-executed counter-stroke and the original trenches were recovered. The Germans showed no further symptoms of passing to the offensive, and neither one nor other of these affairs in any way delayed the preparations for the grand attack shortly to be undertaken.

It has been seen how successful the Somme operations were. The pressure on Verdun had been relieved, the main German Army had been pinned to the Western front of operations and its strength had been considerably worn down. The sketch annexed shows graphically the gain of ground made, but this was not the only gauge by which success was to be estimated; rather was it to be found in the captures of prisoners and in the large number of weapons won. From July 1 to November 18, when active operations practically ceased, 38,000 officers and men had been taken besides 29 heavy guns, 96 field guns and howitzers, 136 trench mortars and 514 machine guns.

Still more important was the great damage which had been inflicted on the German *moral.* The evidence as to this point was indubitable. Time after time in the various encounters it had been noticed that the Germans no longer fought as well as they had done earlier in the war. It is certain that this is to be attributed to the fact that in hand-to-hand encounters they found they were opposed by better men.

No soldiers can go on for any considerable time recognizing this fact without suffering deterioration.

But there were other reasons for the Allies' great success. In the contest of nations

SKETCH MAP SHOWING THE GROUND GAINED BY THE BRITISH AND FRENCH IN THE BATTLE OF THE SOMME.

which began in 1914 the destructive power of fire had been enormously developed. It had been remarked in former wars of recent date that they had become less bloody. For this the main reason was that, while improved weapons had increased losses at the actual points of contact, the same intensity along the whole line of battle which characterized the encounters of earlier time was no longer seen. Moreover, the great sources of loss, disease and hardship, due to want of food and exposure, were better in hand. But in this titanic struggle, although medical science had practically abolished epidemic disease from the armies and largely diminished the loss from exposure, the unprecedented progress in the power of weapons had enormously increased the destruction of life on the battlefield. Moreover, there was another contributing factor—the continuous nature of the struggle. Before the supply of food and ammunition had been rendered so much easier by the increased facility of loco-motion due to liberal construction of railways, good roads and the introduction of the auto-mobile, there were constantly occurring pauses

THE STOKES BOMB-THROWER.

in the fighting, and battles were comparatively infrequent. In this war, whether during the time the operations took place in the open country or during those which were made up of the attack and defence of a fortified position, there was hardly any intermission. Day after day, unless the weather entirely stopped operations, there were encounters of a more or less ardent nature, and always there was some artillery work.

The struggle on the ground was supplemented by the struggle in the air, which had a very important influence on the conduct of war. If two large armies are in juxtaposition with one another, both sides have great difficulty in concealing their strategic movements from one another. For the aeroplanes, with their long range, can ascertain easily what movements of troops are going on behind the enemy's front, provided they are not stopped by the enemy's machines. The reconnoitring duties in front of the army had been largely transferred from the cavalry to the aviators, and it is just as important in the employment of airmen as formerly in the employment of horsemen to ensure the predominance of the recon-noitring arm—*i.e.*, the resistance of the other side must be disposed of just as, formerly,

FITTING FUSES TO STOKES BOMBS.

the enemy's cavalry had to be torn away
before the duties of reconnaissance could be
properly carried out. It is plain that under
modern conditions the difficulty of executing
strategical movements such as Napoleon employed in the Marengo campaign, or Wellington
in 1813, must be very much greater, besides
which the size of armies, when whole nations
are in arms, makes such brilliant movements
still more difficult. Fortunately for the Allies
both British and French airmen at the time of
the Battle of the Somme proved themselves
superior on the whole to those of Germany.

When we entered on the scene of action in the
year 1914 our soldiers were necessarily armed
and trained on the ideas then in vogue. They
had a good rifle, a moderate equipment of
machine-guns, possessed in their guns weapons
which were more powerful than those of other
field artilleries, and rather more numerous than
the officially published endowment of the
German Army. But hardly had the war
begun when it was seen that Germany had
given to her army far more machine-guns,
and had brought far heavier guns into the
field and in greater numbers than we had
expected to meet. This put us at first at a
great disadvantage, but the almost superhuman exertions we made in order to overcome
it brought about in due time a complete
change. Our heavy guns were more numerous
and more copiously provided with ammunition : we had brought the factory on to the

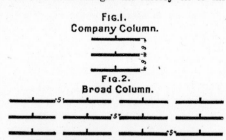

FIG.1.
Company Column.

FIG.2.
Broad Column.

GERMAN INFANTRY COLUMNS.

In the Company Column the three sections are
one behind the other at nine paces distance. The
Broad Column consists of the four Company
Columns of the Battalion with intervals of five
paces between them.

battlefield to take part in the struggle. The
number of machine-guns had been enormously
increased, and the infantry had been provided
with the Lewis gun, technically a machine-
gun, but in reality an automatic rifle which
one man can carry and manipulate, and which
yet gives a fire equal to that of 25 rifles. This

THE STOKES BOMB-THROWER AND
ITS INVENTOR.

This illustration shows how easily the arm can be
carried.

weapon was also largely used in our aeroplanes,
for which its light weight rendered it peculiarly
suitable. The cavalry, too, was provided
with machine-guns, because so much of its
fighting had to be done on foot. Great use
had been made of grenades in the trench warfare,
and our trench mortars—*i.e.*, the weapons
which hurl bombs of various sizes at a very
high angle of fire for a comparatively short
distance—were distinctly superior to those of
the enemy. Grenadiers had been revived, and
formed an integral part of every company.
The special form known as the Stokes mortar
or howitzer had undoubtedly, by its rapid fire,
produced a great impression on the Germans.
All these inventions and improvements enormously increased the amount of fire on the
modern battlefield. The old doctrine of hus-
banding ammunition had given way to the more
rational view—expend as much as you can,
provided a reasonable effect is obtained from
it. This, of course, involved enormous supplies,
such as in 1914 were undreamt of. War had
become largely a question of material. No
soldiers, however good, could succeed without it.

[*Official photograph.*

TROOPS RESTING BEHIND A SHELTERED BANK.

It is a curious thing that just when fire had been rendered more intense, when the great object of rationally manœuvred infantry was to use formations which offered as little target as possible, compatible with a proper development of fire power, without which it would have been impossible to advance against a well-defended position, the Germans should have harked back to the worst type of French tactics of a hundred years before. Large and dense columns were then found impossible on the battlefield, but they were seen once more in the German Army. There had always been a certain school in it which believed in them, and they were employed fairly frequently on the battlefields in France, causing frightful losses, and never succeeding unless the troops attacked were on the point of going back, and so were unable to bring sufficient fire to bear on them.

The narrative has shown that the Allies really obtained the results they sought for in the Battle of the Somme. But it was scarcely to be expected that the Germans would in any way admit this. On the contrary, the newspapers, the General Headquarters and the German people claimed that they had won the battle.

The German Headquarter Staff at the end of December declared that "the great battle of the Somme was actually ended. Since the last infantry attacks failed lamentably over four weeks ago the fire of the French and British artillery had also dimini hed to such an extent that it became possible for the defenders to rebuild their defences, which at places only consisted of shattered trenches and shell craters. These four weeks of relative calm, which the exhausted assailants were forced to allow the defenders, have, once and for all, sealed the fate of the Somme Battle!" A few months later the Germans were scuttling back as hard as they could from a position which, according to their own statements, had been restored to its pristine strength!